The Chinese Vegan Kitchen

PERIGEE TITLES BY DONNA KLEIN

The Mediterranean Vegan Kitchen

The PDQ (Pretty Darn Quick) Vegetarian Cookbook

Vegan Italiano

The Gluten-Free Vegetarian Kitchen

The Tropical Vegan Kitchen

Supermarket Vegan

The Chinese Vegan Kitchen

THE
Chinese
Vegan
Kitchen

**More Than
225 Meat-Free, Egg-Free,
Dairy-Free Dishes
from the
Culinary Regions of China**

DONNA KLEIN

A PERIGEE BOOK

A PERIGEE BOOK
Published by the Penguin Group
Penguin Group (USA) Inc.
375 Hudson Street, New York, New York 10014, USA

Penguin Group (Canada), 90 Eglinton Avenue East, Suite 700, Toronto, Ontario M4P 2Y3, Canada
(a division of Pearson Penguin Canada Inc.) • Penguin Books Ltd., 80 Strand, London WC2R 0RL,
England • Penguin Group Ireland, 25 St. Stephen's Green, Dublin 2, Ireland (a division of Penguin
Books Ltd.) • Penguin Group (Australia), 250 Camberwell Road, Camberwell, Victoria 3124, Australia
(a division of Pearson Australia Group Pty. Ltd.) • Penguin Books India Pvt. Ltd., 11 Community
Centre, Panchsheel Park, New Delhi—110 017, India • Penguin Group (NZ), 67 Apollo Drive,
Rosedale, Auckland 0632, New Zealand (a division of Pearson New Zealand Ltd.) • Penguin Books
(South Africa) (Pty.) Ltd., 24 Sturdee Avenue, Rosebank, Johannesburg 2196, South Africa

Penguin Books Ltd., Registered Offices: 80 Strand, London WC2R 0RL, England

While the author has made every effort to provide accurate telephone numbers, Internet addresses,
and other contact information at the time of publication, neither the publisher nor the author assumes any
responsibility for errors, or for changes that occur after publication. Further, the publisher does not have
any control over and does not assume any responsibility for author or third-party websites or their content.

First edition: December 2012

Library of Congress Cataloging-in-Publication Data

Klein, Donna (Donna M.)
The Chinese vegan kitchen : more than 225 meat-free, egg-free, dairy-free dishes from
the culinary regions of China / Donna Klein.—First edition.
pages   cm
"A Perigee book."
Includes index.
ISBN 978-0-399-53770-7 (pbk.)
1. Cooking, Chinese.   2. Vegan cooking.   I. Title.
TX837.K5447   2012
641.5'636—dc23   2012029883

The recipes contained in this book are to be followed exactly as written. The publisher is
not responsible for your specific health or allergy needs that may require medical supervision.
The publisher is not responsible for any adverse reactions to the recipes contained in this book.

To

The Yali "Nanya" Middle School

Class of 2013

Wǒ ài nǐmen!

—TEACHER DONNA

• ACKNOWLEDGMENTS •

First and foremost, many thanks to my literary agent, Linda Konner, and the staff and crew at the Penguin Group, namely John Duff, who enabled this cookbook, my lucky number 7, to be published—yes!

Sincere thanks to WorldTeach, a nonprofit affiliate of the Center for International Development at Harvard University, which made my volunteer year in China possible.

Special thanks to Yali "Nanya" Middle School in Changsha, Hunan Province, The People's Republic of China, for affording me the honor, privilege, and pleasure of teaching oral English to the Senior One students during the 2010–11 school year.

Heartfelt thanks to all my students at Yali, in the classroom and at English corner, and their families, who contributed recipes, ideas, and endless inspiration for this book.

Thank you, Emma and Sarah, my gorgeous grown-up girls; Jeff, their devoted father; and Trevor and Cooper, our beloved adopted dogs, for holding down the fort while China was my home away from home for eleven months.

Thank you, Karen, my fabulous friend since our St. Joseph's University days, for getting up early on Sunday mornings to Skype from suburban Philadelphia to Changsha and keeping my spirits way up.

Finally, eternal gratitude to the countless Chinese cooks who have fed their families during the best and worst of times in a remarkable country with the longest continuous history in the world, who have produced the most creative cuisine on Earth, and who have passed their secrets on.

• CONTENTS •

Much has been written about the breathtaking beauty of China. If my experiences as a traveler to Beijing, Hong Kong, Macau, Shanghai, Xi'an, and throughout Hunan Province—such as Mount Heng, Shaoshan, Yuelu Mountain, and the amazing Zhangjiajie, whose Wulingyuan Scenic Area, a UNESCO World Heritage Site, is said to have been an inspiration for the scenery in the movie *Avatar*—are any indication, it's all true. Much has also been written about the breathtaking effects of state-sponsored atheism in China, as well. Many claim that communism has essentially stifled—even snuffed out—spirituality, as the majority of Chinese citizens profess to be agnostics, nonreligious, or atheists. If my experiences as a WorldTeach volunteer living and teaching oral English in China for eleven months are any indication, however, it's not at all true. In China, I found the Spirit of God everywhere I looked. Its sacred breath was manifested in the eyes of my students welcoming me every single day to class, in the smiles of the locals greeting me on the streets, in the voices of their children calling "hello," in the touch of the stranger's hand leading me to exactly where I needed to be when I was lost, in the taste of the apple given as a gift on Christmas Eve, and in the smells of the incense wafting through the streets from the temples on the Lunar New Year. Ah, the temples—Daoist, Buddhist, or Confucian, China is temple heaven. The sublime states of loving-kindness, compassion, balance, and harmony emanating from these pillars of Eastern wisdom and philosophy are woven into the fabric of everyday life in China—showing up in formal attire simply isn't necessary to receive the gift of such bliss, only presence. Climbing into a landscape painting of Chinese tranquility can help.

China is open to Western religions as well. I attended services at Changsha's Roman Catholic Church on a glorious Pentecost Sunday. In this Gothic-style structure with its rose petal–pink walls and arched midnight blue ceilings resembling starry skies, a breathtaking Madonna floats on a heavenly orb above the altar as the Earth's benevolent mother filled with grace, beseeching her Son Jesus to bless all of His Father's children in the human race. There were the traditional offertory gifts of bread and wine, and the unexpected delights of melons, mangoes, and apples—always apples. Received were the twelve fruits of the Holy Spirit, flowing in infinite abundance everywhere I went in China: kindness, joy, peace, patience, goodness, forbearance, gentleness, faith, modesty, self-control, purity, and love—always love. As I sat in the pew in stillness, blown away by the music, listening to a hymn familiar from my childhood but sung in Chinese, I surrendered to the sanctity of the spirit-filled moment—a clear connection to an endless wellspring of love and light. A foreigner, I never felt more at home in my life.

A few weeks later, as I flew back to the States, I counted the many blessings of experiences and friendships I had been graced with in China, and soared with gratitude for all that I had waiting for me—my family, my friends, my dogs, my house, my life, my purpose. I felt enveloped in peacefulness as palpable and still as the apples nestled in the offertory basket that miraculous Pentecost Sunday.

I thought of this book I would write—my seventh one, a fortuitous number for relationships in both the East and West and, in my mind, a symbol of the interconnectedness of all the nations of the world through food. And, finally, I thought of my own modest contributions to this interconnectedness to nourish the body while eschewing the use of animal products and, in turn, attempts to leave the tiniest carbon footprint.

Watching the brilliant sun set through the plane's window, drifting off into contented sleep, I felt the breath of the Spirit blowing in me, and was full and satisfied—my happy heartfelt wish for you as you use this book.

Spirit of God

Spirit of God in the clear running water
Blowing to greatness the trees on the hill.
Spirit of God in the finger of morning:
Fill the earth, bring it to birth,
And blow where you will.
Blow, blow, blow till I be
But the breath of the Spirit blowing in me.

Down in the meadow the willows are moaning
Sheep in the pastureland cannot lie still.
Spirit of God, creation is groaning:
Fill the earth, bring it to birth,
And blow where you will.
Blow, blow, blow till I be
But the breath of the Spirit blowing in me.

I saw the scar of a year that lay dying
Heard the lament of a lone whip-poor-will.
Spirit of God, see that cloud crying:
Fill the earth, bring it to birth,
And blow where you will.
Blow, blow, blow till I be
But the breath of the Spirit blowing in me.

Spirit of God, everyone's heart is lonely
Watching and waiting and hungry until
Spirit of God, man longs that you only
Fulfill the earth, bring it to birth,
And blow where you will.
Blow, blow, blow till I be
But the breath of the Spirit blowing in me.

—Words and music by Sister Miriam Therese Winter

Attractive appearance, pleasing fragrance, satisfying flavor—Chinese dishes have been measured by these three major criteria for centuries. Other important considerations are the texture and the intrinsic healthfulness of the food—any and all auspicious connotations are extrinsic added boons. The harmonious blending of these distinctive elements has made Chinese cuisine a veritable feast for the senses and an enduring source of sustenance. While many of China's ancient inventions—paper, moveable type, and the compass, to name a few—have changed the course of history, its most popular contribution to the modern world is arguably Chinese food, enjoyed in restaurants and homes in every corner of the globe. Now vegans throughout the planet can indulge their passion using *The Chinese Vegan Kitchen*.

How is a vegan diet in China possible? It's easy. As the world's largest producer of fruits and vegetables, grains such as rice and wheat, legumes such as mung beans and peanuts, and the inventor of tofu more than two thousand years ago, China boasts an impressive array of meat-free, egg-free, and dairy-free dishes that is highly conducive to healthy, plant-based eating. Additionally, the effect of Buddhist vegetarian practices upon Chinese culinary art is apparent in specific foods, namely seitan, the quintessential mock meat, which, like tofu, originated in ancient China. From tasty appetizers to mouthwatering desserts, *The Chinese Vegan Kitchen* is a comprehensive collection of easy yet authentic recipes from the

Middle Kingdom's various regional cuisines—such as Cantonese, Hunanese, Mandarin, Shanghainese, Sichuanese—that you can prepare in your own kitchen with ingredients readily available in both standard and Western Asian supermarkets.

Diverse Regional Cuisines

In the Western world, it used to be that Chinese food called to mind a single, homogenous cuisine packaged in cute pint-sized containers known as Chinese take-out. These days, with the proliferation of Asian food markets, TV food shows, and Internet food blogs, it's become increasingly obvious that there is much, much more to Chinese cuisine than egg rolls and chow mein. Moreover, it stands to reason that a country as large and as geographically and ethnically diverse as China would naturally have a wide range of culinary styles. While there are various ways of classifying these regional cuisines, an extensive variety of flavors, ingredients, cooking methods, and cultural influences has evolved over the centuries to distinguish the north, south, east, and west schools of Chinese cooking.

THE NORTH

The northern school of cooking is largely defined by the refined cooking of Beijing (also known as Mandarin or Peking cuisine) and its former palace kitchens; the classic style of Shandong, where the wok is said to have originated; and the hearty, cold-weather food of Tianjin and cities bordering Russia such as Harbin, where a version of borscht made with red cabbage is quite popular. While the areas in the south, east, and west favor rice, the north is China's bread basket—wheat-based noodles, dumplings, steamed buns, breads, and pancakes are popular fare. Foods are typically flavored with the liberal use of vinegar, garlic, scallions, leeks, and salt, and tend to be oily. The preferred methods of northern cooking are boiling, steaming, and stir-frying.

THE SOUTH

The food of the Guangdong and Hainan regions largely define the southern regional school of cooking. The Cantonese food from Guangzhou, located in the subtropical province of Guangdong, is the most commonly defined cuisine outside of China—most Chinese restaurants in the Western world feature Cantonese derivatives. Cantonese food is known for its exotic ingredients and fresh, natural flavors. Fermented black beans, hoisin sauce, and oyster sauce—available in a vegetarian form made with soy sauce and mushrooms—are popular condiments in a Cantonese kitchen. Steaming and stir-frying are the two primary Cantonese cooking techniques. Hainan's tropical island cuisine, while strongly tied to Guangdong's, combines special local characteristics with milder seasonings that make it lighter. Steaming, braising, and boiling are popular Hainanese cooking methods.

THE EAST

The regions of Jiangsu, Zhenjiang, and Shanghai largely define the eastern school of cooking, which is typically characterized as sweet and oily. Sugar, vinegars, and wines are frequently employed to create this sweetness as well as to impart subtlety of flavors. Salt is another common ingredient, particularly in the dishes of Jiangsu, which are often described as salty-sweet. Zhenjiang is famous for its fragrant black vinegar, a popular condiment throughout China. Because of Shanghai's status as the world's largest port and its sizeable international population, a variety of dishes with French and Russian roots dominate menus, as well as dishes originating from China's other three regional cuisines. Favored cooking methods in eastern cooking include steaming, stewing, braising, and frying.

THE WEST

Sichuan and Hunan cuisines are the most well known in China's western regional school of cooking, with Yunnan cuisine increasingly gaining recognition. Both Sichuan and Hunan cuisines derive their notably spicy flavors from the use of chili peppers, both fresh and dried, and the famous Sichuan peppercorn—which is not really a pepper, but a dried berry. Also common in Sichuanese cooking are garlic, ginger, and star anise; broad-bean chili paste is a staple seasoning. Hunan cuisine's liberal use of fresh chili peppers makes it even spicier than Sichuan's; it also tends to be oilier, fresher, and simpler in taste. Pickling, salting, drying, and smoking are used extensively for food preservation in the hot, humid climate of both provinces. Stir-frying, steaming, and braising are common cooking techniques in Sichuan, while stewing, stir-frying, braising, baking, pot-roasting, and smoking are popular in Hunan. The cuisine of Yunnan Province is a unique blend of the different cooking and preparation styles of its numerous ethnic minority groups with the spicy foods of neighboring Sichuan Province. Mushrooms and flowers, namely chrysanthemums, figure prominently in local dishes, while clay pot stewing is a popular cooking method.

Hot in Hunan

Hot, spicy, sweet, sour, bold, beautiful—Hunan cuisine embodies all the enticing facets of Chinese cooking. For me, it also conjures up home—I lived in Changsha, Hunan's modern and bustling capital of 7 million-plus people and skyscrapers, for eleven exciting months. (Indeed, as of this writing, plans to construct the world's tallest building by 2013 are awaiting final approval!) Yet not far outside the city limits, a land of gentle hills and fertile valleys morphs into view, blessed by a subtropical monsoon climate, promising an abundance of fresh fruits and vegetables the whole year through. In fact, Hunan is China's third-largest producer of oranges, second-largest producer of tea, and number-one producer of rice—a veritable embarrassment of riches by global standards. Ask the locals what Hunan's greatest agricultural accomplishment is, however, and most of them will proudly answer it's the hot chili peppers, which grow prolifically throughout the province. After all, what would Hunan cuisine—or Chinese cuisine, for that matter—be without them? Known for its exquisitely hot dishes, Hunan cuisine is even spicier—or "la"—and hotter than Sichuan cuisine, to which it is often compared. It is also purer and more simple, relying almost exclusively on fresh, not dried, chili peppers. While the peppers may burn your palate, they load your system with more vitamin C per gram than citrus fruit and more vitamin A than carrots—and contain compounds that can kill harmful bacteria in the digestive system to boot. Blasts of capsaicin, the active ingredient found only in the pepper family that causes the feeling of spicy heat, release endorphins, the body's biological painkillers, for a natural high. Common physiological effects also include a metabolic boost and heavy sweating—explaining the paradox of how hot chilies can actually cool the body and, as a result, why they are so popular in tropical climates. To the uninitiated, Hunan cuisine is an intoxicating contradiction of pleasure and pain. To the initiated, like me, food simply doesn't get any better. Like it or not, it will always take your breath away!

Glossary of Ingredients

ADZUKI BEAN A small, reddish-brown, sweet-tasting bean that is used frequently in Chinese desserts; also known as aduki bean, red bean, or feijoa bean.

ARROWROOT A root vegetable with a bland taste whose starch is typically ground into powder and used as a thickener in sauces, soups, and puddings, etc. The fibrous root is also cubed and used in soups; when boiled, it has a slightly sweet, nutlike taste. Also known as obedience plant.

BAMBOO SHOOT The edible shoot of the bamboo plant. Spring shoots are larger and tougher than winter shoots, which are considered a delicacy. Bamboo shoots contain toxic concentrations of cyanogens, which cause cyanide poisoning; thus, they must always be cooked before eating. Also known as takenoko, kanile, or labong.

BEAN CURD SHEET Made by skimming and drying the skin that forms on top of heated soy milk and left in sheet form; also known as tofu skin, bean curd skin, dried bean curd, yuba, or bean skin.

BEAN CURD STICK Made by skimming and drying the skin that forms on top of heated soy milk in stick form; also known as dried tofu stick, dried bean stick, or tofu bamboo.

BEAN SPROUT A young sprout of a germinating mung bean having a crisp texture; also known as mung bean sprout, green bean sprout, or Chinese bean sprout.

BITTER MELON A gourd resembling a cucumber with rough, pockmarked skin and bitter flesh; also known as balsam pear.

BLACK BEAN SAUCE An Asian sauce or condiment typically made of fermented black soybeans, sugar, flour, garlic, and soy sauce; also known as black bean sauce with garlic. Black bean sauce with chili also contains hot chilies.

BLACK FUNGUS A brownish, crinkly mushroom with a crunchy, grisly, jellylike texture that is sold mainly in dried form; also known as cloud ear, tree ear, wood fungus, mouse ear, or jelly mushroom.

BLACK MUSHROOM (SHIITAKE) Commonly known as shiitake, a black mushroom is a large and meaty cultivated mushroom that can be light or dark brown or sometimes gray. Dried black mushrooms are often preferred due to their more intense flavor. Also known as black forest mushroom, black winter mushroom, brown oak mushroom, Chinese black mushroom, Oriental black mushroom, forest mushroom, golden oak mushroom, or donko.

BLACK RICE A rice grain that is black when raw and dark purple when cooked, available in long-grain and glutinous, or sticky, form; also known as Chinese black rice, forbidden black rice, forbidden rice, black tribute rice, or emperor's rice.

BOK CHOY A member of the cabbage family with a white stem and dark green leaves; also known as bok choi, pak choi, Peking cabbage, or white cabbage. Shanghai bok choy is a type of baby bok choy.

CELLOPHANE NOODLES A thin, transparent Asian noodle typically made from mung bean starch; also known as mung bean noodles, bean threads, or glass noodles.

CELTUCE A cultivar of lettuce grown primarily for its thick, asparagus-like stem, celtuce has a mild taste and crunchy texture; also known as stem lettuce, celery lettuce, asparagus lettuce, or Chinese lettuce.

CHINESE CABBAGE A large-headed cabbage with firmly packed, pale green leaves; also called Napa cabbage, Chinese leaf, Peking cabbage, or celery cabbage.

CHINESE CELERY Originating from wild Asian celery, Chinese celery has very thin, hollow stalks ranging from white to dark green in color with a stronger flavor than regular celery; also known as Chinese small celery or Oriental celery.

CHINESE CHILI PASTE A fiery blend of hot chili peppers, garlic, oil, and salt; also known as Chinese chili sauce, or chili paste with garlic.

CHINESE CHIVES Like regular Western chives, standard Chinese chives are members of the onion family and have white flowers, long green shoots, and lack of a bulb. Unlike regular Western chives, the shoots are broad and flat and have a strong flavor and odor similar to garlic. Standard Chinese chives are also known as garlic chives, Chinese garlic chives, Oriental garlic chives, Chinese leek, ku chai, jiu cai, gau choy, or nira. There are two other varieties of Chinese chives: flowering chives, which have yellow flowers and an even stronger garlicky flavor, and yellow chives, which are grown out of direct sunlight. All are interchangeable in recipes. Flowering chives are also known as flowering garlic chives, flowering Chinese chives, flowering leek, or Chinese leek flower. Yellow chives are also known as blanched chives.

CHINESE EGGPLANT A narrow, purple variety of Asian eggplant that may be streaked with white. It has thinner skin and less seed than regular eggplant, and is therefore less bitter. Also known as Oriental eggplant.

CHINESE FLOWERING CABBAGE A relative of bok choy with small yellow flowers; medium green leaves; and a sweet, mustardy flavor. Also known as choy sum or choi sum.

CHINESE HOT OIL A fiery condiment typically made from soybean oil that has been infused with dried chili peppers; also known as red oil, hot sauce, hot pepper oil, or chili oil.

CHINESE LONG BEAN A pencil-thin legume that resembles a long green bean, usually picked when eighteen inches or less in length; has a flavor similar to the green bean but is not as sweet. Also called long bean, yard-long bean, asparagus bean, or snake bean.

CHINESE MUSTARD GREENS A peppery variety of the cabbage family that is similar in taste to Western mustard greens but with a less pungent flavor, mature Chinese mustard greens are eaten cooked, while young mustard greens can be eaten cooked or raw. Also known as gai choy, kai choy, Chinese mustard cabbage, Indian mustard, or leaf mustard.

CHINESE OKRA A dull green vegetable with lengthwise ridges with a taste and texture slightly similar to Western okra; also known as silk squash, angled luffa, sing gua, or dishwasher gourd.

CHINESE SESAME PASTE Made from ground toasted sesame seeds, sesame paste has a texture and flavor similar to tahini or peanut butter, which can be used as substitutes; also known as Asian sesame paste.

CHINESE SPINACH A leafy green vegetable with either green or red leaves similar in taste to spinach; also known as amaranth, yeen choy, or xian cai.

CHINESE WHITE RADISH (DAIKON) Commonly known as daikon, Chinese white radish is a long radish resembling a large white carrot with a sharp bite; also known as lo bak, low bak, or Chinese icicle radish.

CHINESE YAM A starchy and bland white tuber with a thick, gluey texture when grated. Unlike regular yams, it can be eaten raw after peeling; peel with a vegetable peeler under running water to avoid any skin sensitivity to its sticky juices. Also known as Japanese mountain yam, Korean yam, or wild yam.

DRAGON FRUIT An exotic tropical fruit, usually scarlet red or pink in color (although some are yellow), with a scaly skin and a red or white sweet pulp with tiny black seeds; also known as pitaya, pitahaya, huo long guo, or strawberry pear.

DRIED LILY BUD Yellow-gold or brown in color, with an earthy taste, a dried lily bud is the unopened flower of a daylily.

DRIED OSMANTHUS FLOWER The dried tiny golden-yellow flower of the osmanthus plant, a member of the olive family that is native to China, with a sweet and pleasant fragrance; popular in teas, desserts, and jellies, and occasionally used in savory dishes. Also known as tea olive, fragrant olive, sweet olive, or gui hua.

DUCK SAUCE (*see* Plum Sauce)

DUMPLING WRAPPER A thin, round, flattened piece of dough primarily made of wheat flour and water (sometimes contains eggs) that is used to make dumplings and pot stickers; also known as dumpling skin, gyoza wrapper/skin, or jiaozi wrapper/skin.

FERMENTED BLACK BEANS Strongly flavored soybeans that have been dried and fermented with salt; other spices such as chilies, wine, and/or ginger may be added. Also known as salted black beans or dried black beans.

FERN ROOT NOODLES Purplish-black colored noodles with a chewy texture made from the starch of the common bracken fern; in dried form, they resemble twigs.

FIVE-SPICE POWDER A pungent Chinese blend of five ground spices, typically consisting of equal parts cinnamon, cloves, fennel seed, star anise, and Sichuan peppercorns.

FUZZY MELON A mild-tasting gourd resembling a zucchini covered with fuzz whose skin must be peeled before stuffing and steaming or using in soups and stir-fries. Also known as hairy melon, fuzzy squash, mo gwa, or mo qua.

GINGER A tropical root plant with a tan skin and gnarled, bumpy appearance. The flavor is peppery and slightly sweet, while the aroma is pungent and spicy. Also known as gingerroot.

GINKGO NUT A buff-colored, mildly sweet nut from the center of the inedible fruit of the maidenhair tree, a native of China; also known as gingko, ginkgo/gingko seed, white nut, or bai guo.

GLUTINOUS RICE A variety of short-grain Asian rice that becomes sticky when cooked; also known as sticky rice, sushi rice, sweet rice, pearl rice, waxy rice, botan rice, biroin chal, mochi rice, or pulut.

GLUTINOUS RICE FLOUR An Asian rice flour made from glutinous, or sticky, rice; also known as sweet rice flour, sticky rice flour, mifen, or mochiko.

GOLDEN NEEDLE MUSHROOM (ENOKI) A small white mushroom growing in clumps that have long, thin stems topped with tiny caps having a mild flavor and crisp texture; also known as enoki, velvet stem, snow puff, or golden mushrooms.

HOISIN SAUCE A sweet-and-spicy condiment, hoisin is a thick, dark sauce made from a combination of fermented soybeans, garlic, vinegar, sugar, chilies, and other spices; also known as Chinese barbecue sauce.

HOT BEAN SAUCE A fermented paste that combines hot chilies with broad beans and/or soybeans and other seasonings; also known as hot bean paste, soybean paste with chili, or chili bean sauce/paste.

HOT MUSTARD A sharp, hot condiment made by mixing dry mustard powder with water. Vegetable oil, sesame oil, and rice vinegar may also be added. Also known as Chinese mustard.

KELP A green, gray, or brown sea vegetable, or seaweed, kelp contains essential iodine and is available in fresh and, more commonly, dried form; one of the most popular types of kelp for culinary uses in both fresh and dried forms is seaweed tangle, or sea tangle, which is strands of kelp that are usually emerald green in fresh form and grayish green in dried form. Also known as haidai, kombu, konbu, or dashima.

KIWIFRUIT Native to China, kiwifruit has a thin, fuzzy brown skin and a fruity aroma. The flesh is green with shiny black seeds and succulent flesh. Also known as kiwi.

KONJAC A gray- to white-colored gelatinous, fiber-rich mass made from the starchy corms of the konjac plant, which grows in southern China. Also known as konjac tofu, moyu, or konnyaku.

KUMQUAT A small, round, or oblong citrus fruit with an edible rind and acid pulp used primarily for preserves and sauces; also known as cumquat or kinkan.

LITCHI A small round to oval fruit having a hard, reddish outer covering and sweet, whitish edible flesh that surrounds a single large seed; also known as lychee or litchi/lychee nut.

LONGAN A small round fruit having a golden brown outer covering and sweet, whitish edible flesh surrounding a single large seed; similar to the litchi but with a more subtly sweet flavor. Also known as dragon's eye.

LOQUAT A small pear-shaped fruit with a yellowish-orange skin and juicy flesh; also known as Japanese plum, Chinese plum, or Japanese medlar.

LOTUS ROOT The thick, tuberous root of the lotus, an aquatic plant similar to the water lily, with a sweet taste and crisp texture.

LOTUS SEED The small, nutlike seed of the lotus plant; also known as lotus nuts.

MANGO A tropical fruit with a firm yellowish-red skin, a hard central stone, and juicy aromatic pulp. Also known as mangou, mangot, or manga.

MI DOU FU A white-colored mass resembling tofu that is made from rice milk boiled to a curd in a method similar to making tofu; also known as rice tofu.

MUNG BEAN A tiny green-skinned bean with a tender texture and slightly sweet flavor, whose sprout (see Bean Sprout) is commonly used in salads and stir-fries. Dried mung beans are used in soups, and ground into flour, which is used to make mung bean, or cellophane, noodles. Also known as green bean, green soy, or mongo bean.

MUSHROOM SOY SAUCE A soy sauce that has been infused with the flavor of straw mushrooms.

OYSTER MUSHROOM A shell-shaped mushroom with white flesh and a gray to brown exterior with a soft texture and robust flavor; also known as oyster caps, angel's wing, tree mushrooms, summer oyster mushrooms, pleurotte, or shimeji.

PANDAN LEAF A long leaf of the screwpine pandanus, a tropical plant that grows in southeast Asia, with a sweet, unique flavor that is used to enhance the aroma and flavor of desserts and, occasionally, savory dishes. Also known as screwpine leaf, pandanus leaf, rampe leaf, kewra, bai toey, or bai touy.

PERSIMMON An edible fruit resembling a large tomato with a sweet flesh. The Fuyu persimmon is slightly tart and is best eaten when firm and crisp, like an apple. The acorn-shaped Hachiya persimmon has a softer, sweeter pulp when fully ripened.

PLUM SAUCE A light brown, sweet-and-sour condiment made from sweet plums or other fruit such as peach or apricot, along with sugar, vinegar, ginger, and chilies; also known as duck sauce.

POMEGRANATE An apple-sized fruit with a leathery reddish outer skin and sweet red gelatinous flesh containing many edible seeds; also known as Chinese apple.

RED DATE A small red, plumlike fruit whose skin becomes crinkly when dried; also known as jujube or Chinese date.

RICE NOODLES Flat (stir-fry or linguine-style) or thin (rice vermicelli) long Asian noodles made from rice flour and water used in soups, spring rolls, cold salads, and stir-fries. Generally sold dried in bundle form, they can be located in most major supermarkets in the international aisle among the Asian foods.

RICE PAPER WRAPPER (*see* Spring Roll Wrapper) Typically, a very thin, semi-transparent large round wrapper made from a mixture of rice flour and water, generally sold in dried form that requires soaking to soften, used to make spring rolls or summer rolls. Also known as rice paper, spring roll skin, or spring roll wrapper.

Occasionally, very thin, soft rice-flour wrappers, which require no soaking, are used to make a vegetable roll known as si wa wa, or silk dolls.

RICE VINEGAR Milder and less acidic than regular vinegar, there are three basic types of Chinese rice vinegar—black, red, and white. Black rice vinegar is an aged product made from rice, wheat, millet, and/or sorghum with an inky black color and a complex, malty flavor similar to balsamic vinegar; Zhenjiang is the most popular variety (for a gluten-free option, substitute with balsamic vinegar). Red vinegar has a sweet-and-sour taste, and white vinegar is the closest in acidity and flavor to regular vinegar. Also known as rice wine vinegar.

RICE WINE A rich-flavored liquid made from fermented glutinous rice that typically contains wheat, millet, or yeast. Shaoxing rice wine, an amber-colored, aromatic, and pleasantly nutty-tasting variety, similar to dry sherry, is the most famous. Also known as yellow wine.

SEITAN A chewy, protein-rich meat substitute made from either whole wheat flour or vital wheat gluten; also known as wheat gluten, wheat meat, or gluten.

SICHUAN PEPPERCORN A mildly hot spice from the prickly ash tree that is not related to the peppercorn, Sichuan berries resemble black peppercorns but contain a tiny seed. They have a fragrant aroma and distinctive flavor, and produce a numbing sensation around the mouth. Also known as Szechuan peppercorn, Sichuan/Szechuan pepper, anise pepper, Chinese pepper, or flower pepper.

SNOW FUNGUS A yellowish-white mushroom that is almost transparent, with a crispy, jellylike texture similar to black fungus; it is most commonly used in dessert recipes. Also known as white fungus, white tree ear fungus, white wood ear, silver fungus, silver ear, or snow ear.

SNOW PEAS A member of the legume family, the snow pea is a sweet, crisp variety of pea eaten whole in its pod while still unripe. Also known as Chinese sugar peas or mangetout.

SOYBEAN Cultivated for thousands of years in China, the soybean is considered one of the five sacred grains along with rice, wheat, barley, and millet. Soybean pods range from tan to black; the bean itself can be green, brown, yellow, red, brown, or black; is bland in taste; and is high in protein and nutrition. The beans are used to make a variety of products, including tofu and soy sauce. Also known as soya bean, soy pea, soja, or soi.

SOYBEAN PASTE A salty, fermented paste made from ground soybeans. There are a number of varieties, including brown bean paste, yellow bean paste, and soybean condiment. Also known as soybean sauce, brown bean sauce, or yellow bean sauce.

SOY SAUCE Made from fermented soybeans, wheat flour, water, and salt, there are two main types of soy sauce—light and dark. Light soy sauce is lighter in color, thinner, and saltier and adds a distinct flavor to dishes; it is the main soy sauce used for seasoning. Aged for a longer period, dark soy sauce is thicker, blacker, and sweeter due to the addition of molasses, and is less salty; it is used in recipes to add color and flavor. Another type, thick soy sauce, is a dark soy sauce that has been thickened with starch and sugar or additional molasses; it is often used as a dipping sauce or poured on food after cooking for additional flavor. Also known as soya sauce.

SPRING ROLL WRAPPER (*see* Rice Paper Wrapper) Though the labels *rice paper wrapper* and *spring roll wrapper* are often used interchangeably, a spring roll wrapper in China is typically made from a mixture of wheat flour and water; in this instance, it is sold in soft form, similar to a wonton wrapper, and requires no soaking.

STAR ANISE A star-shaped, dark brown rust-colored spice with a strong licorice taste; also known as Chinese anise.

STRAW MUSHROOM A long, grayish-brown mushroom with a conical cap over a bulbous stem with a mild flavor, it is cultivated on straw that has been used on a rice paddy; also known as paddy-straw mushrooms or grass mushrooms.

TAPIOCA A starch extracted from the root of the cassava, tapioca comes in several forms, including granules and flour, as well as pellets that are called tapioca pearls. In Chinese cooking, the pearls are used in puddings and bubble tea, while the flour is often used to thicken sauces and soups. Also known as cassava or yucca.

TARO A potatolike root vegetable with a white or pale pink and sometimes purple-tinged flesh; peel with a vegetable peeler under running water to avoid any skin sensitivity to its sticky juices. Toxic in its raw state, taro contains calcium oxalate crystals, so the root (as well as the leaves) must always be boiled to remove the crystals before other preparation. Also known as Chinese taro, elephant ear, Buddha's hand, or kalo.

TOASTED SESAME OIL An Asian variety of sesame oil made from roasted/toasted sesame seeds, with a dark color and an intense, nutty flavor and aroma. Valued as a condiment, it is used sparingly in cooking. Toasted, or dark, sesame oil can be found in the international aisle or condiment and salad dressing section of many large supermarkets. For best results, select those brands consisting only of pure 100 percent sesame oil. Also known as dark sesame oil.

TOFU A bean curd made from soybeans, tofu is high in protein and a popular meat substitute. Although bland in flavor, tofu absorbs other flavors well and is used in both savory and sweet Chinese dishes. There are two types of tofu—regular and silken. Regular tofu comes in a variety of textures, from soft to extra-firm. Silken tofu has a creamy, custard-like texture, and also comes in varying degrees of firmness. Also known as Doufu, Do Fu, soybean curd, or bean curd.

VEGETARIAN OYSTER SAUCE A dark brown condiment made from soy sauce, mushroom extract (often from oyster or shiitake mushrooms), sugar, salt, and usually glucose syrup.

WATER CHESTNUT An aquatic vegetable resembling a chestnut that grows in marshes, the water chestnut has a sweet flavor and crisp texture. Also known as Chinese water chestnut or water caltrop.

WINTER MELON Resembling a large watermelon with dark green, waxy skin, the winter melon has a very mild, sweet taste, and is used in savory dishes such as soups and stir-fries. Also known as Dong Gua, Dong Gwa, or wax gourd.

WONTON WRAPPER A paper-thin square piece of dough primarily made of wheat flour and water (sometimes containing eggs) that is used to make wontons; also known as wonton skin.

WOOD EAR MUSHROOM Similar to cloud ear mushrooms (*see* Black Fungus), wood ears have a firm, thick skin and a jellylike, springy texture when fresh that becomes slightly crunchy when cooked. Also known as tree ear, silver ear, or mook yee.

About the Nutritional Numbers

All of the nutritional analyses in this book were compiled using MasterCook Deluxe 4.06 Software, from SierraHome. As certain ingredients (celtuce, fern root noodles) were unknown to the software at the time of compilation, however, substitutes of equivalent caloric and nutritional value were used in their place. All of the recipes using broth have been analyzed using low-sodium canned vegetable broth. All of the recipes using rinsed and drained canned beans have been analyzed using freshly cooked dried beans. Unless salt is listed as a measured ingredient (versus to taste, with no preceding suggested measurement) in the recipe, or unless otherwise indicated, no salt has been included in the analysis; this applies to other seasonings (black pepper, cayenne, etc.) as well. None of the recipes' optional ingredients, unless otherwise indicated, have been included in the nutritional analyses. If there is a choice of two or more ingredients in a recipe (for example, chopped peanuts or slivered almonds), the first ingredient has been used in the analysis. Likewise, if there is a choice in the amounts of a particular ingredient in a recipe (for example, 2 to 3 tablespoons reduced-sodium soy sauce, plus additional, to serve), the first amount has been used in the analysis. If there is a range in the number of servings a recipe yields (for example, 4 to 6 servings), the analysis has been based on the first amount.

The Chinese Vegan Kitchen

CHAPTER ONE

Appetizers and Snacks

Delicate dumplings, crispy spring rolls, chewy pot stickers, fluffy buns, crunchy wontons, tender pancakes—what's not to love about Chinese appetizers? Not surprisingly, the literal meaning of dim sum, China's beloved assortment of small eats and snacks, translated from the Cantonese, is "to dot, or touch, the heart." While dim sum is traditionally served any time between morning and mid-afternoon, these tasty morsels can hit that spot on our hearts anytime and make great dinner party starters and hors d'oeuvres for company. In addition to the customary dumplings and spring rolls, treat your guests to the unexpected delights of Hunan-Style "Smacked" Cucumbers, Pickled Daikon Radish, Sichuan-Style Marinated Green Bell Peppers, Five-Spice Peanuts, or Baked Tofu Nuggets. Your guests will depart with very happy hearts!

Preserved Apple Rings, Shandong-Style

The Chinese adore apples—the best are said to come from Shandong, famous for its superb apple orchards. While there is nothing better than a fresh apple eaten out of hand, sometimes the next best thing is a preserved apple eaten out of the oven. In fact, a recent study indicated that women who ate dried apples every day for 12 months lowered their total cholesterol by 14 percent and their levels of "bad" LDL cholesterol by 23 percent—not bad for a year's worth of delicious work. This totally good-for-you recipe draws its inspiration from my student whose Chinese name in part— the "果"—creates the Mandarin character for apple, 苹果. This one is for you, Victor, the apple of my eye—really!

MAKES 4 TO 6 SERVINGS

> 2 large apples (Fuji, Gala, Honeycrisp, or
>   other sweet-crisp variety), about
>   8 ounces each, peeled, if desired, left
>   whole, and cored

Preheat oven to 150F (65C). Set a cake rack on a large baking sheet. Alternatively, line a large baking sheet with parchment paper.

Slice each apple into rings about ⅛ inch in thickness. Arrange slices in a single layer on the cake rack or parchment. Bake 8 to 10 hours in the center of the oven, turning over halfway through cooking time if using parchment (turning is not necessary with a cake rack), or until apple slices are leathery and flexible, but not brittle. Let cool completely before placing in a resealable plastic bag and storing at room temperature for several weeks. Alternatively, store in the refrigerator or freezer for several months.

{PER SERVING} Calories 62 · Protein 0g · Total Fat 0g · Sat Fat 0g · Cholesterol 0mg · Carbohydrate 16g · Dietary Fiber 3g · Sodium 0mg

Pickled Chilies

Serve these tangy hot chilies as part of a relish tray, tossed with salads, vegetables, noodles, or rice, or stirred into soups. For a milder taste, omit the seeds.

MAKES ABOUT 1 CUP

> 1 cup distilled white vinegar
> 8 small green and/or red chilies, thinly
>   sliced
> 1 tablespoon sugar (optional)
> ½ teaspoon salt

In a small saucepan, bring ½ cup of the vinegar to a boil over medium heat; add the chilies and boil 15 seconds, stirring a few times. Drain and discard the vinegar. Let cool to room temperature. Transfer to a clean glass jar with a lid and add the remaining ½ cup of vinegar, sugar (if using), and salt; cover tightly and shake until the sugar and salt are dissolved. Refrigerate a minimum of 24 hours, or up to several weeks before serving chilled or at room temperature.

{PER SERVING} (about 2 tablespoons, or ⅛ of recipe) Calories 20 · Protein 1g · Total Fat 0g · Sat Fat 0g · Cholesterol 0mg · Carbohydrate 5g · Dietary Fiber 1g · Sodium 137mg

Steamed Buns with Cabbage, Shallots, and Ginger

Based on a family recipe submitted by Alba, one of my most ambitious students at the Yali Middle School in Changsha, these steamed buns take time and practice to make, but the results are worth it. Feel free to experiment with your favorite fillings, or see the variations, below.

MAKES 24 BUNS

1 package (about 1 tablespoon) active dry yeast
1 cup warm water (105–115F; 40–45C)
4½ cups all-purpose flour
¼ cup plus 2 teaspoons sugar
2 tablespoons canola oil
½ cup boiling water
2 tablespoons peanut oil
1 cup chopped shallots or red onion, chopped
4 large cloves garlic, finely chopped
1 tablespoon finely chopped fresh ginger
4 cups shredded cabbage
4 scallions, white and green parts separated, thinly sliced
6 tablespoons reduced-sodium soy sauce
2 tablespoons Shaoxing rice wine, sake, dry sherry, or dry white wine
2 tablespoons cornstarch blended with ½ cup water
2 teaspoons toasted (dark) sesame oil
Freshly ground black pepper, to taste
Basic Dipping Sauce (page 9) (optional)

In a large bowl, dissolve yeast in the warm water. Add 1 cup of flour and mix thoroughly with a whisk. Cover with a damp kitchen towel and let rise 1 hour, or until bubbles appear.

In a small heat-proof bowl, place ¼ cup sugar and canola oil; add the boiling water, stirring until the sugar is dissolved. Let cool until lukewarm. Add to yeast mixture and mix well. Add remaining 3½ cups flour, mixing until dough holds together. Place dough on a lightly floured work surface and knead until smooth and elastic, 8 to 10 minutes. Place dough in an extra-large, lightly oiled clean bowl; cover with a damp kitchen towel and leave to rise in a warm place until doubled in bulk, 1½ to 2 hours.

Meanwhile, in a wok or large nonstick skillet, heat the peanut oil over medium-high heat. Add the shallots, garlic, and ginger; cook, stirring, until fragrant and softened, about 1 minute. Add the cabbage and white parts of the scallions; cook, stirring, until cabbage is wilted, about 2 minutes. Add the soy sauce, wine, and remaining 2 teaspoons sugar and stir well to combine. Reduce the heat to medium and add the cornstarch mixture; cook, stirring, until thickened and bubbly, 1 to 2 minutes. Add the scallion greens, sesame oil, and pepper and stir well to combine. Remove from heat and let cool to room temperature.

Turn dough out onto a lightly floured work surface and divide into 2 portions. Knead each portion for 2 minutes. Roll each portion into a cylinder about 12 inches long. Cut each cylinder into 12 pieces for a total of 24 pieces. Flatten each piece with your palm and, using a rolling pin, roll into a round, about 3½ inches in diameter. Using your fingers, press outside edge of each round to make it slightly thinner than the rest of the dough, like a "flying saucer." Place 1½ to 2 tablespoons of the filling in the center of each round. Pull edges of dough up and around filling and twist to seal.

Place each bun, twisted side down, on a 2-inch square of aluminum foil and place on a large baking sheet. Cover with a damp kitchen towel and let rise in a warm place until puffy and dough springs back when lightly touched with a finger, 30 minutes to 1 hour. Remove towel.

Place a steaming basket in a medium stockpot set over about 1½ inches of water. Working in batches, place the risen buns in a single layer about 1 inch apart in the steaming basket, avoiding the edges; bring water to a boil over medium heat. Cover tightly and steam 10 to 12 minutes, or until cooked through. Remove from heat and let stand, covered, 5 minutes. Uncover and serve at once, with the dipping sauce, if using. (Completely cooled buns can be stored in resealable plastic freezer bags and frozen up to 3 months before thawing and re-steaming a few minutes.)

{PER SERVING} (per bun, without dipping sauce) Calories 135 · Protein 3g · Total Fat 3g · Sat Fat 0g · Cholesterol 0mg · Carbohydrate 24g · Dietary Fiber 1g · Sodium 154mg

{VARIATIONS}

For plain buns, omit the filling and brush the inside of each round lightly with some toasted (dark) sesame oil. Fold each round in half to make a half moon. Press edges together with the tines of a fork to tightly seal. Place on a 3½-inch square of aluminum foil and proceed as otherwise directed in the recipe.

For scallion buns, omit the filling and brush the insides of each round lightly with some toasted (dark) sesame oil and sprinkle with chopped scallion greens. Fold each round in half to make a half moon. Press edges together with the tines of a fork to tightly seal. Place on a 3½-inch square of aluminum foil and proceed as otherwise directed in the recipe.

Hunan-Style Spicy Pickled Chinese Cabbage

This is wonderful tossed with rice or noodles, or spooned over grilled eggplant or veggie burgers. For a milder taste, omit the seeds from the chili peppers.

MAKES 8 SERVINGS

> ½ pound Napa cabbage leaves, washed, dried, cut into about 2½-by-¾-inch pieces
> 1 tablespoon salt
> ¼ cup sugar
> ¼ cup plain rice vinegar
> 3 small fresh red chili peppers, seeded, if desired, and finely chopped
> ½ tablespoon finely chopped fresh ginger
> 1 tablespoon canola oil, heated until very warm

In a medium bowl, toss together the cabbage and salt until well combined. Let stand, uncovered, 1 hour. Drain well in a colander, pressing down with the back of a large wooden spoon.

Meanwhile, in another medium bowl, combine the sugar and vinegar. Add the drained cabbage, chili peppers, and ginger, tossing well to thoroughly combine. Transfer to a clean glass jar and add the warm oil, swirling the jar to combine. Let stand 10 minutes, or until completely cooled. Cover tightly and refrigerate a minimum of 2 days, or up to several weeks. Serve chilled or at room temperature.

{PER SERVING} Calories 70 · Protein 2g · Total Fat 2g · Sat Fat 0g · Cholesterol 0mg · Carbohydrate 14g · Dietary Fiber 2g · Sodium 809mg

Pickled Daikon Radish

This crunchy side dish or relish is perfect for a buffet, as it holds up well at room temperature. If you are watching your sodium, note that most of the salt is rinsed off.

MAKES 4 SERVINGS

3 cups chopped daikon radish (about
    1 pound)
½ tablespoon salt
2 tablespoons plain rice vinegar
½ teaspoon toasted (dark) sesame oil
Freshly ground black pepper, to taste

In a medium mixing bowl, toss the radish with the salt. Cover and refrigerate 30 minutes, or until 2 to 4 tablespoons of water are released. Transfer to a colander and rinse under cold running water. Drain well and pat dry with paper towels.

Place the vinegar and oil in the mixing bowl and stir until thoroughly blended. Add the radish and pepper; toss well to combine. Cover and refrigerate a minimum of 8 hours, stirring a few times, or up to 5 days. Serve chilled or return to room temperature.

{PER SERVING} (based on ½ teaspoon total salt in recipe) Calories 22 · Protein 1g · Total Fat 1g · Sat Fat 0g · Cholesterol 0mg · Carbohydrate 4 · Dietary Fiber 1 · Sodium 285mg

Chinese Corn Flour Flatbread

This northern-style flatbread is delicious served with Rice Congee with Shiitake Mushrooms and Peas (page 41) for a rib-sticking meal. Not to be confused with cornstarch, corn flour is finely ground cornmeal—in a pinch, coarse-ground yellow cornmeal can be further ground in a spice grinder or food processor fitted with the knife blade.

MAKES 3 (5-INCH) FLATBREADS; 6 SERVINGS

1½ cups corn flour
½ cup all-purpose flour
1 teaspoon active dry yeast
½ teaspoon salt
1¼ cups warm water (105–115F; 40–45C)
Flour, for dusting
1 tablespoon peanut oil

In a large bowl, combine the dry ingredients. Add the water, mixing with a wooden spoon and then kneading with your hands to combine. Turn mixture out onto a floured work surface and continue kneading until soft and smooth, 5 to 10 minutes. Place in a lightly oiled clean bowl, cover with a damp kitchen towel, and place in a warm place to double in bulk, 1 to 1½ hours.

Punch down the dough and divide into 3 equal portions. Roll each portion into a 5-inch round about ½ inch in thickness.

In a 12-inch nonstick skillet, heat the oil over medium heat, swirling to evenly coat. Add the bread rounds and cook until golden and cooked through, about 5 minutes per side. Serve warm or at room temperature.

{PER SERVING} (per ⅙ of recipe) Calories 155 · Protein 3g · Total Fat 2g · Sat Fat 0g · Cholesterol 0mg · Carbohydrate 31g · Dietary Fiber 4g · Sodium 180mg

Hunan-Style Spicy Pickled Carrots

The heat of this simple pickling recipe can be increased by including the seeds of the chili peppers.

MAKES 6 SERVINGS

¾ pound baby carrots
1 to 2 fresh red chili peppers, seeded and thinly sliced
1 cup plain distilled white vinegar
½ cup water
½ cup sugar
¼ teaspoon salt

In a medium stockpot, cook the carrots in boiling water to cover for 10 minutes, adding the peppers during the last 2 minutes of cooking; drain in a colander. Rinse under cold running water until cooled; drain again.

Meanwhile, in a small saucepan, bring the vinegar, water, sugar, and salt to a brisk simmer over medium heat, stirring until the sugar is dissolved. Remove from heat and set aside to cool.

Place drained carrots and peppers in a 26- to 32-ounce clean glass jar. Add the vinegar mixture, seal tightly, and refrigerate a minimum of 2 days, or up to several weeks. Serve chilled or at room temperature.

{PER SERVING} Calories 96 · Protein 1g · Total Fat 0g · Sat Fat 0g · Cholesterol 0mg · Carbohydrate 25g · Dietary Fiber 2g · Sodium 108mg

Cilantro and Hot Pepper Salad

Known as "tiger salad" in China, this highly popular and fiery appetizer is not for the fainthearted. Omit the hot oil for a milder variation.

MAKES 4 TO 6 SERVINGS

2 tablespoons reduced-sodium soy sauce, or more, to taste
2 large cloves garlic, finely chopped
½ tablespoon plain rice vinegar
½ tablespoon toasted (dark) sesame oil
1 teaspoon Chinese hot oil, or to taste
¼ teaspoon salt, or to taste
Freshly ground black pepper, to taste
2 large bunches fresh cilantro, trimmed, cut into 2-inch lengths
2 medium green and/or red bell peppers (about 6 ounces each), cut into thin 2-inch lengths
4 scallions, white and green parts, cut into thin 2-inch lengths
1 to 2 fresh red or green chili peppers, seeded, cut into very thin 2-inch lengths

In a large bowl, whisk together the soy sauce, garlic, vinegar, sesame oil, hot oil, salt, and black pepper. Add the remaining ingredients, tossing well to combine. Serve at once.

{PER SERVING} Calories 69 · Protein 3g · Total Fat 3g · Sat Fat 0g · Cholesterol 0mg · Carbohydrate 9g · Dietary Fiber 3g · Sodium 446mg

Pot Stickers with Cabbage and Shiitake Mushrooms

Pot stickers are dumplings that are typically pan-fried on one side and steamed on the other. Pre-cooking the filling lends these delectable little pouches a rich, slightly sweet flavor. The completely cooled filling can be stored, covered, in the refrigerator up to 1 day before assembling the pot stickers. The assembled pot stickers can be covered securely and refrigerated up to 1 day before cooking. They can also be stored in the freezer in a resealable plastic freezer bag up to 1 month; in this instance, prepare as per the boiled variations, below.

MAKES 48 POT STICKERS; SERVES 8 TO 12

3 tablespoons canola oil

1 cup chopped shallots or red onion

1 tablespoon finely chopped fresh ginger

1 cup coarsely chopped stemmed fresh shiitake, oyster, cremini, or fresh cultivated white mushrooms

2 cups coleslaw mix

1 cup chopped scallions, green parts only

Salt and freshly ground black pepper, to taste

¼ cup chopped cilantro or flat-leaf parsley

1 teaspoon toasted (dark) sesame oil

1⅓ cups water

½ teaspoon cornstarch

48 egg-free dumpling wrappers or gyoza skins (about 10 ounces) (see Cook's Tip, below)

Basic Dipping Sauce, below

In a 12-inch nonstick skillet with a lid, heat ½ tablespoon of the canola oil over medium-high heat. Add the shallots and ginger and cook, stirring, until softened, about 2 minutes. Add the mushrooms and cook, stirring, until softened and just beginning to release their liquid, 2 to 3 minutes. Add the coleslaw mix, scallion greens, salt, and pepper; cook, stirring, until cabbage in coleslaw mix is softened and beginning to wilt, 2 to 3 minutes. Remove from heat and add the parsley and sesame oil, tossing well to thoroughly combine. Let cool about 15 minutes, stirring a few times.

Meanwhile, in a small bowl, combine ⅓ cup water and the cornstarch until thoroughly blended. Set aside.

Lay a wrapper on a flat work surface and place 1 heaping teaspoon of the vegetable mixture in the center. Dip your finger in the cornstarch water and wet the edges of the wrapper (this will help the pot stickers seal when cooking). Fold the wrapper over the filling and pinch the edges to seal, forming a pouch. Press lightly to form a flat bottom.

Wipe out the skillet and heat 1½ tablespoons of the remaining oil over medium-high heat for 1 minute. Swirl to evenly coat the bottom of the skillet, and carefully add half the pot stickers in a single layer, flat sides down (touching one another is okay). Cook without turning until lightly browned on the undersides, about 2 minutes, shaking the skillet a few times to prevent sticking. Add ½ cup of the remaining water, cover, and reduce heat to medium; continue cooking without turning until tops of pot stickers are tender and filling is heated through, 2 to 3 minutes. Uncover, return heat to medium-high, and continue cooking without turning until the bottoms are golden brown and the water has evaporated, 1 to 2 more minutes, shaking the skillet a few times. Transfer to a warmed serving platter (lined with paper towels, if desired) and keep warm.

Add the remaining 1 tablespoon of oil to the skillet (do not wipe out the skillet) and heat about

30 seconds. Swirl to evenly coat the bottom of the skillet; repeat the cooking process with the remaining pot stickers and ½ cup water. Serve hot, with the dipping sauce passed separately.

{PER SERVING} (per pot sticker, without sauce) Calories 36 · Protein 1g · Total Fat 1g · Sat Fat 0g · Cholesterol 0mg · Carbohydrate 6g · Dietary Fiber 0g · Sodium 47mg

BASIC DIPPING SAUCE

For a spicier sauce, add a few drops of Chinese hot oil or pinches of cayenne red pepper, to taste.

MAKES ABOUT ¾ CUP

½ cup reduced-sodium soy sauce

¼ cup plain rice vinegar

1 tablespoon thinly sliced scallion greens (optional)

½ tablespoon finely chopped fresh ginger (optional)

In a small bowl, stir together all ingredients. If using optional ingredients, let stand about 15 minutes at room temperature to allow the flavors to blend. Stir again and use at room temperature. Sauce can be stored, covered, in refrigerator up to 1 day before returning to room temperature and using in the recipe.

{PER SERVING} (per tablespoon) Calories 7 · Protein 1g · Total Fat 0g · Sat Fat 0g · Cholesterol 0mg · Carbohydrate 1g · Dietary Fiber 0g · Sodium 400mg

{COOK'S TIP}

Dumpling wrappers or gyoza skins are available in Asian markets and some well-stocked supermarkets, next to the wonton wrappers. Unlike wonton wrappers, they are round rather than square, and tend to be thicker. A 10-ounce package typically contains about 50 wrappers, approximately 3¼ inches in diameter. Check the label carefully, as the yellow wrappers usually contain egg, while the white ones are usually egg-free.

{VARIATIONS}

To make Boiled Pot Stickers with Cabbage and Mushrooms, bring a large pot of water to a boil over medium-high heat. Add half the pot stickers (freshly assembled or frozen), giving them a gentle stir so they don't stick together. When the water returns to a boil, add ½ cup of cold water. Cover and return to a boil; uncover and add a second ½ cup of cold water. Cover and return to a boil; uncover and add an additional ½ cup of cold water. Cover and return to a boil; uncover and remove the pot from heat. Using a slotted spoon, transfer the pot stickers to a colander to further drain. Repeat the cooking process with the remaining pot stickers. Serve as directed in the above recipe (do not line the serving platter with paper towel), with the dipping sauce.

If desired, the boiled dumplings can also be lightly pan-fried like traditional pot stickers. Working in two separate batches, using a 12-inch nonstick skillet, cook each batch of boiled pot stickers on their flat sides (without turning) in about 1 tablespoon of oil over medium-high heat until nicely browned, 3 to 5 minutes. Serve as directed in the main recipe, with the dipping sauce.

To make Toasted Pot Stickers with Cabbage and Mushrooms, preheat the oven to broil. Boil and drain the pot stickers as directed in the first variation, above. Arrange the drained pot stickers, flat sides down, in a single layer on a large, lightly oiled baking sheet. Brush the tops evenly with about 1 tablespoon of canola oil mixed with 1 teaspoon of toasted (dark) sesame oil. Broil 6 to 8 inches from heat source until tops are lightly browned, 3 to 5 minutes, turning the baking sheet a few times to promote even browning. Serve as directed in the main recipe, with the dipping sauce.

Hunan-Style "Smacked" Cucumbers

This is a popular appetizer throughout Hunan Province, nicknamed after the method of striking the cucumbers with the flat side of a chef's knife to allow maximum absorption of the flavorful dressing. A wooden mallet or tenderizer can be used in lieu of the knife, if desired.

MAKES 4 SERVINGS

1 large cucumber (about 12 ounces)
Salt (about ½ teaspoon), plus additional,
   to taste
2 tablespoons plain rice vinegar
2 cloves garlic, finely chopped
1 teaspoon toasted (dark) sesame oil
1 teaspoon sugar
1 teaspoon Chinese hot oil, or to taste
Freshly ground black pepper, to taste

Place cucumber on a cutting board and position the flat side of a chef's knife over top. Using your palm, strike the knife until the cucumber splinters open with jagged cracks. (Alternatively, the flat side of a wooden mallet or tenderizer can be used.) Coarsely chop into bite-size pieces. Transfer to a colander set over a plate and sprinkle lightly with salt. Set aside for 30 minutes to drain; blot dry with paper towels.

Meanwhile, in a medium bowl, stir together the vinegar, garlic, sesame oil, sugar, hot oil, and pepper. Let stand 5 minutes to allow the flavors to blend. Stir again and add the cucumber, tossing well to combine and adding salt, if necessary. Let stand 10 minutes to allow the flavors to blend, tossing a few times. Serve at room temperature. Alternatively, cover and refrigerate up to 2 days, tossing a few times, and serve chilled.

{PER SERVING} (based on ½ teaspoon total salt in recipe) Calories 38 · Protein 1g · Total Fat 2g · Sat Fat 0g · Cholesterol 0mg · Carbohydrate 4g · Dietary Fiber 1g · Sodium 268mg

Tibetan Potato-Cabbage Momos

Tibetan food is heavily influenced by the cuisines of Nepal and India, as evidenced by the Tibetan people's fondness for momos, a type of dumpling or stuffed bun. The comforting potato and cabbage filling makes a tasty side dish on its own.

MAKES 10 BUNS

1½ cups all-purpose flour
¼ cup wheat germ
1 tablespoon sugar
½ teaspoon quick-rise yeast
½ cup plus 2 tablespoons (10 tablespoons)
   warmed soy milk (105–115F; 40–45C)
½ pound boiling potatoes, peeled and cut
   into bite-size chunks
½ tablespoon toasted (dark) sesame oil
¼ teaspoon paprika
¼ teaspoon salt
Freshly ground black pepper, to taste
½ tablespoon canola oil
1 cup chopped onion
1 cup shredded Napa or green cabbage
¼ cup finely chopped cilantro
Cilantro-Tomato Dipping Sauce, below

In a large bowl, combine flour, wheat germ, sugar, and yeast. Add the soy milk, mixing with a wooden spoon and then kneading with hands until combined. Turn mixture out onto a floured work surface and continue kneading until soft and smooth, 5 to 10 minutes. Place in a lightly oiled clean bowl, cover with a damp kitchen towel, and place in a warm place to double in bulk, about 1½ hours.

Meanwhile, in a medium saucepan, bring the potatoes and enough salted water to cover to a boil over high heat; reduce the heat slightly and cook, uncovered, until potatoes are tender, about 15 minutes. Drain well and transfer to a medium bowl. Add the sesame oil, paprika, salt, and black pepper and mash well. Set aside.

In a small nonstick skillet, heat the canola oil over medium heat. Add the onion and cook, stirring, until softened, about 2 minutes. Add the cabbage and cook, stirring, until mixture is golden, about 5 minutes. Remove from heat and let cool a few minutes. Add the cooled cabbage mixture and cilantro to the potato mixture; mix well to combine.

On a lightly floured work surface, knead the risen dough 2 minutes and form into a long cylinder. Cut the dough in half. Cut each half into 5 equal disks, for a total of 10 disks. Flatten each disk with your palm and, using a rolling pin, roll each disk to make a circle 3½ to 4 inches in diameter. Place about 2 tablespoons of the filling into the center of each circle and pull up the edges, twisting to seal. Place each momo, twisted side down, on a 2-inch square of foil, wax paper, or parchment and place on a cookie sheet. Cover with a damp kitchen towel and let rise in a warm place until puffy and light, 30 to 60 minutes.

Place a steaming basket in a medium stockpot set over about 1½ inches of water. Working in batches, as needed, place the risen buns in a single layer about 1 inch apart in the steaming basket, avoiding the edges; bring to boil over medium heat. Cover and steam until the dough is cooked through, 10 to 12 minutes. Remove from heat and let stand, covered, 5 minutes. Uncover and serve at once, accompanied by the Cilantro-Tomato Dipping Sauce. (Completely cooled buns can be stored in resealable plastic freezer bags and frozen up to 3 months before thawing and resteaming a few minutes.)

{PER SERVING} (per bun, without sauce) Calories 123 · Protein 4g · Total Fat 2g · Sat Fat 0g · Cholesterol 0mg · Carbohydrate 22g · Dietary Fiber 2g · Sodium 59mg

CILANTRO-TOMATO DIPPING SAUCE

For a milder sauce, use half the amount of chili paste or omit entirely, if desired.

MAKES ABOUT 1¼ CUPS

  1 cup tomato puree, preferably fire-roasted
  1 cup fresh cilantro leaves
  ½ tablespoon reduced-sodium soy sauce, or to taste
  ½ tablespoon toasted (dark) sesame oil, or to taste
  1 to 2 large cloves garlic, finely chopped
  1 teaspoon Chinese chili paste, or to taste
  ¼ teaspoon salt, or to taste

In a food processor fitted with the knife blade, or in a blender, process all ingredients until thoroughly blended. Serve at room temperature. Alternatively, heat over low heat and serve slightly warm. Sauce can be refrigerated, covered, up to 4 days before returning to room temperature or heating over low heat and serving.

{PER SERVING} (per 1/5 recipe, or about ¼ cup) Calories 35 · Protein 1g · Total Fat 2g · Sat Fat 0g · Cholesterol 0mg · Carbohydrate 5g · Dietary Fiber 1g · Sodium 367mg

Baked Vegetable Eggless Egg Rolls

While egg rolls are standard fare in Chinese restaurants and markets across America, Western-style egg rolls are actually a variant of fried spring rolls in mainland China, where "egg rolls" typically refer to egg-based, flute-shaped pastry eaten as a snack or dessert. In any case, the following baked vegan egg rolls are perfect for stress-free entertaining, as the filling can be made up to 24 hours ahead of assembling the rolls and baking. Feel free to experiment with your own favorite fillings—you will need about 2 cups of cooked filling for 14 egg rolls. Egg-free egg roll wrappers can be found at most Asian markets in the frozen section next to the regular egg roll wrappers—try to use the 7-inch size; otherwise, adjust the filling amount accordingly.

MAKES 14 EGG ROLLS

1 tablespoon peanut oil

2 cloves garlic, finely chopped

2 cups shredded Napa or green cabbage

2 cups shredded carrots

2 cups mung bean sprouts

½ cup finely chopped rinsed and drained canned water chestnuts (about 3 ounces)

½ tablespoon finely chopped fresh ginger

2 scallions, white and green parts, thinly sliced

2 tablespoons finely chopped fresh cilantro (optional)

1 tablespoon cornstarch mixed with ¼ cup water

2 tablespoons reduced-sodium soy sauce

½ teaspoon Chinese chili paste, or to taste (optional)

Salt and freshly ground black pepper, to taste

14 (7-inch) egg-free egg roll wrappers

1 tablespoon cornstarch mixed with 1 tablespoon water

2 teaspoons toasted (dark) sesame oil

Duck sauce, sweet chili sauce, or other dipping sauce

In a large nonstick skillet, heat the peanut oil over medium heat. Add the garlic and cook, stirring constantly, 1 minute. Add the cabbage, carrots, sprouts, water chestnuts, and ginger and cook, stirring often, until vegetables are largely reduced in volume, 4 to 5 minutes. Add the scallions, cilantro (if using), cornstarch mixture, soy sauce, chili paste (if using), salt, and pepper; cook, stirring constantly, until sauce thickens, 1 to 2 minutes. Remove from heat and let cool about 30 minutes (at this point, completely cooled mixture can be refrigerated, covered, up to 24 hours before continuing with the recipe).

Preheat the oven to 375F (190C). Lightly oil a baking sheet.

Lay an egg roll wrapper in front of you so that it forms a diamond shape. Using your finger, wet all the edges with the cornstarch mixture. Place about 2 tablespoons of filling near the bottom. Fold the lower corner edge up to cover the filling. Fold in the sides, and roll up tightly, burrito-style. Seal the top with the cornstarch mixture. Cover with a damp kitchen towel or plastic wrap to prevent drying out. Repeat with remaining wrappers and filling.

Place the egg rolls, seam side down, on the prepared baking sheet. Brush the tops evenly with half of the sesame oil. Bake in the center of the oven until tops are browned, 10 to 12 minutes. Turn over and brush with remaining 1 teaspoon sesame oil.

Bake an additional 7 to 10 minutes, or until crisp and golden. Serve at once, with the dipping sauce passed separately. Alternatively, egg rolls may be kept warm in a preheated 200F (95C) oven for up to 1 hour. (Completely cooled egg rolls can be placed in resealable plastic freezer bags and frozen up to 3 months before reheating in a moderate oven for 10 to 15 minutes.)

{PER SERVING} (per roll, without sauce) Calories 59 · Protein 2g · Total Fat 2g · Sat Fat 0g · Cholesterol 0mg · Carbohydrate 9g · Dietary Fiber 1g · Sodium 140mg

Hunan-Style Marinated Wood Ear Mushrooms with Chili Pepper

This popular appetizer is also delicious tossed with hot cooked rice. Wood ear mushrooms have a unique jellylike texture that becomes slightly crunchy when cooked; cloud ear mushrooms, or black fungus, are interchangeable. For a milder version, omit the Chinese hot oil and seed the chilies.

MAKES 4 TO 6 SERVINGS

2½ ounces dried shredded wood ear mushrooms, soaked in hot water to cover 20 minutes, or until softened, drained and rinsed

1 tablespoon plain rice vinegar

1 tablespoon reduced-sodium soy sauce

½ tablespoon toasted (dark) sesame oil

½ to 1 teaspoon Chinese hot oil

1 teaspoon finely chopped fresh ginger

1 teaspoon sugar

2 cloves garlic, finely chopped

¼ teaspoon salt, or to taste

Freshly ground black pepper, to taste

¼ cup finely chopped red onion

2 scallions, white and green parts, thinly sliced

1 to 2 fresh red chili peppers, seeded, if desired, thinly sliced

Bring a large saucepan of water to a boil over high heat; add the mushrooms and boil 3 to 4 minutes, or until tender yet crunchy. Drain in a colander and rinse under cold running water until cool; drain well.

In a large bowl, stir together the vinegar, soy sauce, sesame oil, hot oil, ginger, sugar, garlic, salt, and black pepper. Let stand about 10 minutes to allow the flavors to blend. Stir again and add the mushrooms, onion, scallions, and chili pepper, tossing well to thoroughly combine. Cover and refrigerate a minimum of 3 hours, or up to 3 days. Toss and serve chilled, or return to room temperature.

{PER SERVING} Calories 95 · Protein 3g · Total Fat 3g · Sat Fat 0g · Cholesterol 0mg · Carbohydrate 19g · Dietary Fiber 3g · Sodium 289mg

Butter Lettuce Cups with Tofu and Shiitake Mushrooms

These appetizing lettuce cups also make a light and satisfying supper for 2 or 3.

MAKES 4 TO 6 SERVINGS

6 dried shiitake mushrooms, soaked in 1 cup hot water to cover 20 minutes, or until softened

1 tablespoon peanut oil

10 ounces extra-firm tofu, drained and chopped

2 scallions, white and green parts separated, thinly sliced

3 large cloves garlic, finely chopped

1 tablespoon finely chopped fresh ginger

1 tablespoon Shaoxing rice wine, dry sherry, sake, or dry white wine

1 medium carrot (about 2 ounces), chopped

½ cup drained and chopped canned water chestnuts

1 tablespoon reduced-sodium soy sauce

½ tablespoon toasted (dark) sesame oil

Salt and freshly ground black pepper, to taste

1 head butter lettuce or red leaf lettuce, washed, leaves separated, and patted dry

Hoisin Sauce (page 116), or prepared hoisin sauce, to serve

Fresh Chili Garlic Sauce (below), to serve

Drain the mushrooms, reserving ¼ cup of the soaking liquid. Strain the reserved soaking liquid through a coffee filter or paper towel to remove any grit. Rinse the mushrooms; remove and discard the stems. Chop the caps and set aside.

In a wok or large nonstick skillet, heat half the peanut oil over medium-high heat. Add the tofu and cook, stirring, until lightly browned, about 5 minutes. Transfer tofu to a holding plate and set aside. Heat the remaining ½ tablespoon of peanut oil and add the mushrooms, white parts of the scallions, garlic, ginger, and wine; cook, stirring, 30 seconds. Add the carrot and reserved soaking liquid and cook, stirring, 3 minutes, or until carrot and mushrooms are tender. Return the tofu to the skillet and add the water chestnuts and reserved scallion greens; cook, stirring, 1 minute. Remove from heat and stir in the soy sauce, sesame oil, salt, and pepper; let cool about 10 minutes, stirring a few times.

To serve, fill each lettuce leaf with 2 to 3 tablespoons of the filling. Serve at once, with Hoisin Sauce and Fresh Chili Garlic Sauce, below, passed separately.

{PER SERVING} (per ¼ of recipe, without sauces) Calories 167 · Protein 9g · Total Fat 8g · Sat Fat 1g · Cholesterol 0mg · Carbohydrate 16g · Dietary Fiber 5g · Sodium 175mg

FRESH CHILI GARLIC SAUCE

This fresh hot sauce is also a fat-free way to spice up plain rice, noodles, and vegetables.

MAKES ABOUT ½ CUP

10 to 12 small fresh red chili peppers, stemmed, cut crosswise in half

6 tablespoons distilled white vinegar

6 large cloves garlic, finely chopped

2 to 3 teaspoons sugar

1 teaspoon salt

In a food processor fitted with the knife blade, or in a blender, process or blend all ingredients until smooth. Transfer to a covered glass jar and refrigerate a minimum of 1 day, or up to 2 weeks.

{PER SERVING} (about 1 tablespoon, or ⅛ of recipe) Calories 39 · Protein 2g · Total Fat 0g · Sat Fat 0g · Cholesterol 0mg · Carbohydrate 10g · Dietary Fiber 1g · Sodium 272mg

Classic Chinese Pancakes

While good-quality frozen moo shu wrappers are readily available at Asian markets, nothing compares to freshly made Chinese pancakes.

MAKES 12 (7-INCH) PANCAKES; 4 TO 6 SERVINGS

1¾ cups all-purpose flour, plus additional
    for dusting
¼ teaspoon salt
¾ cup just-boiled water
1½ tablespoons toasted (dark) sesame oil

In a large bowl, combine the flour and salt. Slowly add boiled water in a steady stream while stirring constantly in one direction with a wooden spoon (to keep bowl in place, wrap a kitchen towel around the bottom). When the flour absorbs the water and cools, knead the dough with floured fingers directly in the bowl into a slightly sticky ball. Alternatively, combine the flour and salt in a food processor fitted with the knife blade; with the motor running, slowly add boiled water and process until a slightly sticky ball forms. Transfer to a large bowl and knead briefly with floured fingers. Cover with a damp kitchen towel and let rest 30 minutes.

Transfer dough to a lightly floured work surface. With floured fingers, knead until the dough is smooth, about 2 minutes. Place in a clean bowl, cover with a damp kitchen towel, and let rest 30 minutes.

Transfer dough to a lightly floured work surface. Shape into a 12-inch-long cylinder and divide into 12 (1-inch) pieces. Using your palm, flatten each piece into a disk and cover with a damp kitchen towel. Working with two disks of dough at a time, lightly brush 1 side of each disk with sesame oil. Place one disk on top of the other, oiled sides together, to create a pair. Roll the pair into a 2-layer, 7-inch pancake. Cover with a damp kitchen towel and repeat process with remaining 10 disks of dough for a total of 6 (2-layer, 7-inch) pancakes.

Heat a large nonstick skillet over medium heat 1 minute. Place a pancake in the hot, dry skillet and cook until it begins to bubble up, about 1 minute (adjust the heat slightly higher, as needed). Using a fork, turn the pancake over and cook until a few brown spots appear, about 1 minute. Remove from the wok and separate into 2 layers. You will have 2 pancakes, each browned lightly on 1 side and white on the other. Stack the pancakes, brown sides down, on a plate and cover with foil to keep from drying out. Repeat process with remaining 2-layer pancakes for a total of 12 (single-layer) 7-inch pancakes. Serve at once.

{PER SERVING} (per pancake) Calories 81 · Protein 2g · Total Fat 2g · Sat Fat 0g · Cholesterol 0mg · Carbohydrate 14g · Dietary Fiber 1g · Sodium 45mg

{VARIATION}
To make Chinese Dessert Crepes, add 2 tablespoons sugar when you combine the flour and salt. Replace the sesame oil with canola oil. Prepare as otherwise directed in the recipe. Fill with Sweet Red Bean Paste (page 182), Coconut Jam (page 177), or your other favorite fillings and fruit, etc.

Scallion Pancakes

I adore these savory pancakes. Serve them with soups, stews, and salads to create a light supper, or use them as a bed for your favorite stir-fries and tofu dishes in lieu of rice or noodles.

MAKES 4 PANCAKES; 8 TO 12 APPETIZER SERVINGS

2 cups all-purpose flour
¼ teaspoon table salt
1 cup just-boiled water
3 tablespoons canola oil, plus additional, as needed
1 tablespoon toasted (dark) sesame oil
½ cup thinly sliced scallions, green parts only
2 tablespoons black or regular sesame seeds, toasted, if desired (optional)
1 teaspoon finely ground sea salt
Freshly ground black pepper, to taste
Garlic Chive–Ginger Dipping Sauce (below)

In a large bowl, combine the flour and table salt. Slowly add just-boiled water in a steady stream while stirring constantly in one direction with a wooden spoon (to keep bowl in place, wrap a kitchen towel around the bottom). When the flour absorbs the water and cools, knead the dough with floured fingers directly in the bowl into a slightly sticky ball. Cover with a damp kitchen towel and let rest 30 minutes. Alternatively, combine the flour and table salt in a food processor fitted with the knife blade; with the motor running, slowly add just-boiled water and process until a slightly sticky ball forms. Transfer to a large bowl and knead briefly with floured fingers. Cover with a damp kitchen towel and let rest 30 minutes.

Meanwhile, in a small bowl, combine 1 tablespoon of the canola oil and sesame oil. Set aside.

On a lightly floured work surface, roll out dough into a thin rectangle, about the size of a standard baking sheet. Brush on oil mixture; sprinkle evenly with the scallions, sesame seeds (if using), sea salt, and pepper. Starting at one long side, carefully roll up the dough to encase the filling. Cut into 4 equal pieces. Using your hands, roll and stretch each piece into a longer cylinder. Take one piece and twist in 3 places, keeping the filling in place; reshape into a cylinder. Coil each piece to form a spiral, pinching end in to keep in place. Press spiral with your palm to flatten it; using a rolling pin, roll out into a pancake 5 to 6 inches in diameter. Repeat process with remaining pieces.

Line a baking sheet with paper towels. In a large nonstick skillet, heat ½ tablespoon of remaining canola oil slightly above medium heat. Working with 1 pancake at a time, place pancake in skillet and cook until golden, about 2 minutes each side. Transfer to prepared baking sheet and cover with foil to keep warm. Repeat process with remaining canola oil and pancakes, adjusting the heat as needed.

Cut each pancake into 6 pieces. Serve immediately with Garlic Chive–Ginger Dipping Sauce on the side.

{PER SERVING} (per ½ pancake without sauce) Calories 176 · Protein 3g · Total Fat 7g · Sat Fat 1g · Cholesterol 0mg · Carbohydrate 24g · Dietary Fiber 1g · Sodium 335mg

GARLIC CHIVE–GINGER DIPPING SAUCE

Use this dipping sauce for dumplings, pot stickers, steamed buns, and spring rolls. Scallion greens can replace the Chinese garlic chives, if desired.

MAKES ABOUT ¾ CUP

¼ cup reduced-sodium soy sauce

¼ cup plain rice wine vinegar

¼ cup chopped garlic chives or green parts of scallions

2 teaspoons finely chopped fresh ginger

2 teaspoons sugar

½ teaspoon crushed red pepper flakes, or to taste

1½ teaspoons toasted (dark) sesame oil

¼ teaspoon salt, or to taste

1 tablespoon finely chopped scallion greens

1 to 1½ teaspoons Chinese chili paste

1 tablespoon peanut oil

Basic Dipping Sauce (page 9) or other dipping sauce

In a small bowl, combine all ingredients, stirring until the sugar is dissolved. Serve at room temperature. Sauce can be stored, covered, in refrigerator up to 1 day before returning to room temperature and serving.

{PER SERVING} (per tablespoon) Calories 8 · Protein 0g · Total Fat 0g · Sat Fat 0g · Cholesterol 0mg · Carbohydrate 2g · Dietary Fiber 0g · Sodium 201mg

Crispy Noodle Pancake

Serve this crispy noodle pancake on its own as a snack or appetizer, or as a bed for countless stir-fried vegetable and tofu dishes. If at all possible, try to use fresh eggless lo mein noodles, available in the refrigerated or frozen section of Asian markets, often labeled "plain noodles." Dried lo mein noodles, known as lao mian or ban mian in Mandarin, or lou mihn in Cantonese, are typically egg-free.

MAKES 4 TO 6 SERVINGS

⅓ pound lo mein or other thin, egg-free Chinese wheat noodles, cooked according to package directions until al dente, drained and rinsed under cold running water, drained well

In a large bowl, combine the noodles, 1 teaspoon of the sesame oil, and salt, tossing until noodles are thoroughly coated. Add the scallion greens and chili paste, tossing well to combine.

Preheat the oven to broil. Set the oven rack 6 to 8 inches from the heating element.

In a 10-inch nonstick ovenproof skillet (preferably cast iron), heat the peanut oil over medium-low heat, swirling to evenly coat the bottom. Add the noodle mixture, pressing down firmly with a spatula or the back of a large wooden spoon to form a pancake. Raise the heat to medium and cook until crisp and golden on the bottom, 7 to 9 minutes, brushing the top with the remaining ½ teaspoon of sesame oil the last few minutes. Place the skillet under the broiler; broil until top is crisp and golden, 5 to 7 minutes, turning the skillet occasionally to promote even browning.

Loosen the underside of the pancake, working a spatula carefully under and around the entire circumference; carefully slide onto a large serving plate. Using a sharp knife or pizza cutter, cut into desired number of slices. Serve at once, with the dipping sauce passed separately.

{PER SERVING} (per ¼ of recipe, without sauce) Calories 186 · Protein 5g · Total Fat 6g · Sat Fat 1g · Cholesterol 0mg · Carbohydrate 29g · Dietary Fiber 1g · Sodium 137mg

Pickled Chinese Long Beans

These appetizing pickled long beans, or snake beans, are based on a family recipe for "sour pods" submitted by Ecksyoo, whose bright smile and blithe spirit lit up English corner on Tuesdays and Wednesdays during my first semester at Yali. These beans make piquant and crunchy additions to relish trays, stir-fries, rice, noodles, soups, and congees. Green beans can replace the long beans, if necessary.

MAKES 8 SERVINGS

½ pound Chinese long beans, trimmed, cut
   into ½-inch pieces
1 cup cider vinegar
¾ cup water
½ cup sugar
1 teaspoon salt
2 to 4 fresh red chili peppers, seeded and
   thinly sliced (optional)

In a large pot of boiling salted water, blanch the long beans 30 seconds; drain and rinse under cold running water until cool. Drain and set aside.

Bring the vinegar, water, sugar, and salt to a brisk simmer over medium heat, stirring until the sugar is dissolved. Remove from heat and set aside to cool.

Place drained long beans and peppers, if using, in a 26- to 32-ounce clean glass jar. Add the vinegar mixture, seal tightly, and refrigerate a minimum of 5 days, or up to several weeks. Serve chilled or at room temperature.

{PER SERVING} (per ⅛ of recipe) Calories 68 · Protein 1g · Total Fat 0g · Sat Fat 0g · Cholesterol 0mg · Carbohydrate 18g · Dietary Fiber 1g · Sodium 270mg

Roasted Five-Spice Peanuts

Jazz up countless rice, noodle, and stir-fried dishes with these tasty morsels. Almonds or cashews can replace the peanuts, if desired.

MAKES 2 CUPS

2 tablespoons orange marmalade,
   preferably a Chinese variety
4 teaspoons water
2 teaspoons reduced-sodium soy sauce or
   gluten-free tamari sauce
1 teaspoon five-spice powder
2 cups unsalted peanuts, without skins

Preheat oven to 250F (120C). Lightly grease a large rimmed baking sheet and set aside.

In a small bowl, mix together the marmalade, water, soy sauce, and five-spice powder until thoroughly blended. Place the peanuts in a medium bowl and add half the marmalade mixture; toss until thoroughly coated. Transfer peanuts to the prepared baking sheet and spread in a single layer. Bake on the middle oven rack 30 minutes, stirring halfway through baking time. Remove baking sheet from oven and drizzle peanuts with the remaining marmalade mixture; toss well to thoroughly coat. Return to oven and bake an additional 15 minutes, or until golden and dry. Toss the peanuts well and immediately transfer to a plate, spreading in a single layer to cool. Serve at room temperature. Completely cooled peanuts can be stored in an airtight container for a few weeks at room temperature, or for several weeks in the refrigerator.

{PER SERVING} (per ¼ cup) Calories 223 · Protein 10g · Total Fat 18g · Sat Fat 3g · Cholesterol 0mg · Carbohydrate 11g · Dietary Fiber 4g · Sodium 55mg

Sichuan-Style Marinated Green Bell Peppers

Serve these scrumptious peppers by themselves as an appetizer or side dish, or toss them with hot cooked rice or noodles, garnished with chopped peanuts or cashews, for a satisfying main meal.

MAKES 4 TO 6 SERVINGS

1 tablespoon peanut oil

4 large green bell peppers (about 8 ounces each), cut into bite-size chunks

1 tablespoon reduced-sodium soy sauce

2 tablespoons plain rice vinegar

½ teaspoon Chinese hot oil, or to taste (optional)

½ teaspoon sugar

½ teaspoon salt

Freshly ground black pepper, to taste

In a wok or large nonstick skillet, heat the peanut oil over medium-high heat. Add peppers and cook, stirring frequently, 7 to 10 minutes, or until browned and slightly charred. Add soy sauce and cook, stirring constantly, 30 seconds. Transfer to a large shallow bowl and add the remaining ingredients, tossing well to thoroughly combine. Let cool to room temperature, stirring a few times. Cover and refrigerate a minimum of 3 hours or up to 3 days and serve chilled, or return to room temperature.

{PER SERVING} Calories 91 · Protein 2g · Total Fat 4g · Sat Fat 1g · Cholesterol 0mg · Carbohydrate 13g · Dietary Fiber 3g · Sodium 420mg

Baked Tofu Nuggets

While these make excellent appetizers to dip in hoisin and other savory sauces, you can also use this basic recipe whenever plain baked tofu is required. Feel free to toss the tofu with your favorite spices—such as Chinese five-spice, cumin, or fennel—before baking, or your favorite herbs—such as cilantro, basil, or chives—after baking.

MAKES 6 TO 8 APPETIZER SERVINGS OR 4 MAIN DISH SERVINGS

1 pound extra-firm tofu, drained

½ tablespoon canola oil

½ tablespoon toasted (dark) sesame oil

Salt, to taste (optional)

Hoisin Sauce (page 116), Quick Spicy Hoisin Sauce (page 140), prepared hoisin, or other favorite dipping sauce, to serve

Place the tofu on a deep-sided plate or shallow bowl. Top with a second plate and weight with a heavy can. Let stand for a minimum of 15 minutes (preferably 1 hour). Drain off the excess water. Cut tofu into 1-inch cubes and set aside.

Meanwhile, preheat oven to 400F (205C). Lightly oil a baking sheet and set aside.

In a medium bowl, combine the canola oil and sesame oil. Add the tofu cubes and salt, if using, tossing well to thoroughly coat. Arrange the tofu cubes in a single layer on the prepared baking sheet. Bake until golden brown and crisp, 35 to 40 minutes, turning the tofu halfway through cooking time. Serve warm, with the hoisin sauce passed separately for dipping.

{PER SERVING} (without sauce) Calories 78 · Protein 6g · Total Fat 6g · Sat Fat 1g · Cholesterol 0mg · Carbohydrate 1g · Dietary Fiber 1g · Sodium 5mg

Saffron-Scented Coconut Rice Cakes with Sesame Seeds

The Asian-Indian influence upon Southwestern China is apparent in these savory saffron-scented little cakes, delicious dipped in your favorite sauce as a snack, or as an accompaniment to tofu or vegetable dishes in lieu of steamed rice or noodles.

MAKES ABOUT 24 CAKES

2 cups water

¾ cup plus 2 tablespoons (14 tablespoons) coconut milk

2 pinches saffron threads

¼ teaspoon ground turmeric

1½ cups basmati rice, rinsed and drained

1 teaspoon toasted (dark) sesame oil

½ teaspoon salt

Freshly ground black pepper, to taste

4 scallions, white and green parts, thinly sliced

⅓ cup sesame seeds

2 tablespoons canola oil

Basic Dipping Sauce (page 9) or other dipping sauce (optional)

In a medium saucepan with a tight-fitting lid, bring the water, coconut milk, saffron, and turmeric to a boil over high heat. Add the rice, sesame oil, salt, and pepper; cover, reduce heat to low, and cook until the rice is tender and has absorbed the liquid, 17 to 20 minutes.

Meanwhile, lightly oil a 9-by-12-inch baking dish. Add the scallions to the hot rice and toss well to combine. Transfer the rice mixture to the prepared baking dish; using a spatula or the back of a large wooden spoon, press the rice to evenly spread. Sprinkle the sesame seeds evenly over the rice. Let cool to room temperature.

Place a piece of plastic wrap over the cooled rice mixture and press firmly. Refrigerate a minimum of 3 hours, or up to 1 day. Uncover and cut into about 24 squares, triangles, diamonds, etc.

To make the rice cakes, in a large nonstick skillet, heat half the canola oil over medium heat. Add half the rice cakes and cook until golden, 2 to 3 minutes per side. Transfer to a holding plate and cover with foil to keep warm. Repeat with remaining oil and rice cakes. Serve at once, seed-coated side up, with Basic Dipping Sauce, if desired.

{PER SERVING} (per cake, or ¹⁄₂₄ of recipe) Calories 83 · Protein 2g · Total Fat 5g · Sat Fat 2g · Cholesterol 0mg · Carbohydrate 9g · Dietary Fiber 0g · Sodium 54mg

{VARIATION}
To enjoy Saffron-Scented Coconut Rice to serve 6, steam the rice as directed in the recipe. Stir in half the amount of scallions and remove the saucepan from heat; let stand, covered, 5 minutes. Uncover, fluff with a fork, and serve at once.

Baked Taiwanese-Style Five-Spice Tofu and Vegetable Spring Rolls

A healthful blend of ready-made five-spice tofu, vegetables, and spices, these baked spring rolls are delicious and crunchy without the standard deep-frying. Well-drained regular extra-firm tofu can replace the baked flavored variety, if necessary; in this instance, add ¼ teaspoon of five-spice powder after the sugar. Sauerkraut, which is pickled cabbage, can replace the pickled turnips, if desired. Peanut powder is available in Asian markets and health food stores—in a pinch, make your own by grinding skinned unsalted roasted peanuts in a food processor or spice grinder, or pounding in an old-fashioned mortar and pestle, as I do.

MAKES 12 SPRING ROLLS

1 tablespoon peanut oil

1 tablespoon finely chopped fresh ginger

2 large cloves garlic, finely chopped

4 ounces packaged baked flavored five-spice tofu or Baked Five-Spice Seasoned Tofu (page 113), finely diced

1 cup coleslaw mix

1 cup mung bean sprouts

2 tablespoons chopped pickled turnips or other pickled vegetables, rinsed and drained

2 scallions, white and green parts, thinly sliced

2 tablespoons finely chopped fresh cilantro

1 tablespoon peanut powder

½ tablespoon vegetarian oyster sauce or mushroom soy sauce

1 teaspoon Chinese chili paste, or to taste (optional)

3 teaspoons sesame oil

1 teaspoon sugar

Salt and freshly ground black pepper, to taste

12 (5-inch-square) soft wheat flour spring roll wrappers, thawed if frozen

½ tablespoon cornstarch mixed with ½ tablespoon water

Duck sauce, plum sauce, sweet chili sauce, or other dipping sauce, to serve

Preheat oven to 400F (205C). Lightly oil a baking sheet. Set aside.

In a wok or large nonstick skillet, heat the peanut oil over medium heat. Add the ginger and garlic and cook, stirring constantly, 1 minute. Add the tofu, coleslaw mix, sprouts, and pickled vegetables; cook, stirring often, until vegetables are largely reduced in volume, 4 to 5 minutes. Add the scallions, cilantro, peanut powder, oyster sauce, chili paste (if using), 1 teaspoon of sesame oil, sugar, salt, and pepper; cook, stirring often, 1 minute. Remove from heat and let cool about 15 minutes, stirring a few times.

Lay a spring roll wrapper in front of you so that it forms a diamond shape. Using your finger, wet all the edges with the cornstarch mixture. Place 1 heaping tablespoon of filling near the bottom. Fold the lower corner edge up to cover the filling. Fold in the sides, and roll up tightly, burrito-style. Seal the top with the cornstarch mixture. Repeat with remaining wrappers and filling.

Arrange spring rolls in a single layer, seam side down, on the prepared baking sheet. Brush tops evenly with 1 teaspoon sesame oil. Bake in the center of the oven until tops are lightly browned, 7 to 9 minutes. Turn over and brush with remaining 1 teaspoon sesame oil. Bake an additional 4 to 6 minutes, or until crisp and golden. Serve at once, with the dipping sauce passed separately. Alternatively, spring rolls may be kept warm in a preheated 200F (95C) oven for up to 1 hour. (Completely cooled spring rolls can be placed in resealable plastic freezer bags and frozen up to 3 months before reheating in a moderate oven for 10 to 15 minutes.)

{PER SERVING} (per roll, without sauce) Calories 67 · Protein 2g · Total Fat 3g · Sat Fat 1g · Cholesterol 0mg · Carbohydrate 8g · Dietary Fiber 1g · Sodium 79mg

Fried Cantonese-Style Tofu and Vegetable Spring Rolls

I like to serve these dark, meaty, Cantonese-style spring rolls with leftover packets of hot mustard and duck sauce from Chinese take-out. Feel free to use this recipe as a model for your favorite fillings—coleslaw mix, broccoli slaw, cilantro, water chestnuts, bamboo shoots, pickled vegetables, and canned straw mushrooms are some suggestions. You'll need about 1 cup of cooked filling per 1 dozen spring rolls.

MAKES 24 SPRING ROLLS

2 tablespoons vegetarian oyster sauce or mushroom soy sauce

2 tablespoons dark soy sauce

1 tablespoon Shaoxing rice wine, dry sherry, sake, or dry white wine

½ tablespoon toasted (dark) sesame oil

1 teaspoon cornstarch

1 tablespoon peanut oil, plus additional for deep-frying

½ pound extra-firm tofu, drained well, patted dry, and finely diced

1 tablespoon chopped fresh ginger

2 large cloves garlic, finely chopped

6 dried shiitake mushrooms, soaked in hot water to cover 20 minutes, or until softened, rinsed, drained, squeezed dry, stemmed, chopped

½ medium red bell pepper (about 3 ounces), chopped

1 cup shredded Napa or green cabbage

1 cup mung bean sprouts

4 Chinese garlic chives or 2 scallion greens, chopped

¼ cup shredded carrots

24 (5-inch) soft wheat flour spring roll wrappers, thawed if frozen

1 tablespoon cornstarch mixed with 1 tablespoon water

Duck sauce, hot mustard, sweet chili sauce, or other dipping sauce, to serve

In a small bowl, stir together the oyster sauce, soy sauce, rice wine, sesame oil, and cornstarch until well blended; set aside. Line a baking sheet with several layers of paper towel; set aside.

In a wok or large nonstick skillet, heat 1 tablespoon of the peanut oil over medium-high heat. Add the tofu and ginger and cook, stirring constantly, 2 minutes. Add the garlic and cook, stirring constantly, 30 seconds. Add the mushrooms and bell pepper and cook, stirring constantly, 1 minute. Reduce the heat to medium and add the cabbage, bean sprouts, garlic chives, and carrots; cook, stirring constantly, until largely reduced in volume, 4 to 5 minutes. Add the oyster sauce mixture; cook, stirring constantly, until heated through and thickened, about 3 minutes. Remove from heat and let cool about 15 minutes, tossing a few times.

Lay a spring roll wrapper in front of you so that it forms a diamond shape. Using your finger, wet all the edges with the cornstarch mixture. Place 1 heaping tablespoon of filling near the bottom, leaving any accumulated liquid behind in the wok. Fold the lower corner edge up to cover the filling. Fold in the sides, and roll up tightly, burrito-style. Seal the top with the cornstarch mixture. Repeat with remaining wrappers and filling.

In a small, heavy-bottomed, deep-sided skillet, heat about ½ inch of oil over medium heat. When a small bit of filling can sizzle (after about 5 minutes of preheating), reduce the heat to medium-low and add about 6 rolls. Cook until light golden and crispy, about 2 minutes per side. Remove with tongs or a slotted spoon and transfer to the prepared baking sheet to drain. Repeat with remaining rolls. Serve at once, with the dipping sauce passed separately. Alternatively, spring rolls may be kept warm in a preheated 200F (95C) oven for up to 1 hour. (Completely cooled spring rolls can be placed in resealable plastic freezer bags and frozen up to 3 months before reheating in a moderate oven for 10 to 15 minutes.)

{PER SERVING} (per roll, without sauce, based on ¼ cup peanut oil absorbed during frying) Calories 68 · Protein 2g · Total Fat 4g · Sat Fat 1g · Cholesterol 0mg · Carbohydrate 7g · Dietary Fiber 1g · Sodium 149mg

Stir-Fried Water Chestnuts in Sichuan Sauce

Water chestnuts are aquatic vegetables that grow in marshes. Sweet and crunchy, they make a delightful contrast to the spicy and smooth Sichuan sauce in the following recipe, perfect as a party appetizer or first course. If possible, purchase the fresh variety for a special taste sensation.

MAKES 4 TO 6 SERVINGS

- 2 cups sliced fresh water chestnuts (see Cook's Tip, below) or rinsed and drained canned sliced water chestnuts
- 2 teaspoons peanut oil
- 2 scallions, white and green parts separated, thinly sliced
- 3 large cloves garlic, finely chopped
- 2 tablespoons Sichuan sauce
- 2 tablespoons low-sodium vegetable broth
- 1 teaspoon sugar
- Salt and freshly ground black pepper, to taste
- 3 cups torn or shredded Napa cabbage leaves or shredded green cabbage
- 1 cup shredded carrots

In a medium stockpot filled with boiling salted water, add the water chestnuts (fresh or canned) and cook 2 minutes. Drain and set aside.

In a wok or large nonstick skillet, heat the oil over medium-high heat. Add the white parts of the scallions and garlic and cook, stirring constantly, 1 minute, or until fragrant. Reduce the heat to medium and add the water chestnuts, Sichuan sauce, broth, sugar, salt, and pepper; cook, stirring constantly, 2 minutes. Remove from heat and keep warm.

In a medium bowl, toss together the cabbage and carrots until well combined. To serve, line a serving platter or 4 individual serving plates with the cabbage mixture and top with equal amounts of the water chestnut mixture. Garnish with the reserved scallion greens and serve at once.

{PER SERVING} Calories 124 · Protein 3g · Total Fat 3g · Sat Fat 0g · Cholesterol 0mg · Carbohydrate 23g · Dietary Fiber 4g · Sodium 48mg

{COOK'S TIP}

If using fresh water chestnuts, they should be firm, with a smooth skin and no soft spots. To remove the skin or soft outer shell, cut off the top and bottom of each water chestnut with a sharp knife, and then cut around the sides until all the skin is removed. Peeled water chestnuts can be immersed in fresh water and refrigerated, covered, up to one week; however, the water must be changed daily.

Chinese Summer Vegetable Rolls

These no-cook delights are popular in southern China, where the summer heat often reaches tropical levels. Use the following recipe as a model for your favorite vegetable combinations. For a gluten-free version, use gluten-free tamari sauce in lieu of standard soy sauce, which contains wheat. Dry round rice paper wrappers, also known as spring roll skins, are available in Asian markets and some well-stocked supermarkets; they need to be rehydrated in water before using.

MAKES 16 TO 18 ROLLS

2 tablespoons rice vinegar

1½ tablespoons reduced-sodium soy sauce

1 tablespoon peanut oil

½ tablespoon sugar

1 large clove garlic, finely chopped

1 teaspoon toasted (dark) sesame oil

½ teaspoon Chinese chili paste

4 cups shredded Napa or green cabbage

4 scallions, white and green parts, thinly sliced

1 cup shredded carrots

1 medium seedless cucumber (about 10 ounces), julienned

½ medium red bell pepper (about 3 ounces), julienned

½ cup finely chopped cilantro

16 to 18 (8½-inch) dry round rice paper wrappers

Basic Dipping Sauce (page 9) or other dipping sauce, to serve

In a large bowl, whisk together the vinegar, soy sauce, peanut oil, sugar, garlic, sesame oil, and chili paste. Add the remaining ingredients except the rice papers, tossing until thoroughly combined. Let stand about 15 minutes to allow the flavors to blend (alternatively, cover and refrigerate up to 3 hours); toss again.

Fill a shallow bowl large enough to comfortably hold a rice paper wrapper with cold water. Working with one wrapper at a time, soak a wrapper in the water until softened, about 30 seconds. Place on a clean kitchen towel and arrange ¼ to ⅓ cup of the vegetable mixture about 2 inches from the lower edge of the wrapper. Fold the lower edge up to cover the filling. Fold in the sides, and roll up gently. Place on a large serving platter, seam down, and cover with plastic wrap. Repeat with remaining wrappers and filling. Serve at once, or refrigerate up to 24 hours before serving chilled, accompanied by dipping sauce.

{PER SERVING} (per roll, without sauce) Calories 49 · Protein 2g · Total Fat 1g · Sat Fat 0g · Cholesterol 0mg · Carbohydrate 8g · Dietary Fiber 1g · Sodium 109mg

{VARIATION}

To make Vegetable Silk Dolls, or Si Wa Wa, a popular summer snack sold on the streets in southern China, substitute about 32 soft, thin, round rice-flour wrappers or pancakes, available in Asian markets, for the dry variety and omit the soaking step. Prepare the filling as directed in the recipe. To assemble the rolls, place about 2 tablespoons of the filling to one side of each wrapper; gently form a cone-shape bundle by bringing the opposite side up over the filling and rolling sideways, creating a "doll." Serve immediately. For best results, assemble on demand or have diners assemble their own rolls.

Baked Tofu Skin Rolls with Shiitake Mushrooms and Seitan

Not only do these crispy baked tofu skin rolls have less fat, calories, and carbs than their deep-fried spring roll–wrapper counterparts, they can easily be made gluten-free by using extra-firm tofu and tamari sauce in lieu of the seitan and regular soy sauce, respectively. Packaged sheets of dried bean curd skin, also called yuba, are available in Asian markets. Since the sizes of the sheets vary, you may need to adjust the size of the rolls accordingly. For a sweet-and-sour effect, I like to serve these tasty rolls with two dipping sauces—the tangy Ginger–Black Vinegar Sauce, below, and prepared duck sauce. These are also delicious chilled, with the vinegar sauce, or all alone.

MAKES ABOUT 18 ROLLS

6 tablespoons water

2½ tablespoons reduced-sodium soy sauce or gluten-free tamari sauce

1½ tablespoons toasted (dark) sesame oil

¾ teaspoon plain rice wine vinegar

¾ teaspoon sugar

½ teaspoon Chinese chili paste, or to taste (optional)

½ tablespoon cornstarch

½ tablespoon peanut oil

4 dried shiitake mushrooms, soaked in hot water to cover 20 minutes, or until softened, rinsed, drained, stemmed, and chopped

½ tablespoon chopped fresh ginger

2 cloves garlic, finely chopped

3 cups shredded Napa or green cabbage

½ cup shredded carrots

½ cup drained and chopped seitan (about 3 ounces), baked flavored tofu, or well-drained extra-firm tofu

1 scallion, white and green parts, thinly sliced

2 tablespoons finely chopped fresh cilantro

3 to 4 (about 12-by-7½-inch) sheets dried bean curd skin (about 3 ounces), stacked, soaked in hot water to cover in a large baking dish 3 minutes, or until pliable, water carefully drained off (leave sheets in dish)

Ginger–Black Vinegar Dipping Sauce, below, duck sauce, or favorite dipping sauce

In a small bowl, combine the water, soy sauce, ½ tablespoon sesame oil, vinegar, sugar, chili paste (if using), and cornstarch until thoroughly blended; set aside.

In a wok or large nonstick skillet, heat the peanut oil over medium-high heat. Add the mushrooms and ginger and cook, stirring constantly, 2 minutes. Add the garlic and cook, stirring constantly, 30 seconds. Reduce the heat to medium and add the cabbage and carrots; cook, stirring constantly, until vegetables are greatly reduced in volume, 4 to 5 minutes. Add the seitan and scallion and cook, stirring constantly, 1 minute. Add the soy sauce mixture and cook, stirring constantly, until thickened, about 3 minutes. Remove from heat and add the cilantro, stirring well to combine. Let cool to room temperature, about 30 minutes, stirring a few times.

Preheat oven to 400F (205C). Lightly oil a large baking sheet and set aside.

Working carefully (the sheets are fragile and tear easily), using a sharp knife, cut the stacked sheets of bean curd skin (while still in the baking dish) in half lengthwise, then cut crosswise into thirds, for a total of 18 (4½- to 5-inch) squares. Working in batches, carefully arrange the squares in front of you so that they form diamond shapes. Place 1 heaping tablespoon of filling toward the bottom of each square. Fold the lower edge up to cover the filling. Carefully fold in the sides, and roll up as snuggly as possible without tearing the skin, burrito-style. Repeat with remaining bean curd skin and filling.

Place the tofu skin rolls, seam side down, on the prepared baking sheet. Brush the tops evenly with half of the remaining sesame oil. Bake in the center of the oven until tops are lightly browned, 7 to 9 minutes. Turn over and brush with remaining ½ tablespoon of sesame oil. Bake an additional 4 to 6 minutes, or until crisp and golden. Serve warm or at room temperature, with the dipping sauce passed separately. Alternatively, completely cooled rolls can be refrigerated, covered, up to 3 days and served chilled, or returned to room temperature.

{PER SERVING} (per roll, or 1/18 of recipe, without sauce) Calories 38 · Protein 2g · Total Fat 2g · Sat Fat 0g · Cholesterol 0mg · Carbohydrate 3g · Dietary Fiber 1g · Sodium 88mg

GINGER–BLACK VINEGAR DIPPING SAUCE

Try to use Zhenjiang black vinegar, available in Asian markets, for this tangy dipping sauce. For a gluten-free option (Chinese black vinegar typically contains wheat or millet), use balsamic vinegar and substitute gluten-free tamari sauce for the standard soy sauce.

MAKES ABOUT ½ CUP

¼ cup Chinese black vinegar or balsamic vinegar

2 tablespoons reduced-sodium soy sauce or gluten-free tamari sauce

1 tablespoon chopped fresh ginger

½ tablespoon toasted (dark) sesame oil

1 to 2 teaspoons Chinese hot oil

1 scallion, thinly sliced

In a small bowl, combine all ingredients. Serve at room temperature. Sauce can be stored, covered, in refrigerator up to 3 days before returning to room temperature and using in the recipe.

{PER SERVING} (Per tablespoon, or ⅛ of recipe) Calories 17 · Protein 0g · Total Fat 1g · Sat Fat 0g · Cholesterol 0mg · Carbohydrate 1g · Dietary Fiber 0g · Sodium 151mg

Yunnan-Style Tomato Jam with Chilies, Cilantro, and Mint

The influence of Thai cuisine is apparent in this hot and spicy tomato jam, typically eaten with freshly cooked bamboo shoots in Yunnan Province. I like to use it as a bread or cracker spread, bruschetta topping, or condiment for veggie burgers or grilled vegetables. Leftovers are wonderful mixed with rice or tossed with noodles.

MAKES ABOUT 1 CUP

2 tablespoons canola oil

1 fresh hot red or green chili pepper, seeded and finely chopped

1 large shallot, finely chopped, or 2 to 3 tablespoons finely chopped red onion

1 tablespoon finely chopped fresh ginger

2 large cloves garlic, finely chopped

1 (14-ounce) can fire-roasted diced
tomatoes, liquid included

2 tablespoons plain rice vinegar

2 tablespoons light brown sugar

½ tablespoon reduced-sodium soy sauce

½ teaspoon salt

¼ teaspoon crushed red pepper flakes

¼ cup finely chopped fresh cilantro

2 tablespoons chopped fresh mint or basil

1 tablespoon fresh lime juice

In a small heavy-bottomed saucepan, heat the oil over medium heat. Add the chili pepper, shallot, ginger, and garlic and cook, stirring constantly, until softened and fragrant, 2 to 3 minutes. Add the tomatoes with their liquid, vinegar, brown sugar, soy sauce, salt, and red pepper flakes; bring to a brisk simmer over medium-high heat. Reduce the heat to medium-low and cook, mashing and stirring occasionally, until thick and jamlike, 25 to 35 minutes. Remove from the heat and stir in the cilantro, mint, and lime juice. Serve slightly warm or at room temperature. Completely cooled mixture can be refrigerated, covered, up to 5 days before returning to room temperature and serving.

{PER SERVING} (per tablespoon, or 1/16 of recipe) Calories 31 · Protein 0 · Total Fat 2g · Sat Fat 0g · Cholesterol 0mg · Carbohydrate 4g · Dietary Fiber 0g · Sodium 143mg

Chinese Sweet Walnuts

Scientific studies are confirming what the Chinese have known since the first walnut trees from Persia were planted in Sichuan Province—walnuts are better than good for you. Revered as a brain food and kidney tonic in Chinese medicine, the walnut is an excellent source of omega-three essential fatty acids and has recently been dubbed the "heart nut" because of its antioxidant, phytonutrient, and nutritional value. Whole blanched almonds or cashews will work in this delicious recipe as well.

MAKES 2 CUPS

1 tablespoon light corn syrup, brown rice
syrup, or maple syrup

1 tablespoon water

2 cups walnut halves (about 1 pound)

2 tablespoons light brown sugar

2 tablespoons granulated white sugar

2 teaspoons ground cinnamon

1 teaspoon ground ginger

Preheat oven to 250F (120C). Lightly grease a baking sheet with sides.

In a medium bowl, combine syrup and water; add walnuts, stirring well to thoroughly coat. In a small bowl, combine sugars, cinnamon, and ginger until thoroughly blended. Add the sugar mixture to the walnut mixture, tossing well to thoroughly coat.

Place nuts in a single layer on prepared baking sheet. Bake on the center oven rack about 45 minutes, stirring and turning every 10 to 15 minutes, or until nuts are toasted and dry. Remove from oven and immediately transfer to a plate to cool to room temperature. Store tightly covered for a few weeks at room temperature, or for several weeks in the refrigerator.

{PER SERVING} (per ¼ cup) Calories 223 · Protein 8g · Total Fat 18g · Sat Fat 1g · Cholesterol 0mg · Carbohydrate 12g · Dietary Fiber 2g · Sodium 2mg

Easy Fried Vegetable Wontons

Precooking the filling is not necessary to make these super-quick, super-delicious fried wontons, a perennial party favorite. The trick is to make sure the filling ingredients are finely chopped.

MAKES 4 TO 6 SERVINGS (24 WONTONS)

1 cup finely chopped coleslaw mix (about 4 ounces)

¼ cup finely chopped fresh cilantro

¼ cup finely chopped scallions (about 2 scallions)

1 tablespoon reduced-sodium soy sauce

1 tablespoon toasted (dark) sesame oil

1 clove garlic, finely chopped

¼ teaspoon Chinese chili paste, or more, to taste

Salt and freshly ground black pepper, to taste

24 egg-free wonton wrappers, thawed if frozen

1½ tablespoons peanut oil

¼ cup water

Basic Dipping Sauce (page 9)

In a medium bowl, toss the coleslaw mix, cilantro, scallions, soy sauce, sesame oil, garlic, chili paste, salt, and pepper until thoroughly combined.

Fill a small container with some water. Lay a wonton wrapper on a flat work surface and place 1 heaping teaspoon of the vegetable mixture in the center. Dip your finger in the water and wet the edges of the wrapper. Seal into a triangle, removing as much air as possible from the dumpling. Make sure edges are secured. Wet the corners and fold in like an envelope, pressing to seal. Repeat with remaining wontons and filling, tossing the filling frequently to redistribute the liquid at the bottom of the bowl.

In a 12-inch nonstick skillet with a lid, heat the peanut oil over medium-high heat for 1 minute. Add the wontons, seam sides up, and cook without turning until lightly browned on the undersides, 2 to 3 minutes, shaking the skillet a few times to prevent sticking. Reduce the heat to medium, add ¼ cup water, cover, and cook until the tops of the wontons are tender and the filling is heated through, about 2 minutes. Serve at once, with the dipping sauce passed separately.

{PER SERVING} (per wonton, without dipping sauce) Calories 38 · Protein 1g · Total Fat 2g · Sat Fat 0g · Cholesterol 0mg · Carbohydrate 5g · Dietary Fiber 0g · Sodium 72mg

CHAPTER TWO

Soups

Soup has been revered in China for countless generations. Indeed, in late 2010, the year I was living in China, archaeologists excavating a tomb near the ancient capital of Xi'an discovered the remains of soup sealed in a bronze pot for 2,400 years. Fortunately, for vegetarians, all soups in China were not created equal. While the imperial court feasted on shark's fin soup as a first course, resourceful Chinese peasants made a meal of water flavored with soybean curd and whatever seasonal vegetables and, often, fruits were available to sustain their families. Contemporary health-conscious, middle-class cooks continue to honor their ancestors' wisdom. To this day, soup is the only liquid, save for tea, served at mealtime—cold drinks are considered unhealthy to consume with meals. Many Chinese begin their day with a warm bowl of congee, a watery yet nourishing rice gruel resembling porridge. Sweet soups, often containing fruit, make a satisfying conclusion to a meal or midday snack—you will find a few in Chapter 8. Whether enjoying fresh Bamboo Shoot Soup as a first course, Tibetan Lentil Soup for lunch, or Spicy Hunan Hot Pot for dinner, you'll be raising your soup spoon in homage to one of China's most venerable arts.

· LIGHT SOUPS ·

Hunan-Style Hot-and-Sour Soup

In Hunan, hot-and-sour soup is a popular remedy for the common cold—it may well prevent them, also, as I never had one during the 11 months I lived there. If you can't locate dried cloud ear or wood ear mushrooms, both of which are readily available in Asian markets, substitute with additional shiitake mushrooms. Though optional, dried lily buds, also available in most Asian markets, lend this soup an authentic, earthy flavor.

MAKES 4 SERVINGS

4 cups reduced-sodium vegetable broth

2 cups water

8 ounces soft tofu, drained and chopped

6 medium dried Shiitake mushrooms,
    soaked in hot water to cover 20 minutes,
    or until softened, rinsed, drained,
    stemmed, and thinly sliced

2 dried cloud ear (black fungus) or wood ear
    mushrooms, soaked in hot water to cover
    20 minutes, or until softened, rinsed,
    drained, thinly sliced

½ cup fresh or frozen peas

½ cup dried lily buds, soaked in hot water
    to cover 20 minutes, or until softened,
    rinsed, drained (optional)

1 large tomato (about 8 ounces), chopped

½ tablespoon finely chopped fresh ginger

1 teaspoon sugar

Salt, to taste

¼ teaspoon crushed red pepper flakes, or
    to taste

2 tablespoons Chinese black vinegar or
    balsamic vinegar, plus additional, to
    serve

2 tablespoons reduced-sodium soy sauce,
    or more, to taste

1 tablespoon toasted (dark) sesame oil

Freshly ground black pepper, to taste

2 tablespoons cornstarch mixed with
    2 tablespoons cold water

4 scallions, green parts only, thinly sliced

1 to 2 teaspoons Chinese hot oil, plus
    additional, to serve

In a medium stockpot, bring the broth and water to a boil over high heat. Add the tofu, mushrooms, peas, lily buds (if using), tomato, ginger, sugar, salt, and red pepper and return to a boil; reduce the heat to medium and simmer, uncovered, 3 minutes, stirring occasionally. Add the vinegar, soy sauce, sesame oil, and black pepper and stir 30 seconds. Add the cornstarch mixture and cook, stirring constantly, until thickened, about 3 minutes. Reduce the heat to low and add the scallion greens and hot oil; cook, stirring, 1 minute. Serve warm, with additional black vinegar and chili oil passed separately.

{PER SERVING} Calories 212 · Protein 19g · Total Fat 8g · Sat Fat 1g · Cholesterol 0mg · Carbohydrate 21g · Dietary Fiber 7g · Sodium 851mg

Basic Vegetable Broth

Use this basic broth wherever low-sodium vegetable broth is called for in the book. Leftovers can be frozen up to 3 months. For a richer flavor, add 1 whole star anise to the simmering broth.

MAKES 6 TO 8 CUPS

1 teaspoon canola oil

1 medium carrot (about 2 ounces), peeled and coarsely chopped

1 celery stalk, leaves attached, coarsely chopped

6 dried shiitake mushrooms, soaked in hot water to cover 20 minutes, or until softened, rinsed, drained, stemmed, and thinly sliced

3 scallions, white and green parts, sliced into ½-inch pieces

2-inch piece fresh ginger, peeled, sliced

10 cups water

½ teaspoon salt

½ teaspoon black peppercorns

½ to 1 tablespoon light or dark brown sugar

In a large stockpot, heat the oil over medium-low heat. Add the carrot, celery, mushrooms, scallions, and ginger and cook, stirring often, until softened and fragrant, 3 to 5 minutes. Raise the heat to medium-high and cook, stirring constantly, until sizzling and beginning to brown, 1 to 2 minutes. Add the remaining ingredients and bring to a boil over high heat. Reduce the heat to between medium and medium-low and simmer uncovered, stirring occasionally, 1 hour. Strain through a sieve, pressing on the solids with the back of a wooden spoon to extract the liquid. Discard the solids. Stir the sugar into the broth. Use the broth as directed in the desired recipe. Completely cooled broth can be refrigerated, covered, up to 5 days before using, or placed in freezer bags and stored in the freezer up to 3 months.

{PER SERVING} (about 1 cup, or ⅙ of recipe) **Calories 30 · Protein 1g · Total Fat 1g · Sat Fat 0g · Cholesterol 0mg · Carbohydrate 6g · Dietary Fiber 0g · Sodium 189mg**

Chinese Apple Soup

China produces over one-third of the world's apples—not surprisingly, they often find their way into soups. The following recipe is a popular cough remedy—in Chinese medicine, figs are said to reduce heat while almonds relieve congestion. Of course, a cold doesn't have to be an excuse to enjoy this light, sweet, and nourishing soup.

MAKES 4 SERVINGS

4 cups water

2 cups low-sodium vegetable broth

2 large Fuji apples (about 8 ounces each), unpeeled, cored, each cut into 8 wedges

1 large onion (about 8 ounces), cut into 8 wedges

8 to 12 whole raw almonds

8 pitted dried red dates (jujubes), halved

4 dried figs, halved lengthwise

¼ teaspoon salt, or to taste

In a medium stockpot, bring all ingredients to a simmer over medium-high heat. Reduce the heat to between low and medium-low and simmer, partially covered, stirring occasionally, about 1½ hours, or until the fruits are very tender. Serve warm.

{PER SERVING} Calories 221 · Protein 9g · Total Fat 5g · Sat Fat 1g · Cholesterol 0mg · Carbohydrate 39g · Dietary Fiber 8g · Sodium 397mg

Winter Melon Soup with Shiitake Mushrooms, Green Beans, and Kelp

Cleansing and cooling, with delicate winter white flesh, winter melon is a popular soup ingredient in China. Based on a family recipe submitted by Saimei, my student with the sweetest of smiles, this tasty winter melon soup bears a delightful tang of the sea with the addition of kelp, a nutritious sea vegetable. If dried thin strands of seaweed tangle, a variety of kelp, are unavailable, a toasted nori sheet, torn into small pieces, can be stirred into the soup just before serving. If winter melon is unavailable, fuzzy melon, zucchini, or the white part of a watermelon can be substituted.

MAKES 6 SERVINGS

4 cups low-sodium vegetable broth

4 cups water

2 pounds winter melon, peeled, seeded, cut into ½-inch cubes

4 ounces green beans, trimmed, cut into ½-inch lengths

6 medium dried Shiitake mushrooms, soaked in hot water to cover 20 minutes, or until softened, rinsed, drained, stemmed, and thinly sliced

½ ounce dried kelp, preferably seaweed tangle, rinsed, soaked in cold water to cover 20 minutes, rinsed and drained

2 tablespoons reduced-sodium soy sauce, or more, to taste

1 tablespoon Chinese black vinegar or balsamic vinegar

1 tablespoon chopped fresh ginger

1 tablespoon sugar

Salt and freshly ground black pepper, to taste

2 scallions, white and green parts, thinly sliced

¼ cup chopped fresh cilantro (leaves and stems)

1 tablespoon toasted (dark) sesame oil, or more, to taste

In a medium stockpot, bring the broth and water to a boil over high heat. Add the melon, green beans, mushrooms, kelp, soy sauce, vinegar, ginger, sugar, salt, and pepper and return to a boil. Reduce the heat to medium-low and simmer, partially covered, until melon is tender and transparent, 25 to 30 minutes, stirring occasionally, adding the scallions and cilantro the last few minutes of cooking. Stir in the sesame oil and serve warm.

{PER SERVING} Calories 102 · Protein 10g · Total Fat 3g · Sat Fat 0g · Cholesterol 0mg · Carbohydrate 12g · Dietary Fiber 5g · Sodium 607mg

Green Apple, Carrot, and Sweet Potato Soup with Ginger

Though not traditional, preroasting the apples and vegetables lends this superb soup a luxurious taste. Any tart apple can replace the Granny Smith variety, if desired.

MAKES 4 SERVINGS

½ pound Granny Smith apples, peeled if
   desired, cored, cut into 1½-inch pieces
½ pound carrots, peeled, cut into 1-inch
   pieces
½ pound sweet potato, peeled, cut into
   ½-inch pieces
1 tablespoon canola oil
¼ teaspoon salt
3 cups reduced-sodium vegetable broth
½ cup water, plus additional, as needed
1 tablespoon chopped fresh ginger
2 to 3 teaspoons reduced-sodium soy
   sauce, or to taste
2 to 3 teaspoons toasted (dark) sesame oil,
   or to taste
Freshly ground black pepper, to taste
Chopped garlic chives or green parts of
   scallions (optional)

Preheat oven to 400F (205C).

In a large bowl, combine apples, carrots, sweet potato, canola oil, and salt; toss well to coat. Arrange in a single layer on an ungreased rimmed baking sheet. Bake for 15 to 20 minutes, or until soft and lightly browned.

Transfer roasted vegetables to a medium stockpot and add the broth, water, and ginger; bring to a boil over medium-high heat. Reduce the heat to medium-low and simmer, uncovered, stirring occasionally, until potatoes are tender, 12 to 15 minutes.

Transfer the soup to a food processor fitted with the knife blade, or a blender; process until smooth and pureed. Return to the pot and stir in the soy sauce, sesame oil, and pepper; reheat over low heat, stirring occasionally and thinning with water, as needed. Serve warm, garnished with the chopped garlic chives, if using.

{PER SERVING} Calories 197 · Protein 10g · Total Fat 6g · Sat Fat 1g · Cholesterol 0mg · Carbohydrate 27g · Dietary Fiber 7g · Sodium 648mg

Bamboo Shoot Soup

This simple yet delicious soup is the perfect starter for any Asian-style meal. Chinese chili paste can replace the Sichuan sauce, if desired. Though fresh winter bamboo shoots are preferable, the frozen varieties are close seconds, and blanching the canned ones before using helps eliminate their somewhat tinny taste.

MAKES 4 TO 6 SERVINGS

About 2 pounds fresh winter bamboo
   shoots, prepared and precooked (see
   Cook's Tip, below), coarsely chopped, or
   16 ounces frozen cooked bamboo shoots,
   thawed, drained, coarsely chopped, or
   1 (16-ounce) can bamboo shoots, rinsed,
   drained, and coarsely chopped
½ tablespoon canola oil
2 scallions, white and green parts
   separated, white parts finely chopped,
   green parts thinly sliced
6 cups low-sodium vegetable broth
1 tablespoon black bean sauce with garlic
1 to 2 teaspoons reduced-sodium soy sauce

½ to 1 teaspoon Sichuan sauce, or to taste

1 teaspoon toasted (dark) sesame oil

Freshly ground black pepper, to taste

If using canned bamboo shoots: In a medium saucepan, bring the bamboo shoots and water to cover to a boil over high heat; boil 1 minute. Drain.

In a medium stockpot, heat the canola oil over medium heat. Add the white parts of the scallions and cook, stirring constantly, until lightly browned, 2 to 3 minutes. Add the broth and bamboo shoots and bring to a boil over high heat. Reduce the heat to medium and stir in the black bean sauce, soy sauce, and Sichuan sauce. Simmer, uncovered, 5 minutes, stirring occasionally.

Remove the pot from heat and transfer about ⅔ of the soup mixture to a blender, or a food processor fitted with the knife blade. Blend or process until smooth and pureed. Return to the pot and add the scallion greens, sesame oil, and pepper. Reheat over low heat as needed, stirring occasionally. Serve warm.

{PER SERVING} Calories 130 · Protein 19g · Total Fat 4g · Sat Fat 0g · Cholesterol 0mg · Carbohydrate 8g · Dietary Fiber 7g · Sodium 883mg

{COOK'S TIP}

To prepare fresh bamboo shoots for safe consumption, peel away the outer leaves and trim any fibrous tissue at the base so that about 50 percent of the original weight remains. Slice the flesh into thin strips and boil in lightly salted water 15 to 20 minutes, or until just tender. Drain and use as directed in recipe.

Velvet Corn Soup

A Chinese classic since the 1950s, this retro-style soup, whose integral ingredient is a can of creamed corn, is consistently tasty. Contrary to popular belief, "creamed" corn contains no dairy.

MAKES 4 SERVINGS

½ tablespoon canola oil

2 scallions, white and green parts separated, thinly sliced

2 large cloves garlic, finely chopped

3 cups low-sodium vegetable broth

1 (15-ounce) can creamed corn

1 tablespoon reduced-sodium soy sauce

1 tablespoon Shaoxing rice wine, dry sherry, sake, or dry white wine

Salt and freshly ground black pepper, to taste

1 teaspoon toasted (dark) sesame oil

In a large saucepan, heat the oil over medium heat. Add the white parts of the scallions and cook, stirring constantly, until softened, 1 to 2 minutes. Add the garlic and cook, stirring constantly, 30 seconds. Add broth and bring to a boil over medium-high heat. Add creamed corn, soy sauce, wine, salt, and pepper and let come to a simmer; reduce heat to medium-low and cook, stirring occasionally, 2 to 3 minutes, to allow flavors to blend. Stir in the scallion greens and sesame oil and serve hot.

{PER SERVING} Calories 152 · Protein 11g · Total Fat 3 · Sat Fat 0g · Cholesterol 0mg · Carbohydrate 23g · Dietary Fiber 4g · Sodium 843mg

Butternut Squash Soup with Star Anise and Ginger

This fragrant, pumpkin-colored soup is an excellent opener to Thanksgiving.

MAKES 6 SERVINGS

1 tablespoon canola oil

⅔ cup chopped shallot or red onion

1 tablespoon chopped fresh ginger

3 star anise

2 cloves garlic, finely chopped

1¾ pounds butternut squash, peeled, seeded, and cut into ½-inch pieces (about 20 ounces or 5 cups)

4 cups low-sodium vegetable broth

2 cups water

¼ teaspoon salt, or to taste

Freshly ground black pepper, to taste

1 to 2 teaspoons reduced-sodium soy sauce, or to taste (optional)

1 to 2 teaspoons toasted (dark) sesame oil (optional)

Chopped fresh cilantro or parsley, for garnish (optional)

In a medium stockpot, heat the oil over medium heat. Add the shallot, ginger, and star anise and cook, stirring, until shallot is just softened, about 2 minutes. Add the garlic and cook, stirring, until garlic is softened but not browned, 1 to 2 more minutes. Add squash, broth, water, salt, and pepper; bring to a boil over high heat. Reduce the heat to medium and simmer, uncovered, stirring occasionally, until squash is very tender, about 20 minutes.

Remove and discard star anise. Working in batches, transfer squash mixture to a food processor fitted with the knife blade, or to a blender; process or blend until smooth and pureed. Return to the pot and add the soy sauce and sesame oil, if using; reheat over low heat as needed, stirring occasionally. Serve warm, garnished with the cilantro, if using.

{PER SERVING} Calories 104 · Protein 9 · Total Fat 2g · Sat Fat 0g · Cholesterol 0mg · Carbohydrate 14g · Dietary Fiber 4g · Sodium 439mg

Chinese Cabbage and Fresh Corn Soup with Shiitake Mushrooms

Here is an ideal soup to make in late summer with the last of the season's less-than-perfect corn, when the first nip of fall is in the air.

MAKES 4 SERVINGS

2 fresh ears yellow corn, shucked

4 cups low-sodium vegetable broth, plus additional, as needed

3 cups water, plus additional, as needed

2 cups shredded Napa or green cabbage

8 dried shiitake mushrooms, soaked in hot water to cover 20 minutes, or until softened, rinsed, drained, stemmed, and thinly sliced, or 8 fresh shiitake mushrooms, stemmed and thinly sliced

½ cup chopped fresh carrot

2 scallions, white and green parts, thinly sliced

2 teaspoons sesame oil

1 teaspoon Chinese chili paste (optional)

Salt and freshly ground pepper, to taste

Working one by one, place an ear of corn in a deep-sided bowl and lean against the side. With a serrated knife, carefully cut off the kernels while moving the knife away from you. Set the kernels aside and save the cob.

In a medium stockpot, bring the broth and water to a boil over high heat. Add the corncobs, reduce the heat to between medium and medium-low, and simmer briskly, partially covered, 15 minutes. Remove the cobs and add the corn kernels, cabbage, mushrooms, and carrot; return to a brisk simmer over medium-high heat. Reduce the heat to between medium and medium-low and simmer, partially covered, stirring occasionally, about 10 minutes, or until vegetables are tender, adding additional broth or water, as needed. Stir in the scallions, sesame oil, chili paste (if using), salt, and pepper. Serve warm.

{PER SERVING} Calories 148 · Protein 14g · Total Fat 3g · Sat Fat 0g · Cholesterol 0mg · Carbohydrate 20g · Dietary Fiber 7g · Sodium 538mg

Hunan-Style Tomato, Potato, and Cauliflower Soup with Chili Peppers

Cauliflower is one of the most beloved vegetables in Hunan, where the beautiful white heads grow prolifically. For a delicious meal-in-a-bowl soup, add some cubed tofu to the simmering broth.

MAKES 4 TO 6 SERVINGS

1 tablespoon peanut oil
1 to 2 fresh red chili peppers, seeded and thinly sliced
1 tablespoon chopped fresh ginger
2 large cloves garlic, finely chopped

1 pound boiling potatoes, peeled, cut into small dice
1 pound cauliflower (about ½ medium head), cut into bite-size pieces
2 medium tomatoes (about 6 ounces each), peeled, seeded, and chopped (see Cook's tip, page 112)
4 cups reduced-sodium vegetable broth
2 cups water
1 to 2 tablespoons reduced-sodium soy sauce
1 teaspoon sugar
¼ teaspoon salt, or to taste
Freshly ground black pepper, to taste
2 scallions, white and green parts, thinly sliced
1 tablespoon toasted (dark) sesame oil
1 teaspoon Chinese chili paste, or to taste
2 teaspoons cornstarch mixed with 2 teaspoons water

In a wok or large deep-sided nonstick skillet, heat the oil over medium-high heat. Add the chili pepper, ginger, and garlic and cook, stirring constantly, 1 minute. Add the potatoes, cauliflower, and tomatoes and cook, stirring, 2 minutes. Add the broth, water, soy sauce, sugar, salt, and black pepper and bring to a boil over high heat. Reduce the heat to medium-low and simmer, uncovered, stirring occasionally, until potatoes are tender but not mushy, 20 to 30 minutes. Add the scallions, sesame oil, chili paste, and cornstarch mixture; cook, stirring constantly, until thickened, 1 to 2 minutes. Serve warm.

{PER SERVING} Calories 248 · Protein 17g · Total Fat 7g · Sat Fat 1g · Cholesterol 0mg · Carbohydrate 33g · Dietary Fiber 9g · Sodium 850mg

Harbin-Style Sweet-and-Sour Red Cabbage Borscht

In northern China, particularly in and around the city of Harbin, close to the Russian border, a spicy sweet-and-sour variation of borscht known as hongtang, or red soup, is made primarily with red cabbage, not beets. Though optional, a dollop of plain soy yogurt or nondairy sour cream is simply delicious here. Serve with pumpernickel bread and a tossed spinach and mushroom salad for a hearty cold-weather meal.

MAKES 4 SERVINGS

1 tablespoon canola oil

1 small red onion (about 4 ounces), thinly sliced

1 tablespoon chopped fresh ginger

2 large cloves garlic, finely chopped

4 cups shredded red cabbage

1 to 2 fresh red chili peppers, seeded and chopped

3 cups low-sodium vegetable broth

½ cup water

¼ cup plain rice vinegar

2 tablespoons reduced-sodium soy sauce

2 to 3 whole star anise

¼ cup packed light brown sugar

Salt and freshly ground black pepper, to taste

1 tablespoon toasted (dark) sesame oil

2 scallions, green parts only, thinly sliced

Plain soy yogurt or nondairy sour cream, for garnish (optional)

Toasted sesame seeds or caraway seeds, for garnish (optional)

In a medium stockpot, heat the canola oil over medium heat. Add the onion, ginger, and garlic and cook, stirring, until just softened, 2 to 3 minutes. Add the cabbage and chili pepper and cook, stirring constantly and scraping from the bottom to prevent sticking, until vegetables are softened and cabbage is wilted, about 5 minutes. Add the broth, water, vinegar, soy sauce, and star anise and bring to a boil over high heat, stirring from the bottom to loosen any browned bits. Reduce the heat to medium-low and stir in the brown sugar, salt, and black pepper; simmer, uncovered, until cabbage is very tender and liquid is reduced by about half, about 20 minutes, stirring occasionally and adjusting the heat between medium and medium-low to maintain a simmer. Remove and discard the star anise. Stir in the sesame oil and scallion greens. Serve warm, garnished with a dollop of soy yogurt and sprinkled with sesame seeds, if desired.

{PER SERVING} Calories 198 • Protein 11g • Total Fat 7g • Sat Fat 1g • Cholesterol 0mg • Carbohydrate 26g • Dietary Fiber 5g • Sodium 705mg

Spinach Wonton Soup

Made with both fresh and frozen spinach, this wonton soup is as simple to make as it is superb to eat. Flavored baked tofu or well-drained extra-firm tofu, finely chopped, can replace the seitan, if desired.

MAKES 4 SERVINGS

2 cups water

2 cups reduced-sodium vegetable broth

1 tablespoon thinly sliced peeled fresh
   ginger plus 1 teaspoon finely chopped
   fresh ginger
2 tablespoons plus 1 teaspoon reduced-
   sodium soy sauce
1 tablespoon Shaoxing rice wine,
   dry sherry, sake, or dry white
   wine
2 teaspoons plain rice vinegar
½ tablespoon light brown sugar
Salt and freshly ground black pepper,
   to taste
1 cup fresh baby spinach leaves
2 scallions, white and green parts,
   thinly sliced, plus 1 scallion, green
   part only, finely chopped
3 teaspoons toasted (dark) sesame oil
1 cup frozen chopped spinach, cooked
   according to package directions,
   drained, squeezed dry between paper
   towels, finely chopped
½ cup drained and finely chopped seitan,
   preferably a flavored variety, or
   flavored baked tofu, or regular
   extra-firm tofu
½ teaspoon Chinese chili paste
¼ teaspoon granulated white sugar
16 egg-free wonton wrappers, thawed
   if frozen

In a medium stockpot, bring the water, broth, sliced ginger, 2 tablespoons soy sauce, rice wine, vinegar, brown sugar, salt, and pepper to a boil over high heat. Reduce the heat to low, cover, and simmer 5 minutes. Add the fresh spinach, sliced scallions, and 1 teaspoon sesame oil; cover, and remove from the heat. Let stand, covered, about 10 minutes.

Meanwhile, in a medium bowl, mix cooked frozen spinach, seitan, finely chopped scallion greens, remaining 2 teaspoons sesame oil, remaining 1 teaspoon finely chopped ginger, remaining 1 teaspoon soy sauce, chili paste, white sugar, salt, and pepper until well combined.

Fill a small container with some water. Lay a wonton wrapper on a flat work surface and place 1 heaping teaspoon of the vegetable mixture in the center. Dip your finger in the water and wet the edges of the wrapper. Seal into a triangle, removing as much air as possible from the dumpling. Make sure edges are secured. Wet the corners and fold in like an envelope, pressing to seal. Repeat with remaining wonton wrappers and filling.

Meanwhile, bring a large stockpot filled with salted water to a boil over high heat. Gently lower the filled wontons into the water and reduce the heat to medium; cook, stirring gently, until wontons have floated to the surface and are translucent, 2 to 3 minutes. Using a slotted spoon, carefully transfer wontons to the hot broth (reheat the broth over low heat, if necessary).

To serve, ladle 4 wontons in each of 4 soup bowls. Ladle equal portions of broth and vegetables over the wontons. Serve at once.

{PER SERVING} Calories 231 · Protein 16g · Total Fat 6g · Sat Fat 1g · Cholesterol 0mg · Carbohydrate 30g · Dietary Fiber 4g · Sodium 854mg

Tibetan Vegetable Soup

You can experiment using different combinations of vegetables in this light yet hearty soup, delicious with Chinese Corn Flour Flatbread (page 6) or pita bread. For added punch, stir in a teaspoon of Chinese chili paste.

MAKES 4 SERVINGS

2 tablespoons canola oil

½ cup finely chopped onion

1 tablespoon finely chopped fresh ginger

3 large cloves garlic, finely chopped

¼ cup all-purpose flour

4 cups low-sodium vegetable broth

3 cups water

8 ounces extra-firm tofu, drained, cut into ½-inch cubes

1 cup chopped fresh cauliflower florets

1 medium tomato (about 6 ounces), chopped

4 scallions, white and green parts, thinly sliced

½ cup chopped carrots

¼ cup chopped celery

1 to 2 tablespoons reduced-sodium soy sauce

Salt and freshly ground black pepper, to taste

¼ cup chopped fresh cilantro (optional)

1 tablespoon toasted (dark) sesame oil

1 teaspoon Chinese chili paste, or to taste (optional)

In a medium stockpot, heat the oil over medium heat. Add the onion, ginger, and garlic and cook, stirring constantly, 1 minute. Add the flour and cook, stirring constantly, until lightly browned, 3 to 5 minutes. Gradually add the broth and water, whisking constantly to maintain a smooth consistency. Add the tofu, cauliflower, tomato, scallions, carrots, celery, soy sauce, salt, and pepper and bring to a boil over medium-high heat, stirring often. Reduce the heat and simmer, partially covered, until vegetables are tender, about 10 minutes, stirring occasionally. Stir in the cilantro (if using), sesame oil, and chili paste (if using), and serve hot.

{PER SERVING} Calories 254 · Protein 19g · Total Fat 13g · Sat Fat 1g · Cholesterol 0mg · Carbohydrate 18g · Dietary Fiber 7g · Sodium 698mg

---

· MEAL-IN-A-BOWL SOUPS, STEWS, AND CONGEES ·

Fresh Arrowroot Soup with Corn, Lentils, and Red Beans

This nourishing and mildly sweet soup is often fed to children. A fresh arrowroot looks like a small onion with a large stem, only without the layers—they are generally abundant in Asian markets throughout the winter months. Canned red beans (not to be confused with cans of sweetened red beans/paste), also known as adzuki beans, are available in Asian markets; red kidney beans or pinto beans can replace them in a pinch.

MAKES 6 SERVINGS

1 tablespoon canola oil

1 cup chopped onion

¼ cup chopped carrot

4 cups low-sodium vegetable broth

4 cups water

1 (16-ounce) can red beans (adzuki), rinsed
and drained
12 ounces fresh arrowroot (about 3
medium), peeled and coarsely chopped
1½ cups frozen yellow corn
½ cup dried lentils, rinsed and picked over
1 teaspoon chopped fresh orange peel or
½ teaspoon dried
½ teaspoon salt, or to taste
Freshly ground black pepper, to taste
2 scallions, green parts only, thinly sliced
Soy sauce and toasted (dark) sesame oil, to
serve (optional)

In a medium stockpot, heat the oil over medium heat. Add the onion and carrot and cook, stirring, until softened, about 3 minutes. Add the remaining ingredients except the scallion greens, soy sauce, and sesame oil and bring to a boil over high heat. Reduce the heat to medium-low and simmer, partially covered, until arrowroot and lentils are tender, 45 minutes to 1 hour, stirring occasionally. Stir in the scallion greens and serve warm, with the soy sauce and sesame oil passed separately, if desired.

{PER SERVING} Calories 279 · Protein 19g · Total Fat 3g · Sat Fat 0g · Cholesterol 0mg · Carbohydrate 47g · Dietary Fiber 10g · Sodium 537mg

Rice Congee with Shiitake Mushrooms and Peas

Congee, a savory or sweet stewlike porridge, most commonly made with rice, is the ultimate Chinese comfort food.

MAKES 6 SERVINGS

2 cups long-grain white rice, rinsed under
cold running water, drained
½ teaspoon salt
1 tablespoon toasted (dark) sesame oil
8 dried shiitake mushrooms, soaked in hot
water to cover 20 minutes, or until
softened, rinsed, drained, stemmed, and
chopped
1 cup frozen baby peas, thawed
2 scallions, white and green parts, thinly
sliced
1 to 2 large cloves garlic, finely chopped
Freshly ground black pepper, to taste
Reduced-sodium soy sauce, Chinese black
vinegar, chopped fresh cilantro, chopped
fresh scallions, and/or chopped pickled
vegetables, to serve

In a medium stockpot, place the rice and salt with cold water to cover by 1 inch. Bring to a boil over high heat; boil 2 minutes. Reduce heat and simmer, partially covered, stirring occasionally, about 20 minutes, or until rice is tender and mixture is soupy, adding water as needed and stirring from the bottom to prevent sticking.

Meanwhile, in a medium nonstick skillet, heat ½ tablespoon of oil over medium heat. Add the mushrooms, peas, scallions, and garlic and cook, stirring, until fragrant and softened, about 2 minutes. Add to the rice mixture and season with pepper; cook over low heat, stirring, until heated through, about 5 minutes. Stir in the remaining ½ tablespoon of oil. Serve at once, with soy sauce and additional condiments passed separately.

{PER SERVING} Calories 273 · Protein 6g · Total Fat 3g · Sat Fat 1g · Cholesterol 0mg · Carbohydrate 54g · Dietary Fiber 2g · Sodium 210mg

Buddha's Delight Vegetable Stew

Traditionally served on New Year's Day, this mildly flavored vegetable stew is well suited to most palates. For extra punch, 1 to 2 teaspoons of Chinese chili paste can be added along with the toasted sesame oil. Dried lily buds are available at most Asian markets—if you can't locate these golden-hued unopened flowers, omit them from the recipe. Dried sheets of bean curd or tofu skin, broken into small pieces, can replace the bean curd sticks, or tofu bamboo. Cubed extra-firm tofu can replace either dried variety, if necessary.

MAKES 4 TO 6 SERVINGS

- 4 ounces dried bean curd sticks or tofu bamboo (about 4 sticks, depending on length), broken into 6-inch lengths, soaked in boiling water to cover until softened, about 30 minutes, drained well
- 1 tablespoon peanut oil
- 2 scallions, white and green parts separated, thinly sliced
- 1 tablespoon finely chopped fresh ginger
- 8 dried shiitake mushrooms, soaked in hot water to cover 20 minutes, or until softened, rinsed, drained, stemmed, thinly sliced
- ½ cup dried lily buds, soaked in hot water to cover 20 minutes, or until softened, rinsed, drained well
- ½ pound frozen bamboo shoots, cooked according to package directions, drained, or 8 ounces canned bamboo shoots, cooked in boiling water 1 minute, drained
- 1 cup sliced fresh water chestnuts, or 1 cup sliced, rinsed, and drained canned water chestnuts
- ½ cup shredded carrots
- 4 ounces fresh snow peas, trimmed, halved diagonally
- 1 cup shredded Napa or green cabbage
- ¼ cup canned or vacuum-packed ginkgo nuts, rinsed and drained
- ½ cup low-sodium vegetable broth, plus additional, as needed
- ¼ cup vegetarian oyster sauce or mushroom soy sauce
- 2 tablespoons regular reduced-sodium soy sauce
- 2 tablespoons Shaoxing rice wine, dry sherry, sake, or dry white wine
- 2 tablespoons black bean sauce with garlic
- 1 tablespoon dark soy sauce
- 1 teaspoon sugar
- 1 (3.75-ounce) package cellophane noodles, or mung bean threads, soaked in hot water to cover 10 minutes, or until softened, drained, cut into 6-inch lengths
- 1 tablespoon toasted (dark) sesame oil

Cut the bean curd sticks crosswise into 1-inch pieces and set aside. In a wok or large deep-sided nonstick skillet with a lid, heat the peanut oil over medium-high heat. Add the white parts of the scallions and ginger and cook, stirring, 1 minute. Add the mushrooms and lily buds and cook, stirring, 1 minute. Add the bamboo shoots, bean curd sticks, water chestnuts, and carrots, and cook, stirring, 1 minute. Add the snow peas, cabbage, and nuts and cook, stirring, 1 minute. Add the broth, oyster sauce, regular soy sauce, rice wine, black bean sauce, dark soy sauce, and sugar and let come to a boil. Reduce the heat to low and add the cellophane noodles, scallion greens, and sesame oil; cook, covered, 5 minutes, stirring occasionally, or until noodles and dried bean curd sticks are tender, adding additional broth as needed. Serve warm.

{PER SERVING} Calories 336 · Protein 10g · Total Fat 10g · Sat Fat 2g · Cholesterol 0mg · Carbohydrate 53g · Dietary Fiber 8g · Sodium 878mg

Country-Style Vegetable Stew with Tofu Puffs

Tofu puffs, also known as bean curd puffs or bean kow, are golden squares of soybean curd that have been deep-fried. Their super-absorbency makes them highly popular in stews and braised dishes. Look for them in the refrigerated section of Asian markets, next to the regular tofu products. For a saucier stew, use 1½ packages, or 6 ounces, of tofu puffs. Serve over rice to catch all the delicious sauce.

MAKES 4 SERVINGS

- 1 cup low-sodium vegetable broth, plus additional, as needed
- 1 cup water, plus additional, as needed
- 3 tablespoons all-purpose flour
- 2 tablespoons peanut oil
- 2 medium onions (about 6 ounces each), each cut into 8 wedges
- 1 medium carrot (about 2 ounces), peeled, cut into ½-inch-thick slices
- ¼ cup chopped celery
- 1 tablespoon chopped fresh ginger
- 2 large cloves garlic, finely chopped
- 1 medium sweet potato (about 6 ounces), peeled and cut into bite-size pieces
- 1 cup green beans, trimmed, cut diagonally in half
- 1 teaspoon Chinese chili paste, or to taste
- ½ teaspoon salt, or to taste
- Freshly ground black pepper, to taste
- 2 (4-ounce) packages deep-fried tofu puffs, each piece halved
- 1 cup frozen peas, thawed

In a small container, whisk together the broth, water, and flour until thoroughly blended; set aside.

In a medium stockpot, heat the oil over medium heat. Add the onions, carrot, celery, and ginger and cook, stirring, until fragrant and softened, about 5 minutes. Add the garlic and cook, stirring, 1 minute. Add the broth mixture, sweet potato, green beans, chili paste, salt, and pepper and bring to a boil over medium-high heat; cook, stirring, 1 minute. Reduce the heat to medium-low, stir in the tofu puffs, cover, and simmer 10 minutes, stirring occasionally. Add the peas and cook, covered, until all vegetables are tender, about 5 more minutes, stirring occasionally and adding additional broth or water for a soupier consistency, if desired. Serve warm.

{PER SERVING} Calories 272 · Protein 12g · Total Fat 12g · Sat Fat 2g · Cholesterol 0mg · Carbohydrate 33g · Dietary Fiber 7g · Sodium 429mg

Millet and Sweet Potato Congee

One of the five sacred grains of ancient China, millet is available in Asian markets and health food stores. This traditional, northern-style porridge-like soup, or congee, makes a nourishing breakfast or interesting main dish.

MAKES 4 TO 6 SERVINGS

6 cups water, plus additional, as needed
1 cup millet, rinsed and drained
1 medium sweet potato (about 6 ounces), peeled and chopped
6 pitted dried red dates (jujubes), halved
¼ cup dark brown sugar
1 tablespoon chopped fresh ginger
1 cinnamon stick
½ teaspoon salt, or to taste
Chopped walnuts or chestnuts (optional)

In a medium stockpot, combine all ingredients except walnuts and bring to a boil over high heat. Reduce the heat to between low and medium-low and simmer, partially covered, until millet is tender and mixture is porridge-like, about 45 minutes, stirring occasionally and adding water, if necessary. Remove and discard the cinnamon stick and serve hot, garnished with the optional nuts, if using.

{PER SERVING} Calories 251 · Protein 6g · Total Fat 2g · Sat Fat 0g · Cholesterol 0mg · Carbohydrate 51g · Dietary Fiber 6g · Sodium 275mg

Changsha-Style Fresh Rice Noodle Soup

I still dream about the inspiration of this simple yet delicious soup, always made with the freshest of rice noodles in the streets of Changsha, the capital of Hunan, which is China's—and, likely, the world's—largest rice producer. The secret to my version is letting the cooked noodles steep in the flavorful broth a few minutes before slurping up and savoring. If you don't have access to fresh flat rice noodles, often sold in the refrigerated section of Asian markets in packages labeled rice sticks, use a wheat-based, eggless, linguine-style fresh wheat pasta instead and cook according to package directions.

MAKES 4 SERVINGS

4 cups reduced-sodium vegetable broth
2 cups water
½ tablespoon reduced-sodium regular soy sauce
½ tablespoon dark soy sauce
½ tablespoon vegetarian oyster sauce
½ tablespoon Chinese black vinegar or balsamic vinegar
½ tablespoon chopped fresh ginger
1 teaspoon light brown sugar
1 teaspoon Chinese chili paste, or to taste
½ star anise
¼ cup chopped fresh cilantro, stems included
1 scallion, white and green parts separated, thinly sliced
½ tablespoon toasted (dark) sesame oil
8 ounces fresh rice sticks or other fresh flat rice noodles

Prepared Hunan pepper sauce (duo jiao) or
   Fresh Chili Garlic Sauce (page 14), to
   serve
Pickled Chinese Long Beans (page 18),
   chopped preserved vegetables, or
   chopped fresh cilantro, to serve

In a medium stockpot, bring the broth, water, soy sauces, oyster sauce, vinegar, ginger, sugar, chili paste, and star anise to a boil over high heat. Reduce heat to medium-low and stir in the cilantro and white parts of the scallion; simmer, partially covered, 10 minutes, stirring occasionally. Remove and discard the star anise. Stir in the green parts of the scallion and the sesame oil. Cover and keep warm over very low heat.

Meanwhile, bring a large pot of salted water to a boil over high heat. Add the noodles and cook according to package directions until noodles are just al dente, typically as quickly as 15 seconds to as long as 1 minute, depending on freshness and thickness, stirring once or twice. Drain in a colander and, without rinsing, immediately transfer noodles to the hot broth. Cover, remove from heat, and let steep 5 minutes. Using tongs, place equal portions of the noodles into each of 4 soup bowls. Ladle equal portions of the broth mixture over top. Serve at once, with the garnishes passed separately.

{PER SERVING} (without optional condiments and garnishes) Calories 275 · Protein 12g · Total Fat 2g · Sat Fat 0g · Cholesterol 0mg · Carbohydrate 53g · Dietary Fiber 4g · Sodium 753mg

Instant Ramen Noodle Soup with Vegetables

Ramen noodle soup is endlessly popular in China—small wonder, as the Chinese invented this wonderfully thin and curly noodle. Instant plain dried ramen noodles are available in Asian markets—if necessary, use the packaged flavored variety and omit the seasoning packets.

MAKES 3 TO 4 SERVINGS

4 cups reduced-sodium vegetable broth
2 cups water
1 cup frozen peas and carrots
3 scallions, white and green parts
   separated, thinly sliced
1 tablespoon reduced-sodium soy sauce,
   or to taste
½ tablespoon chopped fresh ginger
1 teaspoon Chinese hot oil, or to taste
4 ounces instant plain ramen noodles
½ tablespoon toasted (dark) sesame oil

In a medium saucepan, bring the broth, water, peas and carrots, white parts of the scallions, soy sauce, ginger, and hot oil to a boil over high heat. Add the noodles and return to a boil. Reduce the heat to medium-high and cook, stirring to break up the noodles, until noodles are al dente, 2 to 3 minutes. Remove from heat and stir in the scallion greens and sesame oil. Serve at once.

{PER SERVING} Calories 276 · Protein 22g · Total Fat 5g · Sat Fat 1g · Cholesterol 0mg · Carbohydrate 38g · Dietary Fiber 8g · Sodium 934mg

Spicy Hunan Hot Pot

Ready in just about 15 minutes, this easy one-pot wonder makes the perfect rush-hour supper. Cremini or cultivated white mushrooms can stand in for the shiitake, if desired.

MAKES 6 SERVINGS

- 2 teaspoons peanut oil
- 2 tablespoons chopped fresh ginger
- 6 cloves garlic, finely chopped
- ¼ pound fresh shiitake mushrooms, stemmed and sliced
- 4 cups low-sodium vegetable broth
- 2 cups water
- 3 to 4 tablespoons reduced-sodium soy sauce
- 1 tablespoon dark brown sugar
- 2 to 3 teaspoons Chinese chili paste, or to taste
- ½ tablespoon toasted (dark) sesame oil
- 8 ounces dried flat rice noodles (stir-fry or linguine-style)
- 1 pound firm tofu, drained and cut into 1-inch cubes
- 4 cups thinly sliced fresh bok choy greens (tender parts only)
- ½ cup chopped fresh cilantro
- 2 scallions, mostly green parts, thinly sliced
- Prepared Hunan pepper sauce (duo jiao) or Fresh Chili Garlic Sauce (page 14), to serve (optional)

In a medium stockpot, heat the peanut oil over medium heat. Add the ginger and garlic and cook, stirring, until fragrant, about 1 minute. Add the mushrooms and cook, stirring, until softened, 2 to 3 minutes. Add the broth, water, soy sauce, sugar, chili paste, and sesame oil; cover and bring to a boil over high heat. Add the noodles and boil until almost cooked al dente, 3 to 4 minutes, pushing them down into the broth and stirring occasionally. Stir in the tofu and bok choy; cover, and reduce heat to medium. Cook, stirring a few times, until bok choy is wilted and noodles are cooked al dente, 2 to 3 minutes. Remove from heat and stir in cilantro and scallions. Serve warm, with the pepper sauce passed separately, if desired.

{PER SERVING} Calories 275 · Protein 16g · Total Fat 7g · Sat Fat 1g · Cholesterol 0mg · Carbohydrate 41g · Dietary Fiber 4g · Sodium 688mg

Tibetan Lentil Soup

This simple and satisfying lentil soup never fails to lift the spirits.

MAKES 6 SERVINGS

- 1½ tablespoons canola oil
- 1 medium onion (about 6 ounces), chopped
- 1 large carrot (about 3 ounces), peeled and chopped
- 1 fresh red or green chili pepper, seeded and finely chopped
- 2 large cloves garlic, finely chopped
- 1 teaspoon whole cumin seed
- 4 cups low-sodium vegetable broth
- 2 cups water
- 1½ cups dried lentils, rinsed and picked over
- 1 medium boiling potato (about 3 ounces), peeled and chopped

1 teaspoon whole coriander, crushed

1 teaspoon sugar

1 teaspoon salt

½ teaspoon ground cumin

1½ (14.5-ounce) cans diced tomatoes, undrained (about 3 cups)

¼ cup chopped fresh cilantro

1 teaspoon Chinese chili paste

1 tablespoon toasted (dark) sesame oil

In a medium stockpot, heat the oil over medium heat. Add the onion, carrot, chili pepper, garlic, and cumin seed; cook, stirring, until vegetables are softened, about 3 minutes. Add the broth, water, lentils, potato, coriander, sugar, salt, and ground cumin; bring to a boil over high heat. Reduce the heat to between low and medium-low and simmer, covered, 30 minutes, stirring occasionally. Stir in the tomatoes with their liquid, half the cilantro, and the chili paste; simmer, covered, until lentils are tender, about 15 more minutes, stirring occasionally. Stir in the remaining 2 tablespoons of cilantro and the sesame oil. Serve warm.

{PER SERVING} Calories 305 · Protein 23g · Total Fat 7g · Sat Fat 1g · Cholesterol 0mg · Carbohydrate 42g · Dietary Fiber 19g · Sodium 969mg

Northern-Style Fresh Noodle Soup with Tofu and Pickled Vegetables

In the north, this soup is made with hand-pulled fresh wheat noodles known as la mian, but any fresh noodle (udon is a good choice) or pasta will work well in this outstanding recipe. Rinsed and drained sauerkraut can replace the pickled Chinese cabbage, if necessary.

MAKES 4 SERVINGS

¼ cup canola oil

2 scallions, white and green parts, coarsely chopped

4 cups reduced-sodium vegetable broth

2 tablespoons chopped fresh cilantro

2 tablespoons reduced-sodium soy sauce

½ tablespoon toasted (dark) sesame oil

½ cup pickled Chinese cabbage, rinsed and chopped

¼ teaspoon crushed red pepper flakes, or to taste

8 ounces extra-firm tofu, drained, cut into ½-inch cubes

Salt and freshly ground black pepper, to taste

1 tablespoon cornstarch mixed with ½ cup water

8 ounces fresh Chinese wheat noodles (la mian) or other fresh egg-free noodles or pasta, cooked according to package directions until just al dente, drained and rinsed under cold running water

Thinly sliced scallion greens and cilantro leaves, for garnish

In a small saucepan, heat the canola oil over medium heat. Add the chopped scallions and cook until fragrant, stirring often, about 10 minutes, reducing the heat to medium-low after a few minutes. Strain into a heat-proof bowl, discarding the scallions, and set aside.

In a medium stockpot, bring the broth and chopped cilantro to a boil over high heat. Reduce the heat to low and add 1 tablespoon soy sauce and the sesame oil; simmer gently, stirring occasionally, about 5 minutes. Cover and keep warm over very low heat.

In a wok or large nonstick skillet, heat 2 tablespoons of the reserved scallion oil over medium heat. Add the pickled cabbage and red pepper flakes and cook, stirring constantly, 30 seconds. Add the tofu, remaining 1 tablespoon of soy sauce, salt, and black pepper; cook, stirring, 2 to 3 minutes. Add the cornstarch mixture and cook, stirring constantly, until thickened, about 3 minutes. Remove from heat and keep warm.

To serve, divide the noodles equally among 4 serving bowls. Ladle the hot broth mixture equally over top. Top with equal portions of the tofu mixture. Drizzle evenly with the remaining scallion oil. Garnish with the sliced scallion greens and cilantro leaves and serve at once.

{PER SERVING} Calories 312 · Protein 16g · Total Fat 13g · Sat Fat 1g · Cholesterol 0mg · Carbohydrate 34g · Dietary Fiber 4g · Sodium 583mg

Yunnan-Style Udon Noodles in Green Tea Broth

On a cold wintry evening, snuggle up with a steamy bowl of thick, long, slippery udon noodles—known as cu mian in China—in a savory green tea broth. Dried chrysanthemum flowers, widely popular in teas throughout China, are used in cooked dishes, as well, particularly those from Yunnan Province. They can typically be found in western Asian markets close to the rock sugar and tapioca pearls; if necessary, omit from the recipe. Though optional, dried seaweed strips add a salty punch. For a more substantial soup, add cubed tofu to the simmering broth. Four green tea bags can be used in lieu of the loose tea leaves; simply remove them from the liquid after steeping and discard. For best results, use fresh udon noodles, available in the refrigerated section of Asian markets—any fresh egg-free pasta can be substituted, if necessary.

MAKES 4 SERVINGS

7 cups water
¼ cup loose green tea leaves
2 dried chrysanthemum flowers
1 (14-ounce) can reduced-sodium vegetable broth (1¾ cups)
4 scallions, white and green parts separated, thinly sliced
1 to 2 tablespoons reduced-sodium soy sauce, or to taste
1 tablespoon finely chopped fresh ginger
½ teaspoon salt, or to taste
8 ounces fresh udon noodles
1½ tablespoons light brown sugar, or to taste
1 tablespoon toasted (dark) sesame oil
Freshly ground black pepper, to taste
2 sheets dried seaweed or nori, cut into thin 1-inch strips (optional)

In a medium stockpot with a lid, bring the water to a boil over high heat. Remove from heat and stir in the tea leaves and flowers; steep, covered, about 7 minutes, or until fragrant and nicely colored. Strain the tea through a strainer and return the liquid to the stockpot. Discard the tea leaves and flowers.

Add the broth, white parts of the scallions, soy sauce, ginger, and salt to the tea and bring to a boil over high heat; stir in the noodles. When the liquid returns to a boil, reduce the heat to medium-high. Simmer briskly, stirring occasionally, until the noodles are just tender, about 5 minutes, depending on thickness. Remove from heat and stir in the scallion greens, sugar, oil, and pepper. Cover and let stand 5 minutes. Uncover and serve at once, garnished with the dried seaweed strips, if using.

{PER SERVING} Calories 250 · Protein 12g · Total Fat 5g · Sat Fat 1g · Cholesterol 0mg · Carbohydrate 40g · Dietary Fiber 4g · Sodium 666mg

* CHAPTER THREE *

Salads

Salads, the unsung actors in Chinese cuisine, actually play a variety of significant roles. Sometimes a salad is a type of appetizer, served with an assortment of other light dishes on a dim sum display. Other times, especially during the summer months, a salad is a type of main course, composed primarily of cold noodles, rice, or tofu mixed with vegetables. Occasionally, a salad is used to clear the palate, usually after a particularly spicy dish. Seldom, if ever, does the common garden-variety salad, a popular opening act in the West, make an appearance. Indeed, a salad's most favored part is that of side dish, providing a contrast or balance of flavor, texture, and color with the other dishes on the menu, fulfilling the primary principle of Chinese cuisine. Whatever the occasion, the following chapter features something for everyone in the audience, whether it's Chilled Asparagus, Mizuna, and Red Leaf Lettuce Salad, Shandong-Style, for an elegant first course; Chinese Potato Salad for a casual picnic; or Warm Tofu and Chinese Spinach Salad for a superb supper—enjoy the show!

Hunan-Style Shredded Tofu Noodle Salad with Carrots, Celery, and Garlic Chives

Shredded tofu was one of my best "finds" in China. These chewy bean curd noodles—also referred to as shredded tofu noodles, tofu strands, or bean curd strands—are an excellent gluten-free alternative to wheat noodles and other pasta. Upon my return, I was delighted to discover them right in my own backyard, at the local Asian market, in the refrigerated section, next to the standard blocks of tofu—yes!

MAKES 3 MAIN DISH OR 4 TO 6 SIDE DISH SERVINGS

1 (8-ounce) packet shredded tofu

2 to 3 tablespoons reduced-sodium soy sauce

2 to 3 tablespoons plain rice vinegar

1 to 1½ tablespoons toasted (dark) sesame oil

2 to 3 teaspoons Chinese hot oil

1 teaspoon sugar, or to taste

¼ teaspoon crushed red pepper flakes, or to taste

¼ teaspoon salt, or to taste

2 to 4 tablespoons finely chopped fresh cilantro

½ tablespoon finely chopped fresh ginger

1 cup shredded carrots

1 small bunch Chinese garlic chives (about 1 ounce), buds removed, cut into 2-inch lengths, or about 4 scallion greens, sliced lengthwise in half, cut into 2-inch lengths

1 to 2 stalks celery, cut into thin 2-inch lengths

In a medium stockpot, cook the shredded tofu in boiling salted water until separated and al dente, 5 to 9 minutes, depending on freshness, stirring occasionally. Drain in a colander and rinse under cold running water; drain well.

In a large bowl, whisk together the soy sauce, vinegar, sesame oil, hot oil, sugar, red pepper flakes, and salt; stir in the cilantro and ginger and let stand a few minutes to allow the flavors to blend. Add the tofu noodles, carrots, garlic chives, and celery and toss well to combine. Let stand about 15 minutes at room temperature to allow the flavors to blend, tossing a few times. Toss again and serve at room temperature. Alternatively, cover and refrigerate a minimum of 1 hour or up to 2 days and serve chilled, or return to room temperature.

{PER SERVING} Calories 160 · Protein 8g · Total Fat 11g · Sat Fat 2g · Cholesterol 0mg · Carbohydrate 9g · Dietary Fiber 3g · Sodium 608mg

Chilled Asparagus, Mizuna, and Red Leaf Lettuce Salad, Shandong-Style

Here is a light and lovely first-course salad to commence any Asian-style meal. Mizuna is a frilly-leafed Asian green with a pleasant, peppery flavor—arugula or young mustard greens may be used instead. Red leaf lettuce provides a pretty contrast of color.

MAKES 4 SERVINGS

> 1 pound thin asparagus, trimmed, cut crosswise on the diagonal into 2-inch pieces
> 1½ tablespoons reduced-sodium soy sauce
> 1½ tablespoons vegetarian oyster sauce
> 1 tablespoon toasted (dark) sesame oil
> ¼ teaspoon Chinese hot oil, or to taste (optional)
> Salt and freshly ground black pepper, to taste
> 2 cups mizuna, coarsely torn
> 2 cups red leaf lettuce, coarsely torn
> ½ teaspoon toasted sesame seeds

Bring a medium stockpot filled with water to a boil over high heat. Prepare an ice water bath. Cook the asparagus in the boiling water until crisp-tender and bright green, 1 to 2 minutes. Drain and immediately place in the ice water bath; let stand 5 minutes to refresh. Drain well.

In a medium bowl, whisk together the soy sauce, oyster sauce, sesame oil, hot oil (if using), salt, and pepper. Add the asparagus, tossing well to combine. Let stand about 10 minutes to allow the flavors to blend.

In a small bowl, toss together the mizuna and red leaf lettuce. Divide salad greens among 4 salad plates or bowls. Toss the asparagus again; arrange equal portions of asparagus and dressing over the salad greens. Sprinkle evenly with the sesame seeds and serve at once.

{PER SERVING} Calories 64 · Protein 3g · Total Fat 4g · Sat Fat 1g · Cholesterol 0mg · Carbohydrate 6g · Dietary Fiber 2g · Sodium 465mg

Raw Beet and Scallion Salad

For a lovely first course, present this delicious raw beet salad over baby spinach.

MAKES 4 TO 6 SERVINGS

> 1½ tablespoons plain rice vinegar
> ½ tablespoon reduced-sodium soy sauce
> ½ tablespoon canola oil
> ½ tablespoon toasted (dark) sesame oil
> ½ teaspoon sugar
> Salt and freshly ground black pepper, to taste
> 2 medium beets (about 5 ounces each), peeled, julienned or shredded
> 4 scallions, green parts only, sliced into thin 2-inch lengths

In a large bowl, whisk together the vinegar, soy sauce, canola oil, sesame oil, sugar, salt, and pepper until the sugar is dissolved. Add the beets and scallions and toss well to combine. Let stand 15 minutes at room temperature to allow the flavors to blend. Toss again and serve at room temperature. Alternatively, cover and refrigerate up to 24 hours and serve chilled, or return to room temperature.

{PER SERVING} Calories 61 · Protein 1g · Total Fat 4g · Sat Fat 0g · Cholesterol 0mg · Carbohydrate 7g · Dietary Fiber 2g · Sodium 115mg

Endive and Green Apple Salad with Orange-Ginger Dressing

This elegant first-course salad hails from Macau, a former Portuguese colony and the current gaming capital of the world, situated opposite Hong Kong facing the South China Sea.

MAKES 6 SERVINGS

¾ cup orange juice, preferably freshly
    squeezed
½ tablespoon sugar
½ tablespoon chopped fresh ginger
¼ teaspoon grated orange peel
1 teaspoon fresh lemon juice
¼ teaspoon Chinese hot mustard
2 tablespoons chopped fresh cilantro
1½ to 2 tablespoons fresh lime juice (about
    1 lime)
½ tablespoon toasted (dark) sesame oil
Salt and freshly ground black pepper, to
    taste

4 large heads Belgian endive (about
    4 ounces each), trimmed, halved
    crosswise, then cut lengthwise into thin
    strips
2 medium Granny Smith apples, peeled, if
    desired, and chopped
1 cup seedless mandarin orange segments,
    fresh (from about 2 mandarin oranges) or
    canned in juice, drained
1 tablespoon toasted pine nuts or sunflower
    seeds (optional)

In a medium saucepan, bring orange juice, sugar, ginger, and orange peel to a boil over medium-high heat. Reduce the heat to medium and simmer, stirring occasionally, until liquid is reduced by half, 5 to 8 minutes. Stir in lemon juice and mustard and return to a boil over medium-high heat. Remove from heat and let cool completely. (At this point, mixture can be covered and refrigerated up to 2 days before continuing with the recipe.)

In a large bowl, whisk together the orange juice mixture, cilantro, lime juice, sesame oil, salt, and pepper. Add the endive and apple and toss well to combine. Divide evenly among 6 salad plates and garnish evenly with the orange segments and pine nuts, if using. Serve at once.

{PER SERVING} Calories 128 · Protein 5g · Total Fat 2g · Sat Fat 0g · Cholesterol 0mg · Carbohydrate 27g · Dietary Fiber 10g · Sodium 80mg

Sesame Broccoli-Stem and Scallion Salad

Ready-made broccoli slaw makes quick work of this tasty salad. While the broccoli stems are traditionally blanched, you can skip this step if a raw version is preferred. In the latter instance, marinate in the refrigerator a minimum of 3 hours before serving.

MAKES 4 TO 6 SERVINGS

1 (12-ounce) package broccoli slaw
2 tablespoons reduced-sodium soy sauce
1 tablespoon toasted (dark) sesame oil
1 tablespoon light brown sugar
½ tablespoon plain rice vinegar
Salt and freshly ground black pepper,
   to taste
4 scallions, mostly green parts, cut into
   very thin 2-inch lengths
1 teaspoon toasted sesame seeds

In a medium stockpot filled with boiling salted water, blanch the broccoli slaw about 30 seconds. Drain in a colander, then rinse under cold running water until cooled. Drain well.

In a medium bowl, whisk together the soy sauce, oil, sugar, vinegar, salt, and black pepper. Let stand a few minutes to allow the sugar to dissolve; whisk again. Add the broccoli slaw, scallions, and sesame seeds, tossing well to thoroughly combine. Let stand 15 minutes at room temperature to allow the flavors to blend, tossing a few times. Serve at room temperature. Alternatively, cover and refrigerate up to 24 hours and serve chilled, or return to room temperature.

{PER SERVING} Calories 82 · Protein 3g · Total Fat 5g · Sat Fat 1g · Cholesterol 0mg · Carbohydrate 9g · Dietary Fiber 1g · Sodium 319mg

Shredded Cabbage, Apple, and Raisin Salad

This tangy, fruity coleslaw is always a hit at a picnic or potluck.

MAKES 6 SERVINGS

6 tablespoons cider vinegar
3 tablespoons sugar
1 tablespoon toasted (dark) sesame oil
1 teaspoon finely chopped fresh ginger
Salt and freshly ground black pepper,
   to taste
1 large Fuji or other crisp red apple (about
   8 ounces), cored and chopped
1 (16-ounce) coleslaw mix
⅓ cup golden raisins
2 scallions, white and green parts, thinly
   sliced
2 tablespoons chopped fresh cilantro
1 tablespoon toasted sesame seeds

In a large bowl, combine vinegar, sugar, oil, ginger, salt, and pepper in a large bowl; stir until sugar dissolves. Stir in the apple. Add coleslaw mix, raisins, scallions, cilantro, and sesame seeds; toss until well combined. Let stand 10 minutes at room temperature to allow the flavors to blend. Toss again, cover, and refrigerate a minimum of 2 hours or up to 1 day and serve chilled, or return to room temperature.

{PER SERVING} Calories 125 · Protein 2g · Total Fat 3g · Sat Fat 1g · Cholesterol 0mg · Carbohydrate 25g · Dietary Fiber 3g · Sodium 16mg

Spicy Shredded Carrot and Garlic Sprout Salad

Don't worry about the sodium, since more than half the salt called for in the recipe is rinsed off before preparing this tasty salad. Mung bean sprouts can replace the garlic variety, if necessary.

MAKES 4 SERVINGS

8 ounces shredded carrots

1½ teaspoons salt, or to taste

2 cups garlic sprouts

2 scallions, white and green parts, thinly sliced

¼ cup finely chopped fresh cilantro

1 tablespoon sugar

2 teaspoons toasted (dark) sesame oil

½ tablespoon Chinese black vinegar or balsamic vinegar

½ tablespoon plain rice vinegar

1 teaspoon Chinese hot oil, or to taste

½ teaspoon Chinese chili paste, or to taste

Freshly ground black pepper, to taste

In a medium bowl, toss the carrots with 1 teaspoon of the salt until thoroughly combined. Transfer to a colander and let drain 30 minutes, tossing a few times. Rinse the salt off under cold running water and drain well.

Squeeze the carrots dry between paper towels and transfer to another medium bowl. Add the remaining ingredients and toss well to combine. Let stand 10 minutes to allow the flavors to blend. Toss again and serve at room temperature. Alternatively, refrigerate a minimum of 1 hour or up to 1 day and serve chilled, or return to room temperature.

{PER SERVING} (based on ½ teaspoon salt) Calories 73 · Protein 1g · Total Fat 4g · Sat Fat 1g · Cholesterol 0mg · Carbohydrate 10g · Dietary Fiber 2g · Sodium 287mg

Taiwanese Pickled Cucumber and Carrot Salad

Here is a refreshing fat-free summer salad to take on a picnic, as it holds up well at room temperature. And not to worry—2 of the 3 teaspoons of salt are virtually washed away before eating. If sodium is still a concern, reduce the final teaspoon of salt by up to half.

MAKES 4 TO 6 SERVINGS

3 medium cucumbers (about 10 ounces each), unpeeled, unseeded, cut lengthwise into quarters, then crosswise into 3-inch lengths

½ cup shredded carrots

3 teaspoons salt

3 tablespoons plain rice vinegar

3 large cloves garlic, finely chopped

1 fresh red chili pepper, seeded, thinly sliced

2 teaspoons sugar

Freshly ground black pepper, to taste

In a medium bowl, toss the cucumbers and carrot with 2 teaspoons salt until thoroughly combined. Cover and refrigerate a minimum of 3 hours, or overnight.

Transfer vegetables to a colander and rinse under cold running water; drain well. Pat dry with paper towels and transfer to a clean bowl. Add remaining 1 teaspoon of salt along with the other remaining ingredients; toss well to combine. Cover and refrigerate an additional minimum of 3 hours, or up to 2 days. Toss well and serve chilled, or return to room temperature.

{PER SERVING} (based on 1 teaspoon salt) Calories 52 · Protein 2g · Total Fat 0g · Sat Fat 0g · Cholesterol 0mg · Carbohydrate 12g · Dietary Fiber 2g · Sodium 543mg

Chinese Potato Salad

This is an excellent accompaniment to Sichuan Grilled Portobello Mushroom Burger with Quick Spicy Hoisin Sauce (page 140). Dijon mustard can be substituted for the hot Chinese variety, if desired.

MAKES 6 SERVINGS

1½ pounds boiling potatoes, peeled, cut
    into 1-inch pieces
3 tablespoons low-sodium vegetable broth
1½ tablespoons canola oil
1 tablespoon plain rice vinegar
1 tablespoon reduced-sodium soy sauce
½ tablespoon toasted (dark) sesame oil
½ to 1 teaspoon extra-hot Chinese
    mustard
Pinch cayenne pepper, or to taste (optional)
Salt and freshly ground black pepper, to taste
½ medium red bell pepper (about 3 ounces),
    chopped
½ medium green bell pepper (about
    3 ounces), chopped
4 scallions, white and green parts, thinly
    sliced
½ cup chopped celery
2 tablespoons chopped fresh cilantro

In a medium stockpot, bring the potatoes and enough salted water to cover to a boil over high heat. Reduce the heat slightly and boil until potatoes are tender but not mushy, 12 to 15 minutes. Drain and let cool until slightly warm, 10 to 15 minutes.

Meanwhile, in a small bowl, whisk together the broth, canola oil, vinegar, soy sauce, sesame oil, mustard, cayenne (if using), salt, and black pepper until thoroughly blended. In a large bowl, combine the warm potatoes with the bell pepper, scallions, celery, and cilantro. Add the dressing, tossing gently yet thoroughly to combine. Let stand about 15 minutes at room temperature to let the flavors blend. Toss again and serve at room temperature. Alternatively, cover and refrigerate a minimum of 2 hours or up to 1 day and serve chilled, or return to room temperature.

{PER SERVING} Calories 124 · Protein 3g · Total Fat 5g · Sat Fat 0g · Cholesterol 0mg · Carbohydrate 19g · Dietary Fiber 3g · Sodium 138mg

Tibetan Chickpea Salad

This tangy, spicy chickpea salad makes a delightful filling for pita or rolled-up Classic Chinese Pancakes (page 15). Fresh lime juice can replace all or part of the lemon juice, if desired.

MAKES 4 SERVINGS

2 tablespoons fresh lemon juice, or to taste
1 tablespoon extra-virgin olive oil
½ tablespoon toasted (dark) sesame oil
½ tablespoon ground cumin
½ teaspoon coarse salt
⅛ teaspoon cayenne pepper, or to taste
Freshly ground black pepper, to taste
1½ cups rinsed and drained canned
    chickpeas
1 medium tomato (about 6 ounces), seeded
    and chopped
1 medium boiling potato (about 4 ounces),
    peeled, boiled, cooled, and cubed

1 ripe avocado, peeled, pitted, and chopped
(optional)

2 scallions, white and green parts, thinly
sliced

1 fresh green chili, seeded and chopped

2 tablespoons chopped fresh cilantro

In a medium bowl, whisk together the lemon juice, olive oil, sesame oil, cumin, salt, cayenne, and black pepper. Add the remaining ingredients, tossing gently to combine. Let stand about 10 minutes at room temperature to allow the flavors to blend. Toss again and serve at room temperature. Alternatively, without the optional avocado, cover and refrigerate a minimum of 1 hour or up to 2 days and serve chilled, or return to room temperature, adding the avocado, if using, shortly before serving.

{PER SERVING} (without avocado) Calories 183 · Protein 7g · Total Fat 7g · Sat Fat 1g · Cholesterol 0mg · Carbohydrate 25g · Dietary Fiber 3g · Sodium 248mg

Napa Cabbage and Bean Sprout Salad

More delicate in flavor than the standard round green Western variety, Napa cabbage, also known as Chinese cabbage, is a symbol of prosperity in China—its graceful image often appears in glass and porcelain figures. The former can be substituted, if necessary.

MAKES 4 SERVINGS

3 tablespoons reduced-sodium soy sauce

3 tablespoons plain rice vinegar

1 tablespoon toasted (dark) sesame oil

1 teaspoon brown sugar

1 teaspoon freshly grated ginger

½ teaspoon Chinese chili paste, or to taste
(optional)

1 large clove garlic, finely chopped

Salt and freshly ground black pepper, to
taste

4 cups thinly sliced Napa or green
cabbage

4 cups fresh mung bean sprouts

½ medium red bell pepper (about 3 ounces),
thinly sliced

2 to 3 scallions, white and green parts,
thinly sliced

In a large bowl, whisk together the soy sauce, vinegar, oil, brown sugar, ginger, chili paste (if using), garlic, salt, and black pepper until blended. Let stand a few minutes to allow the flavors to blend. Add the remaining ingredients and toss well to thoroughly combine. Let stand 10 minutes to allow the flavors to blend. Toss again and serve at room temperature. Alternatively, cover and refrigerate 1 hour or overnight and serve chilled.

{PER SERVING} Calories 102 · Protein 5g · Total Fat 4g · Sat Fat 1g · Cholesterol 0mg · Carbohydrate 15g · Dietary Fiber 4g · Sodium 472mg

Iceberg Lettuce, Cucumber, and Carrot Salad with Sesame-Mustard Vinaigrette

For a milder vinaigrette, substitute the hot Chinese mustard with prepared yellow mustard.

MAKES 4 SERVINGS

¼ cup plain rice vinegar
1 tablespoon toasted (dark) sesame oil
½ tablespoon reduced-sodium soy sauce
½ tablespoon light brown sugar
1 teaspoon Chinese extra-hot mustard
2 cloves garlic, finely chopped
Salt and freshly ground black pepper, to taste
½ small head iceberg lettuce, cut into ¼-inch-wide strips
1 medium cucumber (about 10 ounces), peeled, seeded, cut into thin 2-inch lengths
½ cup shredded carrots

In a small bowl, whisk together the vinegar, sesame oil, soy sauce, brown sugar, mustard, garlic, salt, and pepper until thoroughly blended. Arrange ¼ of the lettuce on each of 4 serving plates, followed by ¼ of the cucumber, then ¼ of the carrots. Drizzle evenly with equal amounts of the vinaigrette (about 1½ tablespoons). Serve at once.

{PER SERVING} Calories 67 · Protein 2g · Total Fat 4g · Sat Fat 1g · Cholesterol 0mg · Carbohydrate 8g · Dietary Fiber 2g · Sodium 104mg

Lotus Root and Scallion Salad

Lotus root was one of my favorite vegetable finds in China. This crunchy, tangy salad showcases this vegetable's pure and refreshing goodness. If serving chilled, use the maximum amount of vinegar.

MAKES 4 SERVINGS

1 tablespoon peanut oil
2 fresh lotus roots, about 4 ounces each, peeled, sliced into ¼-inch-thick rounds
2 scallions, white and green parts separated, thinly sliced
1 teaspoon sugar
½ teaspoon salt
½ cup water
4 to 6 teaspoons plain rice vinegar

In a wok or large nonstick skillet with a lid, heat the oil over medium-high heat. Add the lotus root, white parts of the scallion, ½ teaspoon sugar, and salt and cook, stirring constantly, 3 minutes, or until lotus root is just softened. Add the water, cover, and reduce the heat to medium; cook about 5 minutes, or until lotus root is crisp-tender. Drain the liquid from the wok and add remaining ½ teaspoon sugar; toss gently to combine. Divide the lotus root equally among each of 4 serving plates. Drizzle each serving with 1 to 1½ teaspoons of the vinegar and sprinkle evenly with the scallion greens. Serve at room temperature. Alternatively, toss the cooked lotus root mixture, vinegar, and scallion greens in a bowl and serve at room temperature, or cover and refrigerate a minimum of 2 hours or up to 1 day and serve chilled, or return to room temperature.

{PER SERVING} Calories 70 · Protein 2g · Total Fat 4g · Sat Fat 1g · Cholesterol 0mg · Carbohydrate 12g · Dietary Fiber 2g · Sodium 291mg

Persimmon, Pomegranate, Loquat, and Apple Salad

Here is a beautiful winter fruit salad to serve around the holidays. The Fuyu persimmon is a sweet, slightly tart fruit that resembles an orange-yellow tomato and is best eaten when firm and crisp. The loquat is a tiny pear-shaped fruit with a yellowish-orange skin and juicy flesh that resembles a kumquat but tastes more like a plum, which it is sometimes called in China and Japan.

MAKES 4 SERVINGS

- 3 Fuyu persimmons (about 4 ounces each), peeled, seeds discarded as needed, and chopped into ½-inch pieces
- ¾ cup pomegranate seeds
- 4 loquats, pitted and chopped
- 1 Fuji or other crisp red apple, peeled, cored, and chopped into ½-inch pieces
- 6 to 8 large fresh mint leaves, shredded
- 2 teaspoons lemon juice
- 1 teaspoon light brown sugar

In a medium bowl, gently toss all ingredients until well combined. Let stand 5 minutes before tossing again and serving at room temperature. Alternatively, cover and refrigerate up to 24 hours and serve chilled.

{PER SERVING} Calories 71 · Protein 1g · Total Fat 0g · Sat Fat 0g · Cholesterol 0mg · Carbohydrate 19g · Dietary Fiber 2g · Sodium 2mg

Green Soybean and Carrot Salad with Rice Vinegar Dressing

This crunchy, protein-packed salad can also be prepared with frozen shelled edamame beans, cooked according to package directions, at room temperature. To cook fresh soybeans in their pods, see Fried Short-Grain Brown Rice with Walnuts and Fresh Soybeans (page 84) for the method.

MAKES 4 SERVINGS

- 2 tablespoons plain rice vinegar
- 2 tablespoons fresh lemon juice
- 1 tablespoon canola oil
- 1 large clove garlic, finely chopped
- Salt and freshly ground black pepper, to taste
- 1½ cups shelled cooked green soybeans or edamame beans (from about 1½ pounds of pods)
- 2 cups shredded carrots
- 2 scallions, white and green parts, thinly sliced
- 2 tablespoons chopped fresh cilantro

In a medium bowl, whisk together the vinegar, lemon juice, oil, garlic, salt, and pepper; let stand a few minutes at room temperature to allow the flavors to blend. Add the remaining ingredients and toss well to combine. Serve at room temperature, or cover and refrigerate a minimum of 1 hour or up to 2 days and serve chilled, or return to room temperature.

{PER SERVING} Calories 173 · Protein 12g · Total Fat 9g · Sat Fat 1g · Cholesterol 0mg · Carbohydrate 14g · Dietary Fiber 6g · Sodium 22mg

Hunan Seaweed Salad with Red Peppers, Cilantro, and Garlic

Sea vegetables, such as kelp, are high in iodine, an essential nutrient that helps promote proper thyroid function. Emerald green kelp strands are sold in the refrigerated section of Asian markets—rinse several times in cold water before using them raw in recipes. This tasty side salad will perk up any table with the tang of the sea.

MAKES 4 TO 6 SERVINGS

12 ounces raw green kelp strands, rinsed several times in cold water, drained well
4 cloves garlic, finely chopped
2 teaspoons distilled white vinegar
1 teaspoon toasted (dark) sesame oil
1 teaspoon Chinese hot oil, or more, to taste
½ teaspoon salt
2 tablespoons chopped fresh cilantro
1 to 2 fresh red chili peppers, seeded, if desired, thinly sliced

Place the kelp in a colander set in the sink. Prepare an ice water bath. Slowly pour boiling water over the kelp. Immediately place kelp in ice water to refresh for 5 minutes. Drain well.

In a medium bowl, combine the garlic, vinegar, sesame oil, hot oil, and salt. Let stand a few minutes to allow the flavors to blend. Pat the drained kelp with paper towels to remove excess moisture. Add the kelp, cilantro, and chilies to the bowl and toss well to combine. Let stand about 15 minutes at room temperature to allow the flavors to blend, tossing a few times. Serve at room temperature. Alternatively, cover and refrigerate a minimum of 1 hour or up to 2 days and serve chilled, or return to room temperature.

{PER SERVING} Calories 70 · Protein 2g · Total Fat 3g · Sat Fat 1g · Cholesterol 0mg · Carbohydrate 11g · Dietary Fiber 4g · Sodium 470mg

Cold Tofu and Scallion Salad

Delicious on its own, this no-cook tofu dish also makes an excellent filling for sandwiches or lettuce wraps. For a pretty luncheon salad, serve on a bed of baby spinach and garnish with cherry tomatoes.

MAKES 4 SERVINGS

1 (16-ounce) package medium-firm tofu, drained, cut into ½-inch cubes
2 scallions, green parts only, thinly sliced
1 tablespoon toasted (dark) sesame oil
1 teaspoon reduced-sodium soy sauce
1 teaspoon vegetarian oyster sauce or mushroom soy sauce (optional)
1 teaspoon Chinese hot oil (optional)
½ teaspoon salt
Freshly ground black pepper, to taste

In a medium bowl, gently toss all ingredients until thoroughly combined. Let stand at room temperature 15 minutes before tossing again and serving. Alternatively, cover and refrigerate up to 2 days and serve chilled.

{PER SERVING} Calories 130 · Protein 9g · Total Fat 10g · Sat Fat 1g · Cholesterol 0mg · Carbohydrate 3g · Dietary Fiber 2g · Sodium 326mg

Five-Spice Tofu and Mixed Vegetable Salad

Bring this tasty northern-style cold salad (liang cai) to your next picnic or potluck.

MAKES 4 TO 6 SERVINGS

2 tablespoons reduced-sodium soy sauce

1 tablespoon Chinese black vinegar or
    balsamic vinegar

1 tablespoon toasted (dark) sesame oil

2 cloves garlic, finely chopped

1 teaspoon Chinese chili paste, or to taste

½ teaspoon sugar

Salt and freshly ground black pepper, to
    taste

1 tablespoon peanut oil

8 ounces packaged flavored baked five-
    spice tofu or Baked Five-Spice Seasoned
    Tofu (page 113) or packaged smoked
    tofu, cut into thin strips

1 medium zucchini (about 8 ounces),
    julienned

1 medium cucumber (about 8 ounces),
    seeded and julienned

1 medium red bell pepper (about 6 ounces),
    cut into thin strips

2 stalks Chinese celery or regular celery
    (cut regular celery lengthwise in half),
    cut into thin 2-inch lengths

2 scallions, cut into 1-inch lengths

In a small bowl, combine the soy sauce, vinegar, sesame oil, garlic, chili paste, sugar, salt, and pepper; set aside.

In a wok or large nonstick skillet, heat the peanut oil over medium-high heat. Add the tofu, zucchini, cucumber, red bell pepper, celery, and scallions and cook, stirring constantly, 1 to 2 minutes, or until vegetables are just softened. Remove from heat and add the dressing, tossing well to combine. Let cool to room temperature before tossing again and serving at room temperature. Alternatively, cover and refrigerate a minimum of 2 hours or up to 1 day and serve chilled, or return to room temperature.

{PER SERVING} Calories 148 · Protein 7g · Total Fat 10g · Sat Fat 2g · Cholesterol 0mg · Carbohydrate 11g · Dietary Fiber 4g · Sodium 477mg

Hunan-Style Zucchini Salad

This refreshing side dish can be prepared with seeded cucumbers in lieu of zucchini, if desired.

MAKES 4 SERVINGS

1 pound zucchini (about 2 medium), peeled,
    sliced lengthwise in half, sliced
    crosswise into ⅜-inch-thick pieces

1 to 2 fresh red chili peppers, seeded and
    thinly sliced

1½ tablespoons reduced-sodium soy
    sauce

2 teaspoons plain rice vinegar

2 teaspoons toasted (dark) sesame oil

2 large cloves garlic, finely chopped

½ teaspoon sugar

½ teaspoon coarse salt

Freshly ground black pepper, to taste

In a medium stockpot filled with boiling salted water, blanch the zucchini and chili peppers 30 seconds. Drain and immediately rinse under cold running water until cooled; drain again.

In a medium bowl, whisk together the soy sauce, vinegar, sesame oil, garlic, sugar, salt, and pepper. Let stand a few minutes to allow the sugar to dissolve; whisk again. Add the zucchini and chili peppers, tossing well to combine. Let stand about 15 minutes to allow the flavors to blend. Toss again and serve at room temperature. Alternatively, cover and refrigerate up to 24 hours and serve chilled, or return to room temperature.

{PER SERVING} Calories 49 · Protein 2g · Total Fat 3g · Sat Fat 0g · Cholesterol 0mg · Carbohydrate 6g · Dietary Fiber 2g · Sodium 464mg

Soybean Sprout, Bell Pepper, Cucumber, and Cabbage Salad

Soybean sprouts have more protein and fat than other sprouts, such as the mung bean variety, which can be substituted in the following recipe. In this instance, the initial blanching is not necessary. For best results, serve the salad shortly after preparing—any leftovers are delicious tossed with noodles the next day.

MAKES 4 TO 6 SERVINGS

8 ounces (about 3½ cups) soybean sprouts, rinsed, stringy tails and any bean husks removed

2 tablespoons reduced-sodium soy sauce

1 tablespoon plain rice vinegar

2 teaspoons toasted (dark) sesame oil

1 clove garlic, finely chopped

½ teaspoon Chinese chili paste, or to taste

½ teaspoon sugar

Salt and freshly ground black pepper, to taste

1 tablespoon peanut oil

1 medium cucumber (about 8 ounces), seeded and julienned

1 medium red bell pepper (about 6 ounces), cut into thin strips

2 cups shredded Napa or green cabbage

2 scallions, white and green parts, thinly sliced

In a medium stockpot, cook the soybean sprouts in boiling salted water for 2 minutes. Drain well and set aside. In a small bowl, combine the soy sauce, vinegar, sesame oil, garlic, chili paste, sugar, salt, and black pepper; set aside.

In a wok or large nonstick skillet, heat the peanut oil over medium-high heat. Add the cucumber, bell pepper, cabbage, and scallions and cook, stirring and tossing constantly, 30 seconds, or until vegetables are barely softened. Remove from heat and add the warm bean sprouts and dressing, tossing well to combine. Let cool to room temperature before tossing again and serving. Alternatively, cover and refrigerate a minimum of 2 hours or overnight and serve chilled.

{PER SERVING} Calories 158 · Protein 9g · Total Fat 10g · Sat Fat 2g · Cholesterol 0mg · Carbohydrate 14g · Dietary Fiber 3g · Sodium 318mg

Marinated Thousand-Layer Tofu Salad

In China, frozen tofu is called thousand-layer tofu; through freezing, the large ice crystals that develop within the tofu result in the formation of large cavities that appear to be layered. Frozen tofu has a meatier, chewier texture than regular tofu. Like a sponge, it easily absorbs the flavors of the marinade in this delicious salad.

MAKES 2 MAIN DISH OR 4 SIDE DISH SERVINGS

2 tablespoons reduced-sodium soy sauce

1½ tablespoons sweet chili sauce

1½ tablespoons plain rice vinegar

1 tablespoon plus ½ teaspoon toasted (dark) sesame oil

2 cloves garlic, finely chopped

½ teaspoon finely chopped fresh ginger

Salt and freshly ground black pepper, to taste

8 ounces frozen tofu (½ of a 16-ounce package), thawed, drained, gently pressed to dry, cut into 1-inch cubes (see Cook's Tip, below)

1 cup snow peas, trimmed, cut diagonally in half

1 cup shredded cabbage

½ cup shredded carrots

2 scallions, white and green parts, thinly sliced

¼ cup chopped fresh cilantro

In a large bowl, stir together 1 tablespoon soy sauce, 1 tablespoon sweet chili sauce, 1 tablespoon rice vinegar, 1 tablespoon sesame oil, garlic, ginger, salt, and pepper until thoroughly blended. Add tofu, tossing to thoroughly combine. Let marinate at room temperature 30 minutes, tossing a few times.

Bring a medium stockpot filled with water to a boil over high heat. Meanwhile, prepare an ice water bath. Add the snow peas to the boiling water and cook until just softened, 1 to 2 minutes. Drain the snow peas and immediately immerse in the ice water bath for 5 minutes. Drain and add to the tofu, along with the cabbage, carrots, scallions, cilantro, remaining 1 tablespoon soy sauce, remaining ½ tablespoon sweet chili sauce, remaining ½ tablespoon rice vinegar, and remaining ½ teaspoon sesame oil. Let stand at room temperature about 15 minutes, tossing a few times. Serve at room temperature. Alternatively, cover and refrigerate 1 to 24 hours and serve chilled, or return to room temperature.

{PER SERVING} Calories 222 · Protein 13g · Total Fat 14g · Sat Fat 2g · Cholesterol 0mg · Carbohydrate 16g · Dietary Fiber 5g · Sodium 632mg

{COOK'S TIP}

To freeze tofu, select a medium-firm tofu for a more porous, spongelike consistency or a firm or extra-firm tofu for a denser, firmer consistency. For best results, soft tofu is not recommended, as it does not hold its shape as well. Drain the tofu. If a denser consistency is desired, place on a deep-sided plate or shallow bowl. Top with a second plate and weight with a heavy can. Let stand for a minimum of 15 minutes (preferably 1 hour). Drain off the excess water. For a more porous consistency, do not weight. Place the weighted or unweighted tofu in a freezer bag and press out any excess air before sealing. Freeze a minimum of 2 days, or up to 3 months. Thaw overnight in the refrigerator; drain well. If a drier tofu is desired, press between paper towels before using.

Chinese Short-Grain Brown Rice Salad with Snow Peas and Corn

This wholesome and delicious salad is perfect for a picnic, potluck, or buffet, as it holds up well at room temperature.

MAKES 4 MAIN DISH OR 6 TO 8 SIDE DISH SERVINGS

¼ cup unseasoned rice vinegar

3 tablespoons canola oil

1 tablespoon toasted (dark) sesame oil

1 teaspoon sugar

½ teaspoon salt, or to taste

Freshly ground black pepper, to taste

4 cups cooked short-grain brown rice, slightly warm or at room temperature (see Cook's Tip, below)

4 ounces snow peas, trimmed, sliced diagonally into fourths or sixths, depending on length

3 scallions, white and green parts, thinly sliced

½ cup cooked and cooled fresh or frozen yellow corn kernels

½ medium red bell pepper (about 3 ounces), chopped

1 stalk celery, chopped

2 tablespoons chopped fresh cilantro or flat-leaf parsley

¼ cup roasted pumpkin or sunflower seeds, or slivered almonds (optional)

In a large bowl, combine the vinegar, canola oil, sesame oil, sugar, salt, and pepper, stirring until the sugar dissolves. Add the remaining ingredients, tossing well to thoroughly combine. Let stand about 15 minutes at room temperature to allow the flavors to blend. Toss again and serve at room temperature. Salad can be refrigerated, covered, up to 24 hours before returning to room temperature and serving.

{PER SERVING} Calories 309 · Protein 5g · Total Fat 13g · Sat Fat 1g · Cholesterol 0mg · Carbohydrate 45g · Dietary Fiber 5g · Sodium 228mg

{COOK'S TIP}

To cook 4 cups of short-grain brown rice, bring a large stockpot filled halfway with salted water to a boil over high heat. Add about 1⅓ cups uncooked short-grain brown rice and boil about 25 minutes, stirring occasionally, or until al dente. Drain in a colander and rinse under cold running water until cooled. Drain well. Use as directed in recipe. Long-grain brown rice can be cooked in the same manner; however, unlike the short-grain, glutinous variety, the grains of long-grain brown rice will harden with refrigeration.

Pot Sticker and Fresh Mustard Greens Salad with Hoisin-Lemon Vinaigrette

This simple yet delicious dinner salad is prepared with frozen vegetable pot stickers, available in Asian markets and many well-stocked supermarkets. Any fresh salad green—arugula, dandelion, or spinach are good choices—can replace all or part of the mustard greens, if desired. Though less authentic, chopped pimiento can replace the pickled red chili peppers.

MAKES 4 SERVINGS

1 pound frozen vegetable pot stickers, freshly cooked according to package directions, well drained

4 teaspoons toasted (dark) sesame oil

¼ cup prepared hoisin sauce or Hoisin Sauce (page 116)

2 tablespoons fresh lemon juice

1 to 2 teaspoons sugar

2 cloves garlic, finely chopped

8 cups trimmed and chopped young Chinese mustard greens (gai choy) or stemmed and torn young Western-style mustard greens (about 9 ounces)

2 tablespoons prepared chopped pickled red chili pepper or Pickled Chilies (page 3)

In a large bowl, while still warm, toss the pot stickers with 2 teaspoons sesame oil; set aside to cool to slightly warm or room temperature.

In another large bowl, mix together the hoisin sauce, lemon juice, sugar, garlic, and remaining 2 teaspoons of sesame oil. Add mustard greens to bowl and toss well to thoroughly coat. Divide the greens evenly among each of 4 serving plates and top with equal portions of the pot stickers. Garnish evenly with the pickled chili peppers and serve at once.

{PER SERVING} Calories 340 · Protein 12g · Total Fat 7g · Sat Fat 1g · Cholesterol 0mg · Carbohydrate 60g · Dietary Fiber 5g · Sodium 361mg

Chinese Lentil and Noodle Salad

This protein-packed noodle salad is ideal for a buffet, as it holds up well at room temperature. For a gluten-free dish, substitute rice noodles for the lo mein variety and use gluten-free tamari in lieu of regular soy sauce, which contains wheat.

4 TO 6 SERVINGS

2 cups water

1 cup dried lentils, rinsed, picked over, and drained

1 tablespoon chopped fresh ginger

⅓ cup seasoned rice vinegar

2 tablespoons reduced-sodium soy sauce

1 tablespoon peanut oil

1 tablespoon toasted (dark) sesame oil

1 to 2 large cloves garlic, finely chopped

Salt and freshly ground black pepper, to taste

6 ounces lo mein or other thin Chinese noodles, cooked according to package directions until al dente, drained and rinsed under cold running water until cool, drained again

1 medium cucumber (about 10 ounces), peeled, seeded, and julienned

1 cup shredded carrots

4 scallions, white and green parts, thinly sliced

In a medium saucepan, bring the water, lentils, and ginger to a boil over high heat. Reduce the heat to low, cover, and simmer until lentils are just tender and still crunchy, 20 to 30 minutes, depending on variety and age, stirring occasionally. Drain off any excess liquid and transfer to a large bowl. Add the vinegar, soy sauce, both oils, garlic, salt, and pepper and toss well to thoroughly combine. Let cool to room temperature, stirring a few times. Add the noodles, tossing well to thoroughly combine. Add the remaining ingredients, tossing well to thoroughly combine. Cover and refrigerate a minimum of 2 hours or up to 1 day and serve chilled, or return to room temperature.

{PER SERVING} Calories 417 · Protein 21g · Total Fat 8g · Sat Fat 1g · Cholesterol 0mg · Carbohydrate 68g · Dietary Fiber 18g · Sodium 322mg

Tofu and Noodle Salad with Vegetables, Mandarin Oranges, and Cashews

This is a perfect party salad to prepare in winter when fresh seedless Clementines, the smallest of the Mandarin oranges, are in season. In a pinch, canned mandarin oranges can be substituted. Almonds, peanuts, or walnuts can replace the cashews, if desired.

MAKES 6 MAIN DISH OR 8 TO 10 SIDE DISH SERVINGS

12 ounces firm or extra-firm tofu, drained

6 tablespoons seasoned rice vinegar

4 tablespoons reduced-sodium soy sauce

4 tablespoons canola oil

2 tablespoons toasted (dark) sesame oil

2 tablespoons finely chopped fresh ginger

4 large cloves garlic, finely chopped

2 teaspoons Chinese chili paste, or to taste

Freshly ground black pepper, to taste

12 ounces thin, egg-free Chinese noodles or other thin noodles, broken in half, cooked according to package directions until just al dente, drained, rinsed under cold running water until cooled

4 scallions, white and green parts, thinly sliced

½ medium red bell pepper (about 3 ounces), julienned

½ medium green bell pepper (about 3 ounces), julienned

1 cup shredded carrots

1 cup snow peas, trimmed, cut diagonally in half

1 cup seedless mandarin orange segments (about 2 to 3 mandarin oranges, preferably Clementines)

½ cup chopped fresh cilantro

½ cup toasted cashews, broken into pieces

Place the tofu on a deep-sided plate or shallow bowl. Top with a second plate and weight with a heavy can. Let stand for a minimum of 15 minutes (preferably 1 hour). Drain off the excess water. Cut tofu into small dice. Set aside.

In a large bowl, combine the rice vinegar, soy sauce, canola oil, sesame oil, ginger, garlic, chili paste, and pepper. Add the tofu to the bowl and let stand 15 minutes to allow the flavors to blend, stirring a few times. Add the noodles and toss well to combine. Let stand another 15 minutes to allow the flavors to blend. (At this point, mixture can be refrigerated, covered, up to 24 hours before continuing with the recipe.) Add the remaining ingredients, tossing gently yet thoroughly to combine. Serve at room temperature, or cover and refrigerate up to 24 hours and serve chilled, or return to room temperature.

{PER SERVING} Calories 387 · Protein 13g · Total Fat 17g · Sat Fat 2g · Cholesterol 0mg · Carbohydrate 46g · Dietary Fiber 2g · Sodium 409mg

Cold Rice Noodles with Napa Cabbage in Sesame-Peanut Sauce

You can make this excellent buffet dish with any thin Asian noodle. Regular green cabbage can be substituted for the Napa variety, if desired.

MAKES 4 MAIN DISH OR 6 TO 8 SIDE DISH SERVINGS

8 ounces flat (stir-fry or linguine-style) rice
   noodles
4 cups shredded Napa cabbage (about
   ½ pound) or green cabbage
2 tablespoons reduced-sodium soy sauce
2 tablespoons Shaoxing rice wine, dry
   sherry, sake, or dry white wine
2 tablespoons toasted (dark) sesame oil
1½ tablespoons natural-style peanut
   butter
1½ tablespoons sesame paste, preferably
   the Asian variety
1 tablespoon plain rice vinegar
1 tablespoon sugar
2 large cloves garlic, finely chopped
½ teaspoon Chinese chili paste, or to taste
Salt and freshly ground black pepper, to
   taste
2 scallions, white and green parts, thinly
   sliced
½ cup chopped fresh cilantro
1 to 2 tablespoons Fresh Chili Garlic Sauce
   (page 14), Pickled Chilies (page 3), or
   prepared chopped pickled red chili
   pepper, to taste (optional)

In a medium stockpot, cook the rice noodles according to package directions until al dente. Meanwhile, place the cabbage in a colander set in a sink; drain the cooked noodles over the cabbage to wilt it. Rinse under cold running water until cool; drain again.

In a small saucepan, heat the soy sauce, wine, sesame oil, peanut butter, sesame paste, rice vinegar, sugar, garlic, chili paste, salt, and pepper over medium-low heat until just warm, stirring constantly. Remove from heat and let cool.

Transfer noodle-cabbage mixture to a large serving bowl and add the soy sauce mixture, scallions, half the cilantro, and fresh chili garlic sauce, if using, tossing well to thoroughly coat. Sprinkle with the remaining cilantro and serve at room temperature, or cover and refrigerate a minimum of 2 hours or up to 2 days and serve chilled, or return to room temperature.

{PER SERVING} Calories 371 · Protein 4g · Total Fat 13g · Sat Fat 2g · Cholesterol 0mg · Carbohydrate 61g · Dietary Fiber 3g · Sodium 51mg

Fern Root Noodle Salad with Red Cabbage and Cucumber

Fern root noodles, made from the starch of the common bracken fern, are purplish black in color and have a chewy texture when cooked; in packaged dried form, they resemble twigs. They are rarely available outside of China, though you may be able to find them in Asian markets located in predominately Asian communities. Black rice noodles, white rice noodles, cellophane noodles, or any noodles made from starch—sweet potato, tapioca, yam—can be substituted, as needed. Green cabbage can replace the red variety, if desired.

MAKES 3 TO 4 MAIN DISH OR 5 SIDE DISH SERVINGS

    1 cup shredded red cabbage
    3 tablespoons vegetarian oyster sauce or
        mushroom soy sauce
    1 tablespoon toasted (dark) sesame oil
    1 tablespoon Chinese hot oil
    2 teaspoons Chinese black vinegar or
        balsamic vinegar
    1 teaspoon reduced-sodium soy sauce
    1 large clove garlic, finely chopped
    Salt and freshly ground black pepper, to
        taste
    1 (7-ounce) package fern root noodles,
        cooked according to package directions
        until al dente, drained, rinsed under
        cold running water until cooled, drained
        well
    1 medium cucumber (about 8 ounces),
        julienned
    ½ cup shredded carrots
    ½ cup chopped fresh cilantro
    2 scallions, white and green parts, thinly
        sliced

In a medium saucepan, blanch the cabbage in boiling salted water 30 seconds. Drain and rinse under cold running water until cooled; drain well.

In a large bowl, stir together the oyster sauce, sesame oil, hot oil, vinegar, soy sauce, garlic, salt, and pepper until well blended. Add the noodles and toss well to thoroughly coat. Add the remaining ingredients and toss well to thoroughly combine. Serve at room temperature, or cover and refrigerate a minimum of 2 hours or up to 1 day and serve chilled, or return to room temperature.

{PER SERVING} Calories 356 • Protein 2g • Total Fat 10g • Sat Fat 1g • Cholesterol 0mg • Carbohydrate 66g • Dietary Fiber 3g • Sodium 712mg

Cold Shredded Tofu Noodles with Sesame Sauce and Cucumbers

This creamy and refreshing salad is a lunch favorite of mine. Asian sesame paste is made purely from roasted sesame seeds—if necessary, equal parts sesame tahini, made from unroasted sesame seeds, and natural peanut butter creates a very close approximation. For a gluten-free dish, use wheat-free tamari sauce in lieu of the soy sauce, which contains wheat. Shredded tofu, or bean curd strands, can be found in the refrigerated section of most Asian markets, next to the regular tofu.

MAKES 3 MAIN DISH OR 4 TO 6 SIDE DISH SERVINGS

    8 ounces shredded tofu
    3 tablespoons Asian sesame paste
    2 tablespoons reduced-sodium soy sauce
    1½ tablespoons toasted (dark) sesame oil

1 tablespoon sugar

2 teaspoons plain rice vinegar

1 teaspoon finely chopped fresh ginger

1 large clove garlic, finely chopped

¼ teaspoon salt, or to taste

Freshly ground black pepper, to taste

2 tablespoons hot water, or more, as
needed

1 large cucumber (about 12 ounces), seeded,
cut into thin 2-inch lengths

4 scallions, green parts only, halved
lengthwise, cut crosswise into 2-inch
lengths

In a medium stockpot, cook the shredded tofu in boiling salted water until separated and al dente, 5 to 9 minutes, depending on freshness, stirring occasionally. Drain and rinse under cold running water until cool. Drain well and set aside.

Meanwhile, in a large bowl, whisk together the sesame paste, soy sauce, sesame oil, sugar, rice vinegar, ginger, garlic, salt, and pepper. Thin with hot water, whisking until the consistency of heavy cream. Add the shredded tofu, cucumber, and scallions, tossing well to thoroughly combine. Let stand 15 minutes at room temperature to allow the flavors to blend. Toss again and serve at room temperature. Alternatively, cover and refrigerate a minimum of 1 hour or up to 2 days and serve chilled or return to room temperature.

{PER SERVING} Calories 255 · Protein 11g · Total Fat 18g · Sat Fat 3g · Cholesterol 0mg · Carbohydrate 16g · Dietary Fiber 3g · Sodium 769mg

Warm Tofu and Chinese Spinach Salad

Make sure you select tender young Chinese spinach leaves for this superb salad. Regular baby spinach or other young salad greens can be substituted.

MAKES 4 SERVINGS

1 (14-ounce package) firm or extra-firm tofu,
drained

2½ tablespoons canola oil

2 tablespoons plain rice vinegar

1 tablespoon light brown sugar

2 teaspoons reduced-sodium soy
sauce

½ tablespoon toasted (dark) sesame oil

1 teaspoon finely chopped fresh ginger

½ teaspoon salt, or to taste

Freshly ground black pepper, to taste

8 cups young Chinese spinach leaves

1 large cucumber (about 12 ounces), seeded
and chopped

1 cup shredded carrots

2 scallions, white and green parts, thinly
sliced

Sunflower seeds and/or golden raisins, for
garnish (optional)

Place the tofu on a deep-sided plate or shallow bowl. Top with a second plate and weight with a heavy can. Let stand for a minimum of 15 minutes (preferably 1 hour). Drain off the excess water. Cut tofu into 1-inch cubes. Set aside.

In a large bowl, whisk together the canola oil, rice vinegar, sugar, soy sauce, sesame oil, ginger, salt, and pepper until blended. Let stand a few minutes to allow the sugar to dissolve; whisk again.

Place 2 tablespoons of the dressing in a large nonstick skillet and heat over medium-high heat. Add the tofu and cook, turning often, until golden brown, 6 to 8 minutes. Remove the skillet from the heat and add 1 more tablespoon of the dressing, stirring to coat.

Add the spinach, cucumber, and carrots to the remaining dressing in the bowl and toss well to coat. Divide the salad mixture equally among 4 salad plates or bowls. Top with equal portions of the warm tofu mixture and sprinkle evenly with the scallions and optional garnishes, if desired. Serve at once.

{PER SERVING} Calories 243 · Protein 14g · Total Fat 16g · Sat Fat 2g · Cholesterol 0mg · Carbohydrate 16g · Dietary Fiber 6g · Sodium 477mg

CHAPTER FOUR

Rice Dishes

The high status of rice in Chinese culture could hardly be overstated. A typical friendly greeting in China is "Have you had your rice today?" Lose a job, and you've had your rice bowl broken. Get an "iron rice bowl," the Chinese nickname for a government job with guaranteed security and benefits, and no worries. But leave a grain behind in that bowl and you are not exactly the best-mannered guest at the table. Cultural context aside, it's absolutely impossible to exaggerate the vital role of rice in sustaining life throughout much of the planet. In fact, rice is the single-most important cereal grain with regard to human nutrition and caloric intake, providing more than one-fifth of the calories consumed worldwide. China is the largest producer of rice in the world; little wonder that rice, in steamed, fried, or noodle form, is a fixture at every meal. Long-grain white rice, which produces fluffier rice, is preferred. Short- to medium-grain white glutinous, or "sticky," rice is used mainly for snacks and sweets. As the expanding Chinese middle class becomes more health-conscious, the healthier brown versions are becoming more readily available at major supermarkets. Black, or "forbidden," rice, once reserved exclusively for the imperial court, is a less well-known type that is used mainly in desserts; there is a growing interest, however, in its potential health benefits, particularly the purplish-black variety. Indeed, with the widening appreciation for the potential health benefits of gluten-free grains in general, there is a renewed enthusiasm for rice in the West—catch the wave with the following recipes and enjoy the ride.

Fried Basmati Rice with Black-Eyed Peas and Walnuts

Black-eyed peas and basmati rice are common in southwestern Chinese cuisine, and walnuts are popular everywhere. Long-grain white or brown rice can replace the basmati variety, if desired.

MAKES 4 SERVINGS

1 tablespoon extra-virgin olive oil

1 tablespoon chopped fresh ginger

3 large cloves garlic, finely chopped

3 cups cooked basmati rice, at room temperature, any clumps removed

1 cup rinsed and drained canned black-eyed peas

¼ cup chopped walnuts

2 scallions, white and green parts, thinly sliced

2 tablespoons chopped fresh cilantro

½ tablespoon toasted (dark) sesame oil

In a wok or large nonstick skillet, heat the olive oil over medium heat. Add the ginger and garlic and cook, stirring, until softened and fragrant, about 3 minutes. Add the rice, black-eyed peas, walnuts, and scallions and raise the heat to medium-high; cook, stirring, until rice and black-eyed peas are heated through, 2 to 3 minutes. Add the cilantro and sesame oil and cook, stirring, 30 seconds. Serve at once.

{PER SERVING} Calories 333 · Protein 9g · Total Fat 10g · Sat Fat 1g · Cholesterol 0mg · Carbohydrate 51g · Dietary Fiber 4g · Sodium 7mg

Xi'an-Style Fried Rice with Pickled Chinese Cabbage

In a pinch, rinsed and drained sauerkraut can replace the pickled Chinese cabbage.

MAKES 4 SERVINGS

2 tablespoons reduced-sodium soy sauce

½ tablespoon toasted (dark) sesame oil

1 teaspoon sugar

½ tablespoon peanut oil

3 cups cooked white or brown rice, at room temperature, any clumps removed

2 scallions, white and green parts separated, thinly sliced

½ cup pickled Chinese cabbage, rinsed, drained, and chopped

Salt and freshly ground black pepper, to taste

In a small bowl, stir together the soy sauce, sesame oil, and sugar; set aside.

In a wok or large nonstick skillet, heat the peanut oil over medium-high heat. Add rice and white parts of the scallions; cook, stirring frequently, until lightly browned, 3 to 5 minutes. Add reserved soy sauce mixture and stir to thoroughly blend. Add the pickled cabbage and scallion greens and cook, stirring constantly, until heated through and well combined, about 1 minute. Season with salt and pepper and serve at once.

{PER SERVING} Calories 234 · Protein 5g · Total Fat 4g · Sat Fat 1g · Cholesterol 0mg · Carbohydrate 44g · Dietary Fiber 1g · Sodium 351mg

Cashew Fried Rice

Here is another excellent recipe to prepare with leftover rice. For best results, separate any clumps of rice with oiled fingers before using in the recipe.

MAKES 4 SERVINGS

3 tablespoons reduced-sodium soy sauce
½ tablespoon sugar
1 teaspoon toasted (dark) sesame oil
1 tablespoon peanut oil
½ cup chopped onion
¼ cup chopped carrot
2 large cloves garlic, finely chopped
½ teaspoon finely chopped fresh ginger
3 cups cooked white or brown rice, at room temperature, any clumps removed
4 scallions, white and green parts separated, thinly sliced
¼ cup frozen green peas, thawed
¼ cup chopped roasted cashews
Salt and freshly ground black pepper, to taste

In a small bowl, stir together the soy sauce, sugar, and sesame oil; set aside.

In a wok or large nonstick skillet, heat the peanut oil over medium-high heat. Add the onion and carrot and cook, stirring constantly, until softened, 2 to 3 minutes. Add garlic and ginger and cook, stirring constantly, 30 seconds. Add rice and white parts of scallions and cook, stirring frequently, until rice is lightly browned, 3 to 5 minutes. Add reserved soy sauce mixture and stir to thoroughly blend. Add the scallion greens, peas, and cashews; cook, stirring constantly, until heated through and well combined, about 1 minute. Season with salt and pepper and serve at once.

{PER SERVING} Calories 311 · Protein 7g · Total Fat 9g · Sat Fat 2g · Cholesterol 0mg · Carbohydrate 51g · Dietary Fiber 3g · Sodium 473mg

Basic Steamed Long-Grain White Rice

Rice is a staple at every single serious Chinese meal. The following recipe proves that cooking perfect steamed rice is easy, even without a rice cooker. The general rule for long-grain white rice is to use 2 cups of water for every cup of rice. (For glutinous or sticky white rice, also known as sushi rice, use 1½ cups of water for every 1 cup of rice; this will yield about 2⅔ cups of cooked glutinous rice.) Though optional, the oil ensures that the cooked grains won't stick together, especially as they cool.

MAKES 4 SERVINGS, OR ABOUT 3 CUPS

2 cups water
1 to 3 teaspoons canola oil (optional)
½ teaspoon salt
1 cup uncooked long-grain rice

In a medium saucepan (1½ to 2 quarts) with a tight-fitting lid, bring the water, oil (if using), and salt to a boil over high heat. Add the rice and stir; reduce the heat to low and quickly cover. Cook until the rice is tender but still slightly chewy and has absorbed the liquid, 17 to 20 minutes, adjusting the heat as needed between low and medium-low so that a little steam is always visibly leaking from the lid. Do not uncover before 17 minutes; test a grain and check the absorption level. When rice is done, remove the pan from the heat, fluff the rice with a fork, and serve at once for best results. If not serving immediately, place a paper towel across the top of the pan and replace the lid; let sit up to 20 minutes before serving.

{PER SERVING} (per ¾ cup, or ¼ of recipe) **Calories 169 · Protein 3g · Total Fat 0g · Sat Fat 0g · Cholesterol 0mg · Carbohydrate 37g · Dietary Fiber 1g · Sodium 269mg**

{VARIATIONS}

To make Steamed Sesame Long-Grain White Rice, replace 1 teaspoon canola oil with 1 teaspoon toasted (dark) sesame oil. Prepare as otherwise directed in the recipe. Toss with 1 teaspoon of toasted sesame seeds before serving, if desired.

To make Steamed Green Tea Long-Grain White Rice, replace all or half of the water with regular-strength brewed green tea. Prepare as otherwise directed in the recipe.

Basic Steamed Long-Grain Brown Rice

While brown rice is not commonly served with meals in China, it is gaining the attention of the increasingly health-conscious growing middle class. For short-grain, or glutinous, brown rice, use 2 cups of water per 1 cup of rice, to yield about 3 cups of cooked rice.

MAKES 4 SERVINGS (ABOUT 3½ TO 4 CUPS)

2½ cups water
1 to 3 teaspoons canola oil (optional)
½ teaspoon salt

1 cup uncooked long-grain brown rice,
     rinsed in 2 to 3 changes of cold water,
     drained well

In a medium saucepan (1½ to 2 quarts) with a tight-fitting lid, bring the water, oil, and salt to a boil over high heat. Add the rice and stir; reduce the heat to low and quickly cover. Cook until the rice is tender but still slightly chewy and has absorbed the liquid, 45 to 50 minutes, adjusting the heat as needed between low and medium-low so that a little steam is always visibly leaking from the lid. Do not uncover before 40 minutes; test a grain and check the absorption level. When rice is done, remove the pan from the heat, fluff the rice with a fork, and serve at once for best results. If not serving immediately, place a paper towel across the top of the pan and replace the lid; let sit up to 20 minutes before serving.

{PER SERVING} (per scant 1 cup, or ¼ of recipe) **Calories 171 · Protein 4g · Total Fat 1g · Sat Fat 0g · Cholesterol 0mg · Carbohydrate 36g · Dietary Fiber 3g · Sodium 270mg**

{VARIATIONS}

To make Steamed Sesame Long-Grain Brown Rice, replace 1 teaspoon canola oil with 1 teaspoon toasted (dark) sesame oil. Prepare as otherwise directed in the recipe. Toss with 1 teaspoon of toasted sesame seeds before serving, if desired.

To make Steamed Green Tea Long-Grain Brown Rice, replace all or half of the water with regular-strength brewed green tea. Prepare as otherwise directed in the recipe.

Steamed Rice with Bean Sprouts and Scallions

I really like this quick-cooking white rice—the scallions and sprouts add flavor and fiber without overwhelming the taste of other dishes you might also like to serve with it. To create a delicious main course, stir in a cup of cooked peas and a few tablespoons of chopped fresh cilantro along with the scallions and sprouts.

MAKES 4 SERVINGS

1½ cups water
1 cup uncooked long-grain white rice, rinsed well and drained
½ teaspoon salt, plus additional, to taste
4 scallions, white and green parts, thinly sliced
2 cups mung bean sprouts, rinsed and drained
½ to 1 tablespoon toasted (dark) sesame oil
Freshly ground black pepper, to taste

In a medium saucepan, combine the water, rice, and salt. Cover and bring to a boil over high heat. Uncover, lower heat to medium, and stir. Cover and cook 10 minutes. Uncover and stir. If rice is very moist, continue cooking, uncovered, a few minutes more, or until almost all of the water has been absorbed. Remove the saucepan from the heat and add the scallions, sprouts, oil, and pepper, tossing well to combine. Cover and let stand 10 minutes. Season with additional salt and pepper, if necessary. Toss lightly with a fork and serve.

{PER SERVING} Calories 206 · Protein 5g · Total Fat 2g · Sat Fat 0g · Cholesterol 0mg · Carbohydrate 42g · Dietary Fiber 2g · Sodium 275mg

Chinese Cabbage Rice with Tofu and Shiitake Mushrooms

You can make this using shredded green cabbage in lieu of the Napa variety, if desired—the resulting dish will still be delicious.

MAKES 4 MAIN DISH OR 6 TO 8 SIDE DISH SERVINGS

1 tablespoon peanut oil
4 ounces extra-firm tofu, drained well, pressed between several paper towels to dry, cut into small dice
2 large cloves garlic, finely chopped
8 ounces Napa cabbage (about ½ small), chopped
4 dried shiitake mushrooms, soaked in hot water to cover 20 minutes, or until softened, rinsed, drained, stemmed, and chopped
1 fresh red chili pepper, seeded and chopped (optional)
1 (14-ounce) can low-sodium vegetable broth (1¾ cups)
½ cup water
1 tablespoon reduced-sodium soy sauce
½ tablespoon toasted (dark) sesame oil
Salt and freshly ground black pepper, to taste
1 cup long-grain white rice

In a medium deep-sided skillet with a lid, heat the peanut oil over medium heat. Add the tofu and cook, stirring, until lightly browned, 3 to 4 minutes. Add the garlic and cook, stirring constantly, 1 minute. Add the cabbage, mushrooms, and chili pepper, if using; increase the heat to medium-high. Cook, turning constantly with a wide spatula, until vegetables are softened and reduced in size, about 3 minutes. Add the broth, water, soy sauce, sesame oil, salt, and pepper; bring to a boil over high heat. Stir in the rice and let come to a brisk simmer. Reduce the heat to between low and medium-low, cover, and simmer until all the liquid is absorbed, 17 to 20 minutes. Remove from heat and let stand, covered, 5 minutes. Stir to evenly distribute the ingredients and serve hot.

{PER SERVING} Calories 293 · Protein 12g · Total Fat 7g · Sat Fat 1g · Cholesterol 0mg · Carbohydrate 46g · Dietary Fiber 4g · Sodium 393mg

Eggplant Rice with Soybeans

This hearty rice dish is a meal in itself with a tossed green salad. Salting the eggplant is not necessary if using the long, narrow, often white-streaked Chinese variety, which contains fewer seeds than regular eggplant, and is therefore less bitter. Green peas can stand in for the soybeans, if desired. For best results, use freshly cooked rice.

MAKES 4 TO 6 SERVINGS

- 1 pound of eggplant (about 1 large Western eggplant or 2 medium Chinese eggplants), unpeeled, cut into ½-inch dice, placed in a colander, sprinkled with salt, drained 30 minutes (salting is optional)
- 1 tablespoon peanut oil
- 4 scallions, white and green parts separated, thinly sliced
- 1 to 2 fresh red or green chili peppers, seeded and thinly sliced

- 1 tablespoon finely chopped fresh ginger
- 1 teaspoon whole cumin seeds
- 2 large cloves garlic, finely chopped
- ½ cup low-sodium vegetable broth, plus additional, if necessary
- 1 to 2 tablespoons sweet chili sauce
- 1 to 2 tablespoons reduced-sodium soy sauce
- 1 tablespoon toasted (dark) sesame oil
- ¼ teaspoon Chinese five-spice powder
- ¼ teaspoon salt, or to taste
- 3 cups freshly cooked white or brown rice
- 1 cup frozen shelled soybeans, cooked according to package directions, well drained
- ½ cup chopped fresh cilantro

Rinse the drained eggplant under cold running water. Dry between paper towels and set aside.

In a wok or large nonstick skillet, heat the peanut oil over medium heat. Add the white parts of the scallions, chilies, ginger, and cumin; cook, stirring, 1 minute. Add the eggplant and cook, stirring, until softened, about 3 minutes. Add the garlic and cook, stirring, 2 minutes. Add the broth and cook, stirring, until liquid has mostly evaporated and eggplant is tender, 4 to 5 minutes, adding more broth, if necessary. Add chili sauce, soy sauce, sesame oil, five-spice powder, and salt; cook, stirring, 1 minute. Add rice, soybeans, and scallion greens; cook, tossing and stirring, until heated through, about 2 minutes. Remove from heat and add the cilantro, tossing well to thoroughly combine. Serve warm.

{PER SERVING} Calories 364 · Protein 14g · Total Fat 11g · Sat Fat 2g · Cholesterol 0mg · Carbohydrate 53g · Dietary Fiber 7g · Sodium 361mg

Tibetan-Style Curried Rice with Golden Raisins, Ginger, and Cilantro

This fragrant dish will perfume your kitchen for hours with the smells of the Orient. For added protein, toss the hot cooked rice with 1 cup of rinsed and drained canned chickpeas, cooked peas, or cooked soybeans.

MAKES 4 SERVINGS

2 cups low-sodium vegetable broth

1 cup long-grain white rice

¼ cup golden raisins

1 tablespoon finely chopped fresh ginger

½ tablespoon canola oil

½ teaspoon ground turmeric

½ teaspoon curry powder

½ teaspoon salt

2 scallions, white and green parts, thinly sliced

2 tablespoons chopped fresh cilantro

½ tablespoon toasted (dark) sesame oil

In a medium saucepan with a tight-fitting lid, bring the broth, rice, raisins, ginger, canola oil, turmeric, curry powder, and salt to a boil over high heat, stirring once. Reduce the heat to low, quickly cover, and cook until the rice is tender and all the water is absorbed, 17 to 20 minutes, adjusting the heat as needed between low and medium-low so that a little steam is always visibly leaking from the lid. Uncover, remove from heat, and stir in the scallions, cilantro, and sesame oil. Re-cover and let stand 5 minutes. Uncover, fluff with a fork, and serve at once.

{PER SERVING} Calories 258 · Protein 9g · Total Fat 4g · Sat Fat 1g · Cholesterol 0mg · Carbohydrate 47g · Dietary Fiber 3g · Sodium 499mg

Rice with Green Peppers and Fermented Black Beans

Inspired by a recipe from Ecksyoo, one of my most enthusiastic English corner students at Nanya and current email pal, this simple yet delicious dish is one of my favorites. Fermented black beans, also known as salted black beans or dried black beans, are strongly flavored soybeans that have been dried and fermented with salt; they are available in Asian markets. Green bell pepper can replace half of the chilies, if desired. For best results, use freshly cooked rice.

MAKES 4 SERVINGS

1 tablespoon peanut oil

1 medium green bell pepper (about 6 ounces), cored, seeded, and cut into ½-inch-thick slices

2 jalapeño chili peppers, cut lengthwise in half, seeded, and sliced into ½-inch-thick pieces

½ tablespoon rinsed and drained fermented black beans, chopped

2 large cloves garlic, finely chopped

3 teaspoons toasted (dark) sesame oil

3 cups freshly cooked white or brown rice

1 tablespoon reduced-sodium soy sauce, or to taste

½ tablespoon black bean sauce with garlic, or to taste

Salt and freshly ground black pepper, to taste

In a wok or large nonstick skillet, heat the peanut oil over medium-high heat. Add the bell pepper and jalapeño peppers and cook, stirring often, until softened and beginning to brown, 3 to 4 minutes. Add the beans, garlic, and 1 teaspoon sesame oil;

cook, stirring constantly, 1 minute. Add the rice, soy sauce, black bean sauce, and remaining 2 teaspoons sesame oil; cook, tossing and stirring constantly, until heated through, 1 to 2 minutes. Season with salt and pepper and serve warm.

{PER SERVING} Calories 260 · Protein 5g · Total Fat 8g · Sat Fat 1g · Cholesterol 0mg · Carbohydrate 43g · Dietary Fiber 1g · Sodium 178mg

Pineapple Baked Rice

Boluo fan, or pineapple rice, is a popular dish in Yunnan Province, located in the southwestern region of China. For best results, use freshly cooked rice; if desired, brown rice can replace the white variety.

MAKES 4 MAIN DISH OR 6 SIDE DISH SERVINGS

8 ounces extra-firm tofu, rinsed and
    drained
1 medium pineapple (about 3 pounds), cut
    lengthwise in half, leaves intact
1 tablespoon canola oil
¼ cup finely chopped shallots or red onion
2 tablespoons prepared sweet chili sauce
2 tablespoons reduced-sodium soy sauce
1 tablespoon toasted (dark) sesame oil
3 cups hot cooked white rice
½ cup frozen peas and carrots, cooked
¼ cup frozen yellow corn, cooked
Salt and freshly ground black pepper, to
    taste

Preheat oven to 325F (165C).

Place the tofu on a deep-sided plate or shallow bowl. Top with a second plate and weight with a heavy can. Let stand for a minimum of 15 minutes (preferably 1 hour). Drain excess water. Cut into ½-inch cubes.

Using a tablespoon or melon baller, scoop out the flesh from the pineapple halves, discarding the fibrous core, leaving a thin border of flesh attached to each shell. Divide the flesh in half, saving half for future use. Chop the remaining flesh and set aside.

In a wok or large nonstick skillet, heat the canola oil over medium heat. Add the tofu and cook, stirring occasionally, until lightly browned, 5 to 7 minutes. Add the shallots and cook, stirring, until softened, about 2 minutes. Add the chili sauce, soy sauce, and sesame oil; cook, stirring, about 30 seconds, or until bubbly. Add the rice, peas and carrots, corn, salt, and pepper and cook, stirring, 2 minutes. Add the reserved chopped pineapple and cook, stirring, 1 minute. Remove from heat and let cool a few minutes.

Mound equal portions of the rice mixture into the pineapple shells, lightly packing down. Place the filled shells on large lightly oiled pieces of foil and draw up to loosely yet completely enclose. Transfer to a baking sheet and bake 30 minutes, or until hot through the center. Unwrap and serve immediately, directly from the pineapple shells, family-style. Alternatively, cut each filled pineapple shell crosswise in half and serve on individual serving plates.

{PER SERVING} Calories 353 · Protein 10 · Total Fat 10g · Sat Fat 1g · Cholesterol 0mg · Carbohydrate 56g · Dietary Fiber 3g · Sodium 325mg

Green Tea Fried Rice with Peas

Here is a delicious recipe to use up a leftover pint container of Chinese take-out rice (which usually holds 3 cups once the clumps are separated) and a used green tea bag. Black tea—which recent research indicates may provide many of the same health benefits as green—can be substituted.

MAKES 4 SERVINGS

¼ cup brewed green tea liquid

2 tablespoons reduced-sodium soy sauce

2 tablespoons Shaoxing rice wine, dry sherry, sake, or dry white wine

½ tablespoon toasted (dark) sesame oil

1 teaspoon plain rice vinegar

1 teaspoon brown sugar

1 tablespoon canola oil

½ cup fresh or frozen peas, thawed

2 scallions, white and green parts, thinly sliced

Brewed leaves from a standard green tea bag (about 1 teaspoon)

1 teaspoon chopped fresh ginger

Salt and freshly ground black pepper, to taste

3 cups cooked rice, clumps broken up, as needed, at room temperature

In a small bowl, combine the tea liquid, soy sauce, rice wine, sesame oil, rice vinegar, and sugar; set aside.

In a wok or large nonstick skillet, heat the canola oil over medium heat. Add the peas, scallions, tea leaves, ginger, salt, and pepper; cook, stirring, until peas are tender and scallions are softened, about 3 minutes. Add the rice and cook, stirring, about 2 minutes. Add the tea liquid mixture and cook, stir-

ring, until rice absorbs the liquid, about 2 minutes. Serve at once.

{PER SERVING} Calories 263 · Protein 5g · Total Fat 6g · Sat Fat 1g · Cholesterol 0mg · Carbohydrate 45g · Dietary Fiber 2g · Sodium 307mg

Hunan Fried Rice with Tofu

A meal in itself, this delicious dish is moister than most fried rice recipes. Omit the cayenne for a milder version. For best results, use freshly cooked rice.

MAKES 4 MAIN DISH OR 6 TO 8 SIDE DISH SERVINGS

3 tablespoons reduced-sodium soy or tamari sauce

2 tablespoons Shaoxing rice wine, dry sherry, sake, or dry white wine

1 tablespoon toasted (dark) sesame oil

1 tablespoon light brown sugar

2 large cloves garlic, finely chopped

1 teaspoon finely chopped fresh or pickled ginger

⅛ teaspoon cayenne pepper, or to taste

½ pound extra-firm tofu, drained, cut into small dice

2 teaspoons cornstarch

1 tablespoon canola oil or peanut oil

1 medium red or green bell pepper, chopped

1 cup coleslaw mix or shredded cabbage

½ cup chopped onion

3 cups freshly cooked rice, at room temperature

Salt and freshly ground black pepper, to taste

In a shallow bowl, combine soy sauce, rice wine, toasted sesame oil, sugar, garlic, ginger, and cayenne. Add the tofu and stir well to combine. Cover and marinate 30 minutes to 1 hour at room temperature (or refrigerate 1 to 24 hours), stirring a few times. Drain the tofu, transferring the marinade to a small bowl. Blend the reserved marinade with the cornstarch; add back to the tofu, tossing to coat.

In a wok or large nonstick skillet, heat the canola oil over medium-high heat. Add the bell pepper, coleslaw mix, and onion and cook, stirring constantly, 2 minutes. Add the tofu and marinade and cook, stirring constantly, until the liquid is mostly absorbed, 1 to 2 minutes. Add the rice and cook, stirring constantly, until heated through and well combined, 1 to 2 minutes. Season with salt and pepper and serve at once.

{PER SERVING} Calories 347 · Protein 10g · Total Fat 10g · Sat Fat 1g · Cholesterol 0mg · Carbohydrate 53g · Dietary Fiber 3g · Sodium 464mg

Sticky Rice with Five-Spice Tofu and Scallions

Though typically used in desserts, sticky rice is occasionally used in savory dishes such as this superb one. Any flavored baked tofu can stand in for the five-spice variety, if desired.

MAKES 4 SERVINGS

1 cup glutinous or sticky rice
1½ cups plus 2 tablespoons water
½ teaspoon salt, plus additional, to taste

1 (10-ounce) package baked flavored five-spice tofu, cut into ½-inch cubes
½ tablespoon toasted (dark) sesame oil
½ tablespoon canola oil
2 scallions, white and green parts, thinly sliced
Freshly ground black pepper, to taste

Place rice in a medium heavy-bottomed, deep-sided skillet (about 9½ inches in diameter) with a tight-fitting lid. Add enough cold water to cover and stir well; drain in a fine-meshed colander. Repeat rinsing and draining. Return rice to the pan. Add 1 cup plus 2 tablespoons water and salt; bring to a boil over high heat. Reduce heat to between low and medium-low, cover, and simmer 10 minutes. Add remaining ½ cup water, tofu, and sesame oil, stirring well to combine. Cover and cook until rice has absorbed the liquid and is tender, 8 to 10 minutes. Remove from heat and let stand, covered, 5 minutes. Uncover and fluff with a fork.

Meanwhile, in a small skillet, heat the canola oil over medium heat. Add the scallions and cook, stirring constantly, until sizzling and fragrant, 1 to 2 minutes. Remove from heat and add half the scallion mixture, salt, and pepper to the rice and tofu mixture, tossing to combine. Set remaining scallion mixture briefly aside.

To serve, divide the rice and tofu mixture equally among 4 serving bowls or plates. Sprinkle equally with the remaining scallion mixture and serve at once.

{PER SERVING} Calories 258 · Protein 9g · Total Fat 7g · Sat Fat 1g · Cholesterol 0mg · Carbohydrate 40g · Dietary Fiber 2g · Sodium 276mg

Fried Short-Grain Brown Rice with Walnuts and Fresh Soybeans

Fried rice doesn't get much healthier—or more delicious—than this easy dish. By preparing the rice, walnuts, and soybeans in advance, it cooks up in minutes.

MAKES 4 SERVINGS

1 cup short-grain brown rice
¾ pound green soybean pods (edamame) or 1 cup frozen shelled edamame, cooked according to package directions, drained
¼ cup coarsely chopped walnuts
2 tablespoons reduced-sodium soy sauce
½ tablespoon peanut or canola oil
1 tablespoon finely chopped fresh ginger
2 large cloves garlic, finely chopped
2 scallions, white and green parts, thinly sliced
½ tablespoon toasted (dark) sesame oil
Salt and freshly ground black pepper, to taste

Bring a large stockpot filled halfway with salted water to a boil over high heat. Add the rice and cook, stirring occasionally, until al dente, about 25 minutes. Drain in a colander and rinse under cold running water until cool. Drain well.

If using fresh soybean pods, place a steamer basket in a medium stockpot filled with about 2 inches of water. Add the soybean pods and bring the water to a boil over high heat. Immediately reduce the heat to medium, cover, and steam 5 minutes, or until beans are tender yet crunchy (carefully remove a pod, pop open, and test a bean). Uncover and let cool a few minutes. Carefully remove steamer basket and place soybean pods in a colander; rinse under cold running water until cooled. Pop the beans out of the pods, discarding the pods and placing the beans in a small bowl. Set aside.

In a small heavy-bottomed skillet set over medium heat, place the walnuts and cook, stirring constantly, until lightly toasted and fragrant, about 3 minutes. Drizzle with 1 tablespoon soy sauce and cook, stirring to thoroughly coat, about 45 seconds. Remove skillet from heat and let cool.

In a wok or large nonstick skillet, heat the peanut oil over medium-high heat. Add the ginger and garlic and cook, stirring constantly, 1 minute. Add the rice and shelled cooked soybeans and cook, stirring constantly, 3 minutes. Reduce the heat to medium and add the walnuts, scallions, remaining 1 tablespoon soy sauce, sesame oil, salt, and pepper; cook, stirring, until heated through, about 2 minutes. Serve at once.

{PER SERVING} Calories 335 · Protein 13g · Total Fat 13 · Sat Fat 2 · Cholesterol 0mg · Carbohydrate 44g · Dietary Fiber 4g · Sodium 304mg

Hong Kong–Style Tomato Fried Rice

I love this fried rice recipe for one essential reason—it contains ketchup, 6 whole tablespoons of it! While ketchup isn't typically associated with Chinese food, tomatoes have been around in the Middle Kingdom since the late 16th century; indeed, many etymologists believe that the word ketchup is derived from a Chinese word that means "tomato sauce." Fortunately, this universally popular condiment is a good source of lycopene, an antioxidant that may help prevent some forms of cancer. Moreover, a leading brand recently stopped making ketchup with high-fructose corn syrup—just another excuse to indulge in this delicious fried rice dish.

MAKES 4 SERVINGS

6 tablespoons tomato ketchup
½ tablespoon vegetarian oyster sauce or mushroom soy sauce
1 teaspoon toasted (dark) sesame oil
1 tablespoon peanut oil
½ cup chopped onion
2 to 3 scallions, white and green parts separated, thinly sliced
3 cups cooked white rice, at room temperature, clumps removed
1 medium tomato (about 6 ounces), seeded and chopped
1 cup frozen peas, thawed (optional)
Salt and freshly ground black pepper, to taste

In a small bowl, combine the ketchup, oyster sauce, and sesame oil; set aside.

In a wok or large nonstick skillet, heat the peanut oil over medium-high heat. Add the onion and white parts of the scallions and cook, stirring, until softened, 2 to 3 minutes. Add the rice and cook, stirring, 1 minute. Add the tomato, peas (if using), salt, and pepper; cook, stirring, 2 minutes. Reduce the heat to medium and add the ketchup mixture; cook, stirring, 2 minutes. Remove from heat and add the scallion greens, stirring well to combine. Serve at once.

{PER SERVING} Calories 264 · Protein 5g · Total Fat 5g · Sat Fat 1g · Cholesterol 0mg · Carbohydrate 50g · Dietary Fiber 2g · Sodium 353mg

Rice and Peas with Soy-Ginger Sauce

Plain noodles are also delicious prepared this way.

MAKES 4 SERVINGS

¼ cup reduced-sodium soy sauce
1 tablespoon toasted (dark) sesame oil
1 tablespoon finely chopped fresh ginger
2 scallions, green parts only, thinly sliced
Salt and freshly ground black pepper, to taste
3 cups hot cooked white or brown rice
1 cup fresh or frozen hot cooked peas

In a small bowl, stir together the soy sauce, sesame oil, ginger, half the scallion greens, salt, and pepper until well combined. Let stand 10 minutes at room temperature to allow the flavors to blend.

Place the rice and peas in a warmed serving bowl and add the soy sauce mixture and remaining scallion greens, tossing well to thoroughly combine. Serve at once.

{PER SERVING} Calories 252 · Protein 7g · Total Fat 4g · Sat Fat 1g · Cholesterol 0mg · Carbohydrate 46g · Dietary Fiber 3g · Sodium 645mg

Savory Eight-Treasure Rice Cake

This is a savory Buddhist version of the popular Eight-Treasure Glutinous Rice Cake (page 186), enjoyed at Chinese New Year. As with the latter, feel free to experiment with your favorite vegetables, nuts, and seeds, so long as the total number equals 8. If you can't locate dried lotus seeds, substitute with 2 tablespoons of pumpkin or sunflower seeds and omit the first step of the recipe.

MAKES 8 SERVINGS

½ cup dried lotus seeds (about 2.5 ounces), soaked in cold water to cover 3 hours or overnight, drained

2 tablespoons reduced-sodium soy sauce

1 tablespoon toasted (dark) sesame oil

½ teaspoon five-spice powder

1 teaspoon salt

Freshly ground black pepper, to taste

1 tablespoon peanut oil

½ cup chopped onion

6 dried shiitake mushrooms, soaked in hot water to cover 20 minutes, or until softened, rinsed, drained, stemmed, and chopped

½ cup chopped, rinsed, and drained canned water chestnuts

2 tablespoons slivered almonds

2⅔ cups freshly cooked glutinous rice, slightly warm or at room temperature (see page 76 for method)

2½ cups freshly cooked long-grain white rice, slightly warm or at room temperature (see page 76 for method)

1 cup frozen peas and carrots, thawed

3 scallions, white and green parts, chopped, plus 1 scallion, green parts only, thinly sliced

In a small saucepan, bring drained lotus seeds and enough water to cover to a boil over high heat. Reduce heat to medium and simmer briskly for 15 minutes, or until tender. Remove from heat and drain; rinse under cold running water and drain again. Using your fingers, break each seed apart into two symmetrical halves, removing any green germ. Set aside.

In a small bowl, combine the soy sauce, sesame oil, five-spice powder, salt, and pepper; set aside.

In a wok or large nonstick skillet, heat the peanut oil over medium-high heat. Add the onion and cook, stirring constantly, 1 minute. Add mushrooms, water chestnuts, lotus seeds, and almonds and cook, stirring constantly, until fragrant and mushrooms begin to release their liquid, about 2 minutes. Add the soy sauce mixture and cook, stirring constantly, 30 seconds. Add both types of rice, peas and carrots, and 3 chopped scallions and cook, tossing and stirring constantly, 1 minute. Remove from heat and let stand, covered, 5 minutes.

Lightly oil a steam-proof 8-cup/2-quart bowl. Transfer the rice mixture to the oiled bowl, pressing down firmly with the back of a spoon. (At this point, mixture can be brought to room temperature and refrigerated, covered, up to 24 hours before continuing with the recipe.)

Place a steamer basket in a tall stockpot filled with about 2 inches of water. Place the bowl of rice in the steamer basket and bring the water to a boil over high heat. Immediately reduce the heat to medium, cover, and steam 20 minutes (add 5 minutes if refrigerated). Uncover and let cool a few minutes.

Carefully remove rice bowl from the steamer basket. Let stand 10 minutes to allow rice grains to harden slightly. Pass the tip of a dinner knife around the edge of the rice cake to loosen it. Invert onto a warmed, deep-welled serving platter. (The cake should slip out easily.) Garnish with the sliced scallion greens and serve at once, using a large spoon to divide into pie-like wedges among individual serving bowls.

{PER SERVING} Calories 227 · Protein 5g · Total Fat 5g · Sat Fat 1g · Cholesterol 0mg · Carbohydrate 40g · Dietary Fiber 2g · Sodium 435mg

CHAPTER FIVE

Noodle Dishes

If noodles bring bliss, then China is noodle nirvana. Although noodles have been eaten in many parts of the world for at least 2,000 years, in 2002, archaeologists found an earthenware bowl containing the world's oldest known noodles—4,000 years old!—along China's Yellow River, ending the debate—at least for now—on who first invented these slippery delights. While those well-preserved noodles were made from millet, one of the five sacred grains of ancient China, today's noodles are generally made from wheat flour, rice flour, or mung bean starch. Wheat noodles are more commonly produced and consumed in northern China, while rice noodles are more typical of southern China; cellophane noodles, usually made from mung bean starch and, sometimes, other starches such as yam, potato, and tapioca, are eaten throughout the various regions. In Chinese, miàn (often transliterated as "mien" or "mein") refers to noodles made from wheat, while fěn (often transliterated as "fun") refers to noodles made from rice flour, mung bean starch, or any kind of starch. From Cellophane Noodles in Spicy Peanut Sauce, to Mixed Vegetable Lo Mein, to Rice Noodles with Chinese Broccoli and Shiitake Mushrooms, they're all here, and they're all heavenly!

Chao Fen with Mixed Vegetables and Black Bean Sauce

Known as chow fun on most Chinese restaurant menus across America, chao fen typically refers to a mix of cooked wide rice noodles that are stir-fried with vegetables or tofu. Try to use the widest flat noodles you can find—⅛ to ¼ inch is ideal. Fresh or dried rice sticks, usually a bit wider than the standard stir-fry or linguine-style variety, will suffice. Packaged fresh Asian stir-fry vegetables and packaged fried tofu, available in Asian markets, make quick work of this delicious dish. Packaged baked tofu can replace the fried variety, if desired; alternatively, omit the tofu entirely.

MAKES 4 TO 5 SERVINGS

- 2 tablespoons black bean sauce with garlic
- 2 tablespoons Shaoxing rice wine, dry sherry, sake, or dry white wine
- 2 tablespoons reduced-sodium soy sauce
- 2 tablespoons light brown sugar
- 1 tablespoon Chinese black vinegar or balsamic vinegar
- 3 teaspoons toasted (dark) sesame oil
- 1 teaspoon Chinese chili paste, or to taste (optional)
- 1 tablespoon peanut oil
- 4 scallions, white and green parts, thinly sliced
- 1 tablespoon chopped fresh ginger
- 3 cloves garlic, finely chopped
- 1 (12-ounce) bag fresh Asian stir-fry vegetables (about 5½ cups)
- ½ cup low-sodium vegetable broth
- 8 ounces fried tofu, cut into ½-inch cubes
- 8 ounces fresh or dried wide flat rice noodles, preferably ⅛ to ¼ inch in width, cooked according to package directions until just al dente, drained, and rinsed under cold running water until cool, well drained
- ½ cup chopped fresh cilantro

In a small bowl, combine the black bean sauce, rice wine, soy sauce, brown sugar, vinegar, 1 teaspoon of sesame oil, and chili paste, if using; set aside.

In a wok or large nonstick skillet with a lid, heat the peanut oil over medium-high heat. Add half the scallions, ginger, and garlic and cook, stirring constantly, 1 minute. Add the stir-fry vegetables and broth, stirring to combine. Reduce the heat to medium, cover, and cook, stirring occasionally, until the vegetables are crisp-tender, about 3 minutes. Add the reserved black bean sauce mixture and cook, stirring, 30 seconds. Add the tofu and cook, stirring, 1 minute. Add the noodles and cook, tossing and stirring often with a wide spatula, until heated through, about 2 more minutes. Add the remaining scallions, cilantro, and remaining 2 teaspoons of sesame oil; cook, tossing, 30 seconds. Serve at once.

{PER SERVING} Calories 399 · Protein 10g · Total Fat 10g · Sat Fat 2g · Cholesterol 0mg · Carbohydrate 67g · Dietary Fiber 5g · Sodium 488mg

Quick Chao Fen with Scallions and Peanuts

Similar variations of these fried rice noodles, or chao fen (aka "chow fun"), are invariably slurped up on the streets of Changsha, especially during the wee weekend hours. After midnight, when you're starving and all the restaurants and bars have closed, there is no street food more satisfying. If possible, try to use fresh, wide rice noodles, available in the refrigerated or frozen food section of Asian markets, for this dish. Fresh or dried rice sticks, usually a bit wider than the standard stir-fry or linguine-style variety, will suffice.

MAKES 4 SERVINGS

8 ounces fresh or dried wide flat rice noodles, preferably ⅛ to ¼ inch in width

1 tablespoon regular reduced-sodium soy sauce

½ tablespoon toasted (dark) sesame oil

1 teaspoon Chinese chili paste, or to taste

Salt and freshly ground black pepper, to taste

2 scallions, white and green parts, chopped

½ cup low-sodium vegetable broth

1 to 1½ teaspoons dark soy sauce

1½ tablespoons peanut oil

2 large cloves garlic, finely chopped

¼ cup chopped fresh cilantro

2 tablespoons chopped roasted or whole fried peanuts (optional)

Bring a large pot of water to a boil over high heat. Add the noodles and cook according to package directions, stirring a few times, until just al dente (typically about 15 seconds for fresh noodles, 3 to 5 minutes for dried). Drain in a colander and rinse under cold running water until cool. Drain well.

In a small bowl, combine the regular soy sauce, sesame oil, chili paste, salt, and pepper; stir in half of the scallions and set aside. In another small bowl, combine the broth and dark soy sauce and set aside.

In a wok or large nonstick skillet, heat the peanut oil over medium heat. Add the garlic and cook, stirring constantly, 1 minute, or until softened and fragrant. Add the noodles and toss to coat with the oil, using a pair of chopsticks or fork to separate any clumps. Add the soy sauce–scallion mixture and cook, stirring and tossing constantly with a wide spatula, until noodles are heated through, about 2 minutes. Add the broth and dark soy sauce mixture, remaining scallions, and cilantro and cook, tossing constantly with the spatula, until most of the broth has been absorbed, 1 to 2 minutes. Serve at once, garnished with the peanuts, if using.

{PER SERVING} Calories 274 · Protein 2g · Total Fat 7g · Sat Fat 1g · Cholesterol 0mg · Carbohydrate 51g · Dietary Fiber 1g · Sodium 273mg

Hunan-Style Vegetable Chao Mian

You can tone down the heat of this tasty vegetable chao mian, literally "fried noodles," known in American Asian restaurants as chow mein, by omitting the chili peppers and replacing with a few pinches of cayenne pepper, if desired. You can also omit the Crispy Noodle Pancake and chow mein noodles and serve over plainly cooked noodles or rice for an equally delicious meal.

MAKES 4 SERVINGS

1 tablespoon peanut oil

4 dried shiitake mushrooms, soaked in hot water to cover 20 minutes, or until softened, rinsed, drained, stemmed, and thinly sliced

4 scallions, white and green parts
  separated, thinly sliced
4 large cloves garlic, finely chopped
1 cup shredded cabbage
1 cup chopped cauliflower
1 cup shredded carrot
¼ cup drained and chopped canned
  bamboo shoots
1 to 2 fresh red chili peppers, seeded and
  thinly sliced
½ teaspoon salt, or to taste
Freshly ground black pepper
½ cup tomato sauce
2 teaspoons cornstarch mixed with ¼ cup
  water
½ tablespoon toasted (dark) sesame oil
½ tablespoon sugar
1 to 1½ teaspoons Chinese chili paste
1 Crispy Noodle Pancake (page 17),
  divided into 4 wedges
1 cup crispy chow mein noodles

In a wok or large nonstick skillet, heat the peanut oil over medium-high heat. Add the mushrooms, white parts of the scallions, and garlic and cook, stirring constantly, 1 minute. Add the cabbage, cauliflower, carrot, bamboo shoots, chilies, salt, and pepper and cook, stirring constantly, 2 minutes. Stir in the tomato sauce, cornstarch mixture, sesame oil, sugar, and chili paste and reduce the heat to medium; cook, stirring, until thickened, 2 to 3 minutes, adding the scallion greens toward the end.

To serve, place 1 fried noodle pancake wedge on each of 4 serving plates. Top with equal portions of the vegetable mixture. Sprinkle evenly with the fried chow mein noodles (¼ cup) and serve at once.

{PER SERVING} Calories 362 · Protein 9g · Total Fat 15g · Sat Fat 2g · Cholesterol 0mg · Carbohydrate 52g · Dietary Fiber 5g · Sodium 664mg

Shanghai-Style Noodles with Green Onion Sauce

If you love scallion greens as much as I do, you will love these simple yet flavorful noodles enjoyed everywhere throughout Shanghai.

MAKES 4 SERVINGS

1½ tablespoons peanut oil
1 bunch scallions (6 to 8), green parts only,
  thinly sliced lengthwise, cut crosswise
  into very thin 2-inch-long strips
3½ tablespoons reduced-sodium soy sauce,
  plus additional, to serve
8 ounces egg-free Chinese lo mein or other
  wide-cut Asian noodles, or linguine

In a wok or large nonstick skillet, heat the oil over medium-high heat. Add the scallion greens and cook, stirring constantly, until beginning to wilt and bright green, about 30 seconds. Add 3 tablespoons of soy sauce and cook, stirring constantly, until scallions are wilted but not shriveled, about 1 minute. Transfer the mixture to a large serving bowl and set aside to cool to room temperature.

In a large stockpot filled with boiling salted water, cook the noodles according to package directions until al dente. Drain and rinse under cold running water until cool. Drain well. Add noodles and remaining ½ tablespoon soy sauce to the cooled scallion mixture, tossing well to thoroughly combine. Serve at room temperature, with additional soy sauce passed separately.

{PER SERVING} Calories 253 · Protein 10g · Total Fat 6g · Sat Fat 1g · Cholesterol 0mg · Carbohydrate 46g · Dietary Fiber 1g · Sodium 979mg

Cellophane Noodles in Spicy Peanut Sauce

Perfect for a buffet, this tasty noodle dish is delicious warm or at room temperature. Any Asian noodle can replace the cellophane variety, if desired.

MAKES 4 SERVINGS

8 ounces cellophane noodles, cooked according to package directions until al dente, drained
Spicy Peanut Sauce, below
¼ cup low-sodium vegetable broth
½ cup chopped fresh cilantro
Salt and freshly ground black pepper, to taste

In a large bowl, place the warm noodles and add the peanut sauce, broth, and cilantro, tossing well to combine and cutting the noodles into shorter lengths with the edge of a spatula. Serve warm or at room temperature.

{PER SERVING} Calories 328 · Protein 5g · Total Fat 11g · Sat Fat 2g · Cholesterol 0mg · Carbohydrate 54g · Dietary Fiber 4g · Sodium 267mg

SPICY PEANUT SAUCE

Use this versatile sauce as a dip for vegetables or topping for grilled tofu, as well.

MAKES ABOUT ¾ CUP

¼ cup natural-style peanut butter
¼ cup warm water
2 scallions, green parts only, finely chopped
1 to 2 small fresh red chili peppers, seeded and finely chopped
2 tablespoons cider vinegar
1 tablespoon reduced-sodium soy sauce
1 tablespoon toasted (dark) sesame oil
1 teaspoon Chinese hot oil, or more, to taste
1 to 2 large cloves garlic, finely chopped

In a small bowl, whisk together the peanut butter and water until smooth. Add the remaining ingredients, stirring well to combine. Serve at room temperature. Sauce can be covered and refrigerated up to 5 days before returning to room temperature and using.

{PER SERVING} (per tablespoon, or 1⁄12 of recipe) Calories 49 · Protein 2g · Total Fat 4g · Sat Fat 1g · Cholesterol 0mg · Carbohydrate 2g · Dietary Fiber 1g · Sodium 77mg

Sichuan Hot-and-Sour Cellophane Noodles

A comfort food sought out on the streets of Sichuan Province, these spicy noodles are sophisticated enough to serve up at your next dinner party. Cellophane noodles made from sweet potato flour are available at most Asian markets—the standard mung bean variety, also known as bean threads, can be used as well.

MAKES 6 SERVINGS

½ tablespoon peanut oil
2 tablespoons rinsed and drained chopped preserved vegetables, preferably mustard tubers or greens
1 tablespoon rinsed and drained fermented black beans, chopped
6 large cloves garlic, finely chopped
½ tablespoon chopped fresh ginger

3 tablespoons dark soy sauce

1 tablespoon Shaoxing rice wine, dry sherry, sake, or dry white wine

2 teaspoons hot bean paste/sauce or soybean paste with chili

2 cups reduced-sodium vegetable broth

1 tablespoon cornstarch mixed with 2 tablespoons water

6 very small heads baby bok choy/Shanghai bok choy (about 2 ounces each), root ends trimmed about ⅛ inch

12 ounces cellophane noodles, preferably made from sweet potato flour, cooked according to package directions until al dente, drained, rinsed under cold running water until just cool

4 tablespoons Chinese black vinegar or balsamic vinegar

4 tablespoons reduced-sodium regular soy sauce

4 teaspoons Chinese hot oil, or more, to taste

1 tablespoon toasted (dark) sesame oil

2 teaspoons Sichuan peppercorns, crushed

¼ cup finely chopped scallions, mostly green parts

¼ cup finely chopped fresh cilantro

Chopped roasted peanuts (optional)

In a small nonstick skillet, heat the peanut oil over medium heat. Add the preserved vegetables, fermented black beans, half of the garlic, and ginger and cook, stirring, until softened and fragrant, about 2 minutes. Add 1 tablespoon of the dark soy sauce, wine, and hot bean paste and cook, stirring constantly, 1 minute. Add ½ cup broth and bring to a boil over medium-high heat, stirring often. Reduce heat to medium-low and add the cornstarch mixture; cook, stirring, until thickened, 1 to 2 minutes. Remove from heat, cover, and keep warm.

Meanwhile, in a medium stockpot, cook the bok choy in boiling salted water until just tender, 2 to 3 minutes. Drain and cut lengthwise in half. Arrange in the bottom of each of 6 deep soup bowls; top with equal portions of the noodles. Set briefly aside.

In a small saucepan, bring the remaining 1½ cups broth to a brisk simmer over medium-high heat. Remove from heat and immediately stir in the vinegar, regular soy sauce, remaining 2 tablespoons dark soy sauce, hot oil, sesame oil, remaining garlic, and Sichuan pepper. Ladle equal portions over the noodles. Top with equal portions of the vegetable–black bean mixture. Sprinkle with equal portions of the scallions, cilantro, and peanuts, if using. Serve at once, with diners tossing the contents of their respective bowls until thoroughly combined.

{PER SERVING} Calories 317 · Protein 7g · Total Fat 7g · Sat Fat 1g · Cholesterol 0mg · Carbohydrate 57g · Dietary Fiber 5g · Sodium 926mg

Sichuan-Style "Dan Dan" Noodles with Pickled Vegetables and Peanuts

Called "Dan Dan" (pole pole) noodles after the street vendors who used to carry them across their shoulders on bamboo poles, this popular dish is characterized by a liberal dose of roasted Sichuan peppercorns, which lend it a sharp, distinctive bite. This vegetarian version eschews the traditional pork, of course—Asian sesame paste, made from toasted sesame seeds, adds a rich depth of cholesterol-free flavor, instead. Sesame tahini or natural-style peanut butter can stand in for the sesame paste, if necessary. Any pickled vegetable—sauerkraut, cauliflower, carrots, peppers—can replace the pickled mustard greens, if desired.

MAKES 6 SERVINGS

1 to 1½ teaspoons Sichuan peppercorns

¼ cup low-sodium vegetable broth

3 tablespoons Asian sesame paste or sesame tahini

2 tablespoons reduced-sodium regular soy sauce

1½ tablespoons black or plain rice vinegar

1½ tablespoons toasted (dark) sesame oil

1 tablespoon dark soy sauce

1 to 2 teaspoons Chinese hot oil

1 teaspoon sugar

¼ cup chopped pickled mustard greens, rinsed and drained

12 ounces egg-free Chinese noodles, other thin Asian pasta, or vermicelli, cooked according to package directions until al dente, drained

4 scallions, white and green parts, thinly sliced

⅓ cup chopped roasted peanuts

1 tablespoon toasted sesame seeds (optional)

Salt and freshly ground black pepper, to taste

Heat a dry small heavy-bottomed skillet over medium-low heat. Add peppercorns and cook, stirring often, until lightly toasted and fragrant, 2 to 3 minutes. Immediately remove from skillet and set aside to cool. Crush with a mortar and pestle, or with a rolling pin. Set aside.

In a large bowl, whisk together the broth, sesame paste, regular soy sauce, vinegar, sesame oil, dark soy sauce, hot oil, sugar, and reserved crushed peppercorns until thoroughly blended. Stir in the pickled mustard greens. Let stand about 15 minutes at room temperature to allow the flavors to blend, and stir again. Add the noodles, tossing until thoroughly coated. Add the scallions, peanuts, sesame seeds (if using), salt, and black pepper and toss well again. Serve warm or at room temperature.

{PER SERVING} Calories 357 · Protein 12g · Total Fat 13g · Sat Fat 2g · Cholesterol 0mg · Carbohydrate 49g · Dietary Fiber 3g · Sodium 346mg

Chilled Summer Lo Mein Noodles with Sesame-Ginger Sauce

Chilled noodle dishes are highly popular throughout China during the summer months. For a gluten-free dish, substitute rice noodles for lo mein and use gluten-free tamari sauce and balsamic vinegar in lieu of the soy sauce and black vinegar, which both contain wheat.

MAKES 4 SERVINGS

3 tablespoons reduced-sodium soy sauce

1½ tablespoons finely chopped fresh ginger

1 tablespoon Asian sesame paste, tahini, or
  natural peanut butter

4 large cloves garlic

2 teaspoons Chinese black vinegar or
  balsamic vinegar

2 teaspoons sugar

½ tablespoon toasted (dark) sesame oil

1 teaspoon Chinese hot oil, or to taste

Freshly ground black pepper, to taste

½ pound lo mein or other thin egg-free
  Chinese wheat noodles, cooked
  according to package directions until al
  dente, drained and rinsed under cold
  running water, drained well

1 cup mung bean sprouts

2 scallions, green parts only, thinly sliced

½ cup chopped fresh cilantro

1 tablespoon Fresh Chili Garlic Sauce (page
  14), Pickled Chilies (page 3), or prepared
  chopped red pickled chili peppers, or to
  taste

In a large bowl, combine the soy sauce, ginger, sesame paste, garlic, vinegar, sugar, sesame oil, hot oil, and black pepper. Add the noodles, tossing well to thoroughly combine. Add the remaining ingredients and toss gently to combine. Serve at room temperature. Alternatively, cover and refrigerate a minimum of 1 hour or up to 1 day and serve chilled, or return to room temperature.

{PER SERVING} Calories 303 · Protein 9g · Total Fat 8g · Sat Fat 1g · Cholesterol 0mg · Carbohydrate 50g · Dietary Fiber 3g · Sodium 481mg

Mixed Vegetable Lo Mein

This is an eye-catching, palate-pleasing dish to serve company—try to use fresh, eggless lo mein noodles, available in the refrigerated or frozen food sections of Asian markets, sometimes labeled "plain noodles," if possible. The heat can be toned down by reducing the amount of hot oil—or eliminating it entirely. Coarsely chopped Napa or green cabbage can replace the bok choy, if desired.

MAKES 4 SERVINGS

1 tablespoon peanut oil

1 tablespoon chopped fresh ginger

3 large cloves garlic, finely chopped

4 ounces fresh shiitake, cremini, or
  cultivated white mushrooms, stemmed,
  thinly sliced

1 medium red bell pepper (about 6 ounces),
  thinly sliced

2 cups coarsely shredded bok choy (about
  4 ounces/2 Shanghai bok choy)

4 ounces snow peas, trimmed

½ cup low-sodium vegetable broth

2 tablespoons reduced-sodium soy sauce

2 tablespoons plain rice vinegar

1 to 2 teaspoons Chinese hot oil, or to taste

1 tablespoon toasted (dark) sesame oil

8 ounces lo mein or other thin egg-free
  Chinese noodles, cooked according to
  package directions until al dente, drained

½ tablespoon dark soy sauce

¼ cup chopped roasted peanuts or cashews
  (optional)

In a wok or large nonstick skillet, heat the peanut oil over medium-high heat. Add the ginger and garlic and cook, stirring constantly, 30 seconds. Add mushrooms, bell pepper, and bok choy; cook, stirring often, until softened, about 3 minutes. Add snow peas, broth, soy sauce, vinegar, and hot oil; cook, stirring often, until vegetables are crisp-tender, 3 to 4 minutes. Add sesame oil and stir quickly to combine. Add noodles and cook, tossing and stirring constantly, until heated through, 1 to 2 minutes. Remove from heat and add the dark soy sauce, tossing well to thoroughly coat all the noodles (they will darken). Serve at once, sprinkled with the peanuts, if using.

{PER SERVING} Calories 333 · Protein 12g · Total Fat 9g · Sat Fat 1g · Cholesterol 0mg · Carbohydrate 52g · Dietary Fiber 4g · Sodium 470mg

Pantry Lo Mein

Made entirely of pantry staples, this basic lo mein recipe can be enjoyed on its own or tossed with your favorite stir-fried, steamed, or microwaved vegetables for instant vegetable lo mein any day of the week—see the three variations below for suggestions. If you don't have time to cook vegetables, toss with a few thinly sliced scallions and sprinkle with chopped peanuts for a delicious main dish. Dried lo mein noodles, known as lao mian or ban mian in Mandarin, or lou mihn in Cantonese, are typically egg-free. For a saucier lo mein, double the sauce ingredients.

MAKES 4 SERVINGS

⅛ teaspoon onion powder
⅛ teaspoon garlic powder
⅛ teaspoon crushed red pepper flakes (optional)
Freshly ground black pepper, to taste
8 ounces lo mein or other thin egg-free Chinese noodles, cooked according to package directions until al dente, drained

In a small bowl, combine the soy sauce, oyster sauce, oil, sugar, salt, onion powder, garlic powder, red pepper flakes (if using), and pepper. Let stand a few minutes to allow the flavors to blend; stir again.

Place the hot cooked lo mein noodles in a serving bowl (or return to the cooking pot) and add the sauce mixture, tossing well to combine. Serve at once.

{PER SERVING} Calories 233 · Protein 8g · Total Fat 3g · Sat Fat 0g · Cholesterol 0mg · Carbohydrate 44g · Dietary Fiber 1g · Sodium 288mg

{VARIATIONS}

To make Golden Pepper and Mushroom Lo Mein: In a wok or large nonstick skillet, heat 1 teaspoon peanut oil and 1 teaspoon toasted (dark) sesame oil over medium-high heat. Add 1 (8-ounce) golden bell pepper, thinly sliced, and 8 ounces fresh shiitake mushrooms, stemmed and thinly sliced; cook, stirring constantly, 2 to 3 minutes, or until softened. Add 3 scallion greens, cut into 1-inch lengths, and ¼ cup low-sodium vegetable broth; cook, stirring constantly, 2 to 3 minutes, or until peppers are crisp-tender and liquid is reduced by about half. Add to the hot cooked lo mein noodles immediately after the sauce mixture, tossing well to combine. Serve at once.

To make Spinach and Mushroom Lo Mein: In a wok or large nonstick skillet, heat 1 teaspoon of peanut oil and 1 teaspoon of toasted (dark) sesame oil over medium-high heat. Add 8 ounces fresh shiitake mushrooms, stemmed and thinly sliced, and 2 scallions, white and

½ tablespoon reduced-sodium soy sauce
½ tablespoon vegetarian oyster sauce, dark soy sauce, or mushroom soy sauce
½ tablespoon toasted (dark) sesame oil
1 teaspoon light brown sugar
¼ teaspoon salt

green parts, thinly sliced; cook, stirring constantly, until mushrooms are tender and have released their liquid, about 4 minutes. Add 6 ounces torn baby spinach leaves, ¼ cup low-sodium vegetable broth, and ½ teaspoon sugar; toss and stir 30 seconds, or until spinach begins to wilt. Add to the hot cooked lo mein noodles immediately after the sauce mixture; toss well until the spinach is wilted. Serve at once.

To make Easy Mixed Vegetable Lo Mein: Cook 1 (12-ounce) bag of fresh or frozen stir-fry vegetables according to package directions; drain and toss with ¼ cup low-sodium vegetable broth and ½ tablespoon toasted (dark) sesame oil. Add to the hot cooked lo mein noodles immediately after the sauce mixture. Serve at once.

Hunan Cold Sesame Noodles

This spicy, delicious noodle dish is unusual in that it contains no soy sauce. Duo jiao, a fiery Hunan pepper sauce consisting of chopped red chilies pickled in brine, has a distinctive salty-and-sour taste; it is available in Asian markets. Chinese chili paste, a milder hot sauce flavored with garlic, can be substituted; it is available in most regular supermarkets. If using natural, un-sweetened peanut butter, you may need to add a bit more sugar to the recipe.

MAKE 4 SERVINGS

8 ounces egg-free Chinese noodles, other thin Asian pasta, or vermicelli
2 tablespoons toasted (dark) sesame oil
½ cup low-sodium vegetable broth
¼ cup creamy or crunchy peanut butter
2 teaspoons seasoned rice vinegar
½ tablespoon sugar
1 teaspoon Asian sesame paste or sesame tahini
1 teaspoon Hunan pepper sauce (duo jiao) or Chinese chili paste, or to taste
1 teaspoon finely chopped and seeded green or red chili pepper (optional)
1 medium seedless cucumber (about 8 ounces), julienned or shredded
2 scallions, white and green parts, thinly sliced
¼ cup chopped fresh cilantro and/or basil
Salt and freshly ground black pepper, to taste

In a large stockpot filled with boiling salted water, cook the noodles according to package directions until al dente. Drain and rinse under cold running water until cool. Drain again and transfer to a large bowl. Add the sesame oil, tossing until thoroughly coated. Cover and refrigerate a minimum of 1 hour, or overnight.

In a large bowl, stir together the broth, peanut butter, vinegar, sugar, sesame paste, pepper sauce, and chili (if using) until thoroughly blended. (At this point, sauce can be covered and refrigerated up to 1 day before continuing with recipe.) Add the cold noodles and toss well to thoroughly coat. Add the cucumbers, scallions, cilantro, salt, and black pepper; toss well again, and serve. Alternatively, cover and refrigerate a minimum of 1 hour or up to 1 day and serve chilled or return to room temperature, tossing well before serving.

{PER SERVING} Calories 396 · Protein 13g · Total Fat 17g · Sat Fat 3g · Cholesterol 0mg · Carbohydrate 50g · Dietary Fiber 4g · Sodium 149mg

Shanghai-Style Lo Mein with Fried Tofu and Hot Bean Sauce

Fried tofu is available in Asian markets, usually in the refrigerated section by the other tofu—any precooked tofu can be substituted, if desired. Chinese hot bean sauce or paste, also called soybean paste with chili, is not to be confused with standard black bean paste, which is considerably less spicy. Black bean sauce with chili can be substituted, if necessary. For a whole-grain alternative, replace the Chinese noodles with whole wheat linguine or spaghetti.

MAKES 4 SERVINGS

1 tablespoon peanut oil

1 tablespoon finely chopped fresh ginger

2 large cloves garlic, finely chopped

8 ounces fried tofu, cut into ½-inch cubes

3 tablespoons hot bean sauce or paste

1 teaspoon sugar

2 scallions, white and green parts, finely chopped

3 teaspoons sesame oil

½ pound lo mein or other thin egg-free Chinese wheat noodles, cooked according to package directions until al dente, drained

In a wok or large nonstick skillet, heat the peanut oil over medium-high heat. Add the ginger and garlic and cook, stirring constantly, 30 seconds. Add the tofu and cook, stirring constantly, 1 minute. Add the hot bean sauce and sugar and cook, stirring constantly, 30 seconds. Add the scallions and 1 teaspoon sesame oil and cook, stirring constantly, 30 seconds. Add the noodles and remaining 2 teaspoons sesame oil and toss until thoroughly coated and heated through, 1 to 2 minutes. Serve at once.

{PER SERVING} Calories 337 · Protein 13g · Total Fat 11g · Sat Fat 2g · Cholesterol 0mg · Carbohydrate 48g · Dietary Fiber 3g · Sodium 150mg

Sichuan-Style Lo Mein with Sesame and Garlic

If you're fond of garlic and spice, you'll love this garlicky, spicy noodle dish.

MAKES 4 SERVINGS

3 tablespoons reduced-sodium soy sauce

3 tablespoons plain rice vinegar

3 tablespoons Asian sesame paste, sesame tahini, or natural peanut butter

1 tablespoon toasted (dark) sesame oil

1 tablespoon sugar

1 to 2 teaspoons Chinese chili paste

Salt and freshly ground black pepper

1 tablespoon peanut oil

3 scallions, white and green parts, thinly sliced, plus 2 scallions, green parts only, thinly sliced

8 cloves garlic, finely chopped

½ pound lo mein or other thin egg-free Chinese wheat noodles, cooked according to package directions until al dente, drained and rinsed under cold running water, drained well

2 to 3 teaspoons chopped pickled red chili pepper or Pickled Chilies (page 3), or to taste

In small bowl, combine the soy sauce, vinegar, sesame paste, sesame oil, sugar, chili paste, salt, and pepper; set aside.

In a wok or large nonstick skillet, heat the peanut oil over medium-high heat. Add the 3 scallions, white and green parts, and garlic and cook, stirring constantly, 1 minute. Add the noodles and cook, tossing and stirring constantly, 1 minute. Add the soy sauce mixture and cook, tossing and stirring constantly, 1 to 2 more minutes, or until all ingredients are heated through. Remove from heat and stir in the remaining scallion greens and pickled chili pepper. Serve at once.

{PER SERVING} Calories 372 · Protein 11g · Total Fat 14g · Sat Fat 2g · Cholesterol 0mg · Carbohydrate 53g · Dietary Fiber 3g · Sodium 459mg

Rice Noodles with Tofu and Hot Bean Sauce

This classic hot bean sauce is made from Chinese hot bean paste, also called soybean paste with chili, not to be confused with standard black bean paste, which is considerably less spicy.

MAKES 4 SERVINGS

    8 ounces extra-firm tofu, drained
    3 tablespoons hot bean paste or sauce, or
        soybean paste with chili
    1 teaspoon sugar
    1 tablespoon peanut oil
    1 tablespoon chopped fresh ginger
    2 large cloves garlic, finely chopped
    2 scallions, white and green parts, thinly
        sliced
    3 teaspoons sesame oil
    8 ounces dried flat (stir-fry or linguine-
        style) or thin (vermicelli-style) rice
        noodles, cooked according to package
        directions until just al dente
    3 tablespoons low-sodium soy sauce

Place the tofu on a deep-sided plate or shallow bowl. Top with a second plate and weight with a heavy can. Let stand for a minimum of 15 minutes (preferably 1 hour). Drain off the excess water. Cut into 1-inch cubes.

In a small bowl, mix together 2 tablespoons hot bean paste and sugar; set aside.

In a wok or large nonstick skillet, heat the peanut oil over medium-high heat. Add the tofu and cook, stirring, until lightly browned, 4 to 5 minutes. Add the ginger and garlic and cook, stirring constantly, 2 minutes. Reduce the heat to medium and add the hot bean paste mixture; cook, stirring, 2 minutes. Add the scallions and 1 teaspoon sesame oil and stir quickly to combine. Add the noodles, soy sauce, remaining 1 tablespoon hot bean paste, and remaining 2 teaspoons sesame oil; cook, tossing and stirring constantly with a wide spatula, until coated and heated through, about 2 minutes. Serve at once.

{PER SERVING} Calories 333 · Protein 6g · Total Fat 10g · Sat Fat 2g · Cholesterol 0mg · Carbohydrate 55g · Dietary Fiber 2g · Sodium 602mg

Hunan-Style Green Beans and Tofu Skins with Rice Noodles

Here is an outstanding dish you won't find in the typical Chinese restaurant outside of China. Tofu skins, also known as dried bean curd or yuba, are the yellowish membranes that form on top during the production of tofu. Dried in sheet form, it's known as tofu skin; in stick form, it's known as tofu bamboo. For a milder dish, use half the fresh chili pepper or replace with a pinch or two of crushed red pepper flakes.

MAKES 4 SERVINGS

4 ounces dried tofu skin sheets (about
    4 sheets), soaked in hot water to cover
    until pliable, about 3 minutes, drained
    well, or sticks (about 4 sticks, depending
    on length), broken into 6-inch lengths,
    soaked in boiling water to cover until
    softened, about 30 minutes, drained well
2 tablespoons peanut oil
2 tablespoons dark sesame oil
1 to 2 fresh red chili peppers, seeded, if
    desired, and thinly sliced
1 tablespoon finely chopped fresh ginger
2 large cloves garlic, finely chopped
1 pound green beans, trimmed, cut into
    1-inch pieces
¾ cup reduced-sodium vegetable broth
Salt and freshly ground black pepper, to
    taste
4 ounces flat rice noodles (stir-fry or
    linguine-style), cooked according to
    package directions until just al dente,
    drained well
2 tablespoons reduced-sodium soy sauce,
    or to taste
2 tablespoons vegetarian oyster sauce, or
    to taste
1 teaspoon Hunan pepper sauce (duo jiao) or
    Chinese chili paste, or to taste

Carefully cut the tofu skin sheets into long, wide ribbons, or cut the tofu skin sticks lengthwise in half or in thirds or quarters, depending on width. Set aside.

In a wok or large nonstick skillet, heat the peanut oil and 1 tablespoon sesame oil over medium-high heat. Add the chili pepper, ginger, and garlic and cook, stirring constantly, 1 minute. Add beans, tofu skins, broth, salt, and pepper and bring to a boil. Reduce heat to medium, cover, and cook until

beans and tofu skins are tender, about 5 minutes, stirring occasionally. Add noodles, soy sauce, oyster sauce, remaining 1 tablespoon sesame oil, and pepper sauce to the skillet; cook, tossing and stirring constantly, until heated through and thoroughly combined, about 2 minutes. Serve at once.

{PER SERVING} Calories 306 · Protein 8g · Total Fat 15g · Sat Fat 2g · Cholesterol 0mg · Carbohydrate 38g · Dietary Fiber 5g · Sodium 753mg

Stir-Fried Udon Noodles with Broccoli

The key to the success of this delicious dish is not to fully cook the udon noodles (known as cu mian in China) before stir-frying.

MAKES 4 SERVINGS

12 ounces fresh udon noodles
8 ounces fresh broccoli florets, cut into
    bite-size pieces
2 tablespoons peanut oil
4 scallions, white and green parts,
    separated, thinly sliced
2 to 3 large cloves garlic, finely chopped
¼ teaspoon crushed red pepper flakes, or
    to taste
2 tablespoons vegetarian oyster sauce or
    mushroom soy sauce
2 tablespoons reduced-sodium soy sauce
2 tablespoons Shaoxing rice wine, dry
    sherry, sake, or dry white wine
2 tablespoons rice wine vinegar
1 tablespoon toasted (dark) sesame oil
Salt and freshly ground black pepper, to
    taste

In a large stockpot, cook the noodles and broccoli in boiling salted water according to noodle package directions until almost al dente, about 3 minutes. Drain well in a colander.

In a wok or large nonstick skillet, heat the peanut oil over medium-high heat. Add the white parts of the scallions, garlic, and red pepper flakes; cook, stirring constantly, 1 minute. Add the noodles and broccoli and cook, stirring constantly, 1 minute. Reduce the heat to medium and add the oyster sauce, soy sauce, rice wine, vinegar, sesame oil, salt, and pepper. Cook, tossing and stirring often, until heated through and combined, about 2 minutes. Add the scallion greens and toss well to combine. Serve at once.

{PER SERVING} Calories 300 · Protein 9g · Total Fat 8g · Sat Fat 1g · Cholesterol 0mg · Carbohydrate 47g · Dietary Fiber 3g · Sodium 417mg

Sichuan-Style Cold Udon Noodles with Pickled Vegetables

Pickled vegetables are a specialty of Sichuan Province—the most popular is zha cai (literally "pressed vegetable"), a type of pickled mustard stem. Feel free to use your favorites in the following recipe, perfect for a buffet, as it holds up well at room temperature. To reduce the heat and spiciness, omit the Chinese hot oil and use half the amount of Sichuan peppercorns. Try to use fresh udon noodles—known as cu mian in China—which can be located in the refrigerated section of Asian markets.

MAKES 4 SERVINGS

1 tablespoon toasted (dark) sesame oil
1 tablespoon peanut oil
1 tablespoon reduced-sodium soy sauce
1 tablespoon cider vinegar
½ tablespoon whole Sichuan peppercorns, crushed into small pieces
2 large cloves garlic, finely chopped
1 teaspoon Chinese hot oil
¼ teaspoon coarse salt, or to taste
¼ teaspoon crushed red pepper flakes, or to taste
2 scallions, white and green parts, finely chopped
8 ounces fresh udon noodles, cut in half, cooked according to package directions until al dente, drained and rinsed under cold running water until cool, drained well
½ cup chopped fresh cilantro (leaves and stems)
¼ cup pickled Chinese vegetables, preferably mustard stems or tubers, rinsed, drained, and cut into julienne pieces
¼ cup shredded fresh carrots (optional)

In a large bowl, whisk together the sesame oil, peanut oil, soy sauce, vinegar, Sichuan peppercorns, garlic, hot oil, salt, and red pepper flakes until blended. Stir in the scallions and let stand a few minutes to allow the flavors to blend. Add the noodles, cilantro, pickled vegetables, and carrots (if using); toss well to thoroughly combine. Cover and refrigerate a minimum of 1 hour or up to 2 days and serve chilled, or return to room temperature.

{PER SERVING} Calories 249 · Protein 7g · Total Fat 9g · Sat Fat 1g · Cholesterol 0mg · Carbohydrate 35g · Dietary Fiber 2g · Sodium 324mg

Rice Noodles with Chinese Broccoli and Shiitake Mushrooms

With its long stems and big bluish green leaves, Chinese broccoli, or gai lan, is one of the most sought-after vegetables in Asian markets. Broccolini or regular broccoli can be substituted, if necessary; in this instance, blanch the florets as well.

MAKES 4 SERVINGS

12 ounces Chinese broccoli, tough ends trimmed, leaves and stalks separated, cut into 2-inch pieces

¾ cup reduced-sodium vegetable broth

3 tablespoons reduced-sodium soy sauce, plus additional, to serve

1 tablespoon Chinese black vinegar or balsamic vinegar, plus additional, to serve

1 teaspoon sugar

1 tablespoon peanut oil

8 medium fresh shiitake mushrooms, stemmed and quartered

1 tablespoon finely chopped fresh ginger

3 large cloves garlic, finely chopped

¼ teaspoon crushed red pepper flakes, or to taste

2 teaspoons cornstarch mixed with 2 tablespoons cold water

4 scallions, white and green parts, cut diagonally into 1-inch pieces

1 teaspoon toasted sesame seeds (optional), plus additional, to serve

Salt, preferably the coarse variety, to taste, plus additional, to serve

Freshly ground black pepper, to taste

8 ounces dried flat rice noodles (stir-fry or linguine-style), cooked according to package directions until just al dente

1 tablespoon toasted (dark) sesame oil

In a large pot of boiling salted water, blanch the broccoli stalks until crisp-tender, 1 to 2 minutes. Drain and set aside.

In a small bowl, stir together the broth, soy sauce, vinegar, and sugar; set aside. In a wok or large nonstick skillet, heat the peanut oil over medium heat. Add the mushrooms, ginger, garlic, and red pepper flakes; cook, stirring, until mushrooms are softened, 2 to 3 minutes.

Add the broth mixture to the wok; bring to a simmer over medium-high heat. Stir in the cornstarch mixture and reduce heat to medium; cook, stirring, 1 minute. Add the reserved broccoli stalks, broccoli leaves, scallions, sesame seeds (if using), salt, and black pepper; cook, tossing and stirring constantly, until heated through, about 2 minutes. Add the noodles and sesame oil; cook, tossing with a wide spatula until thoroughly combined and heated through, about 2 minutes. Serve at once, with additional soy sauce, black vinegar, sesame seeds (if using), and coarse salt passed separately.

{PER SERVING} Calories 346 · Protein 7g · Total Fat 8g · Sat Fat 1g · Cholesterol 0mg · Carbohydrate 65g · Dietary Fiber 5g · Sodium 581mg

CHAPTER SIX

Tofu, Seitan, and Other Main Dishes

If such a poll were possible, vegetarians the world over would surely rank tofu as one of China's greatest inventions, right up there with paper and moveable type. Created over 2,000 years ago from the curds of soybeans containing the nine essential amino acids, tofu is a complete protein; consequently, it is universally recognized as the quintessential meat alternative. Though bland on its own, tofu has an uncanny ability to take on the flavors of the other foods and seasonings with which it is cooked; it is used in both savory and sweet dishes. In Chinese cuisine, tofu is eaten in a myriad of ways, including stir-fried, stewed, baked, braised, grilled, deep-fried, in soup, cooked in sauce, stuffed with fillings, and, sometimes, raw. Tofu, of course, isn't the only meat substitute that the Chinese have perfected. Seitan, or wheat gluten, also known as "mian jin" in Chinese (literally, "noodle or dough tendon"), originated in ancient China as an imitation meat for adherents of Buddhism. Made by washing wheat flour dough with water until all the starch dissolves, leaving insoluble gluten as an elastic mass that is then cooked before being eaten, wheat gluten takes three primary forms—fried, steamed, or baked. Other popular tofulike meat substitutes are rice tofu, or "mi dou fu," which is rice milk boiled to a curd in a method similar to tofu, and konjac tofu, or "moyu dou fu," a gelatinous, fiber-rich mass with almost zero calories, which is made from the starchy corm of the konjac plant grown in southern China. As the following flavorful vegan main dishes will validate, meat never again has to be an option.

· TOFU DISHES ·

Poached Tofu with Spicy Kumquat Sauce

This is a speedy yet special dish to serve company during the cold-weather months when kumquats are in season.

MAKES 4 SERVINGS

2 cups low-sodium vegetable broth
2 cups water
1 scallion, thinly sliced
½ star anise
16 ounces firm tofu, drained
Spicy Kumquat Sauce, below

In a medium saucepan, bring the broth, water, scallion, and star anise to a boil over high heat; add the tofu, reduce the heat, and simmer gently, uncovered, 10 minutes.

To serve, remove the tofu from the broth mixture (reserve broth mixture for another use) and cut into thin slices. Divide the slices evenly among each of 4 serving plates and top with equal portions of the Spicy Kumquat Sauce, below. Serve at once.

{PER SERVING} Calories 198 · Protein 13g · Total Fat 9g · Sat Fat 1g · Cholesterol 0mg · Carbohydrate 20g · Dietary Fiber 4g · Sodium 143mg

SPICY KUMQUAT SAUCE

Use this piquant, spicy sauce to enliven countless tofu and seitan dishes.

MAKES ABOUT 1¼ CUPS

½ tablespoon canola oil
6 fresh kumquats, unpeeled, seeded, and chopped
1 fresh green or red chili pepper, seeded and finely chopped
1 shallot, finely chopped, or 2 tablespoons finely chopped red onion
2 tablespoons Chinese black vinegar or balsamic vinegar
1 cup fresh orange juice
¾ cup low-sodium vegetable broth
1 tablespoon brown sugar
½ tablespoon toasted (dark) sesame oil
Salt and freshly ground black pepper, to taste

In a small heavy-bottomed saucepan, heat the canola oil over medium-low heat. Add the kumquats, chili pepper, and shallot; cook, stirring occasionally, until the shallot is softened, 4 to 5 minutes. Add the vinegar and cook, stirring occasionally, until liquid is almost completely evaporated. Add the juice, broth, and sugar; bring to a simmer over medium heat. Simmer, stirring occasionally, until sauce is reduced to about 1¼ cups. Stir in the sesame oil and season with salt and pepper. Serve warm. Completely cooled sauce can be covered and refrigerated up to 3 days before reheating over low heat and serving.

{PER SERVING} (about 3 tablespoons, or ⅙ of the recipe) Calories 72 · Protein 3g · Total Fat 2g · Sat Fat 0g · Cholesterol 0mg · Carbohydrate 12g · Dietary Fiber 2g · Sodium 68mg

Stuffed Acorn Squash with Tofu and Cabbage

Though typically steamed in China, roasting is the more practical way to cook acorn squash in the West. Coleslaw mix can stand in for the shredded cabbage, if desired.

MAKES 4 MAIN DISH SERVINGS

8 ounces extra-firm tofu, rinsed and
    drained
2 medium acorn squash (1½ to 2 pounds
    each), halved lengthwise, seeds removed
2½ teaspoons toasted (dark) sesame oil
½ teaspoon salt, plus extra, to taste
Freshly ground black pepper, to taste
1½ tablespoons canola oil
1 large red onion (about 8 ounces), chopped
1 tablespoon chopped fresh ginger
2 large cloves garlic, finely chopped
10 cups shredded green or Napa cabbage
    (about 1¼ pound)
½ cup water, plus additional, if necessary
¼ cup chopped fresh cilantro or parsley
3 tablespoons toasted sesame seeds
1 tablespoon reduced-sodium soy sauce

Preheat oven to 375F (190C). Lightly oil a large baking sheet and set aside.

Place the tofu on a deep-sided plate or shallow bowl. Top with a second plate and weight with a heavy can. Let stand for a minimum of 15 minutes (preferably 1 hour). Drain excess water. Cut into ½-inch cubes.

Meanwhile, brush the centers of the squash halves evenly with ½ teaspoon sesame oil. Season to taste with salt and pepper. Place cut side down on prepared baking sheet. Bake for 35 to 45 minutes, or until tender.

In a large nonstick skillet, heat 1 tablespoon canola oil over medium heat. Add the tofu and cook, stirring occasionally, until lightly browned, 5 to 7 minutes. Remove from the skillet and set aside. Add remaining ½ tablespoon canola oil, onion, and ginger and cook, stirring, until onion is softened, 4 to 5 minutes. Add the garlic and cook, stirring constantly, 1 minute. Add the cabbage, water, ½ teaspoon salt, and reduce the heat to medium-low; cook, covered, until cabbage is tender, about 10 minutes, stirring occasionally. Uncover and return the heat to medium; cook, stirring occasionally, until deep golden, about 15 minutes, adding water, if necessary, to prevent burning. Add the reserved tofu, half the cilantro, half the sesame seeds, soy sauce, and remaining 2 teaspoons sesame oil; cook, stirring, until heated through, 1 to 2 minutes.

To serve, fill each squash half with equal portions of the tofu-cabbage mixture. Sprinkle evenly with remaining cilantro and sesame seeds. Serve warm.

{PER SERVING} Calories 309 · Protein 11g · Total Fat 15g · Sat Fat 2g · Cholesterol 0mg · Carbohydrate 41g · Dietary Fiber 6g · Sodium 462mg

Black Bean Tofu

This colorful and flavorful tofu dish is one of my favorites. To ensure that the tofu browns nicely, weight it as directed for 1 hour, if possible. Serve over brown rice for a complete meal.

MAKES 4 SERVINGS

1 pound extra-firm tofu, drained
2 tablespoons peanut oil

4 to 6 large cloves garlic, peeled, thinly
    sliced lengthwise

1 tablespoon chopped fresh ginger

⅛ teaspoon crushed red pepper flakes, or
    to taste

½ medium red bell pepper (about 3 ounces),
    cut into thin 1½-inch lengths

4 scallions, green parts only, cut into
    1½-inch lengths

¼ cup black bean sauce

1 tablespoon reduced-sodium soy sauce

1 tablespoon Shaoxing rice wine, dry
    sherry, sake, or dry white wine

1 teaspoon sugar (optional)

1 teaspoon toasted (dark) sesame oil

Place the tofu on a deep-sided plate or shallow bowl. Top with a second plate and weight with a heavy can. Let stand for a minimum of 15 minutes (preferably 1 hour). Drain excess water. Cut into ½-inch cubes.

In a wok or large nonstick skillet, heat 1 tablespoon peanut oil over medium-high heat. Add the tofu and cook, turning often, until browned and crispy, 5 to 7 minutes. Transfer tofu to a holding plate and reduce the heat to medium. Add remaining 1 tablespoon peanut oil, garlic, ginger, and red pepper flakes; cook, stirring constantly, 2 minutes. Add the red bell pepper and cook, stirring constantly, until just softened, about 2 minutes. Reduce heat to medium-low and add the reserved tofu, scallion greens, black bean sauce, soy sauce, wine, sugar (if using), and sesame oil. Cook, stirring and turning constantly, until tofu is heated through, about 2 minutes. Serve at once.

{PER SERVING} Calories 199 · Protein 11g · Total Fat 14g · Sat Fat 2g · Cholesterol 0mg · Carbohydrate 9g · Dietary Fiber 3g · Sodium 350mg

Stir-Fried Five-Spice Tofu with Chinese Flowering Chives

Stir-fries don't get any easier or more delicious than this—serve over rice or toss with noodles for a complete meal. Feel free to substitute the five-spice tofu or smoked tofu with the flavored variety of your choice. Chinese garlic chives or the green parts of about 8 scallions, sliced lengthwise in half before cutting into 2-inch pieces, can stand-in for the flowering chives, if necessary.

MAKES 3 TO 4 SERVINGS

1 tablespoon peanut oil

1 bunch Chinese flowering chives (about
    4 ounces), cut into 2-inch lengths
    (include buds)

1 (10-ounce) package five-spice flavored
    tofu or smoked tofu, cut crosswise into
    thin slices

¼ teaspoon salt, or to taste

Freshly ground black pepper, to taste

Reduced-sodium soy sauce, to taste
    (optional)

In a wok or large nonstick skillet, heat the peanut oil over medium-high heat. Add the chives and cook, stirring constantly, 1 to 2 minutes, or until bright green. Add the tofu, salt, and pepper and cook, stirring constantly, until heated through, 2 to 3 minutes. Serve at once, with the soy sauce passed separately, if using.

{PER SERVING} Calories 129 · Protein 9g · Total Fat 9g · Sat Fat 1g · Cholesterol 0mg · Carbohydrate 6g · Dietary Fiber 3g · Sodium 193mg

Sesame-Orange-Glazed Tofu Nuggets with Broccoli and Red Bell Pepper

This eye-pleasing dish is also one of the most delicious entrées in this book. Serve with brown rice for a totally awesome meal.

MAKES 6 SERVINGS

1 pound extra-firm tofu, drained

1 pound fresh broccoli florets, cut into bite-size pieces

1 large red bell pepper (about 8 ounces), sliced into thin strips

1 cup orange juice, preferably freshly squeezed

½ cup water

3½ tablespoons cornstarch

1 tablespoon Chinese chile paste, or more, to taste

1 tablespoon reduced-sodium soy sauce

1 tablespoon sugar

2 teaspoons plain rice vinegar

½ teaspoon salt, plus additional, to taste

2 tablespoons hoisin sauce

1 teaspoon toasted (dark) sesame oil

⅓ cup sesame seeds

3 tablespoons all-purpose flour

¼ cup peanut oil

Salt and freshly ground black pepper, to taste

2 scallions, white and green parts, thinly sliced

Place the tofu on a deep-sided plate or shallow bowl. Top with a second plate and weight with a heavy can. Let stand for a minimum of 15 minutes (preferably 1 hour). Drain excess water. Cut into 1-inch cubes; set aside.

Place a steamer basket in a medium stockpot filled with about 2 inches of water. Add the broccoli and bring the water to a boil over high heat. Immediately reduce the heat to medium-low, cover, and steam 2 minutes. Carefully uncover and add the bell pepper; cover, and steam 4 minutes, or until all of the vegetables are just crisp-tender. Uncover and let cool a few minutes.

Meanwhile, in a small saucepan, whisk together the orange juice, water, 1½ tablespoons of the cornstarch, chili paste, soy sauce, sugar, vinegar, and salt until thoroughly blended. Bring to a brisk simmer over medium-high heat, stirring often. Reduce the heat to medium and cook, whisking constantly, until glaze bubbles and thickens, 2 to 3 minutes. Remove from heat and stir in the hoisin sauce and sesame oil; set aside.

Line a baking sheet with a few layers of paper towels and set aside. Place the sesame seeds in a small bowl. In another small bowl, combine the flour and remaining 2 tablespoons cornstarch. Roll tofu in the sesame seeds, and then in the flour mixture until well coated; set aside.

In a wok or large nonstick skillet, heat the peanut oil over medium-high heat. Add the tofu and cook, turning with a spatula every few minutes, until nicely browned on all sides, 6 to 8 minutes. Transfer to prepared baking sheet and season with salt and pepper. Set aside to drain a few minutes.

In the same wok (it's not necessary to wipe out), return the tofu and add the steamed vegetables, scallions, and glaze; cook over medium heat, stirring and turning often, until tofu and vegetables are thoroughly coated and heated through, about 2 minutes. Serve at once.

Mixed Mushroom Stir-Fry with Tofu, Green Apple, and Jasmine Tea Leaves

Jasmine tea is the most famous scented tea in China. I was lucky enough to live in Hunan Province, a major producer of this subtly sweet specialty, where I enjoyed it endlessly. Typically, the scent of jasmine flowers is blended with green tea leaves; however, any high-quality jasmine tea variety can be used in this recipe. Serve over jasmine rice for an extra-special treat.

MAKES 4 SERVINGS

12 ounces extra-firm tofu, drained

¼ cup reduced-sodium vegetable broth

2 tablespoons reduced-sodium soy sauce

1 teaspoon jasmine green tea leaves

1 teaspoon sugar

1 teaspoon toasted (dark) sesame oil

1 tablespoon peanut oil

8 dried shiitake mushrooms, soaked in hot water to cover 20 minutes, or until softened, rinsed, drained, stemmed, and sliced

¼ cup dried shredded wood ear mushrooms, soaked in hot water to cover 20 minutes, or until softened, rinsed and drained

2 cloves garlic, finely chopped

1 small Granny Smith apple (about 4 ounces), or other tart apple, unpeeled, cored, thinly sliced

4 scallions, white and green parts, thinly sliced, plus 1 scallion, green part only, thinly sliced

1 (14-ounce) can straw mushrooms, rinsed and drained

Salt and freshly ground black pepper, to taste

2 tablespoons vegetarian oyster sauce or mushroom soy sauce

Place the tofu on a deep-sided plate or shallow bowl. Top with a second plate and weight with a heavy can. Let stand for a minimum of 15 minutes (preferably 1 hour). Drain off the excess water. Cut into ½-inch cubes.

In a small bowl, combine the broth, soy sauce, and tea leaves; microwave on high 25 seconds, or until a boil is reached. Cover and let steep 5 minutes. Uncover (do not strain) and stir in the sugar and sesame oil; set aside.

In a wok or large nonstick skillet, heat the peanut oil over medium-high heat. Add the shiitake mushrooms and cook, stirring constantly, 2 minutes. Add the wood ear mushrooms and cook, stirring constantly, 1 minute. Add the tofu and garlic and cook, stirring constantly, 1 minute. Add the apple and 4 scallions, white and green parts, and cook, stirring constantly, 2 minutes. Add the straw mushrooms and cook, stirring constantly, 1 minute. Reduce the heat to medium-low and add the broth-tea mixture, salt, and pepper; cook, covered, stirring occasionally, until apples are tender, 2 to 3 minutes. Stir in the oyster sauce and remaining scallion greens. Serve at once.

Braised Dry Tofu with Cabbage and Tomatoes

Dry tofu is a compressed tofu with the least amount of moisture of all fresh tofu; it has a rubbery texture similar to fully cooked meat. If necessary, 12 ounces of extra-firm tofu, weighted and drained, can be used in the following recipe. Regular green cabbage can stand in for the Napa variety, if desired. For a more substantial main dish, serve over rice.

MAKES 4 SERVINGS

1½ tablespoons peanut oil

1 (8-ounce) package thick dry tofu, spiced, if desired, soaked in warm water to cover for 10 minutes, drained, cut into 1-inch cubes

1 large Napa cabbage (about 2 pounds), cored, leaves torn into bite-size pieces

2 large tomatoes (about 8 ounces each), peeled, seeded, and cut into small pieces (see Cook's Tip, below)

4 scallions, white and green parts, thinly sliced

3 large cloves garlic, finely chopped

½ cup low-sodium vegetable broth

2 tablespoons reduced-sodium soy sauce, or more, to taste

½ teaspoon sugar

¼ teaspoon crushed red pepper flakes, or to taste (optional)

Salt and freshly ground black pepper, to taste

½ tablespoon toasted (dark) sesame oil

1 teaspoon cornstarch mixed with 1 teaspoon water

In a large nonstick skillet with a lid, heat the peanut oil over medium-high heat. Add the tofu and cook, stirring, until nicely browned on all sides, 3 to 5 minutes. Add the cabbage and cook, tossing and stirring constantly, until softened and beginning to wilt, about 2 minutes. Add the tomatoes, scallions, and garlic; cook, tossing and stirring constantly, 2 minutes. Reduce the heat to medium and add the broth, soy sauce, sugar, red pepper (if using), salt, and pepper, stirring well to combine. Cover and cook 2 minutes, stirring once. Uncover and add the sesame oil and cornstarch mixture, stirring well to combine. Continue to cook, uncovered, stirring occasionally, until liquid is slightly reduced and thickened, about 2 minutes. Serve warm.

{PER SERVING} Calories 217 · Protein 13g · Total Fat 12g · Sat Fat 2g · Cholesterol 0mg · Carbohydrate 20g · Dietary Fiber 7g · Sodium 415mg

{COOK'S TIP}

To peel the tomatoes, bring a medium stockpot filled with water to a boil over high heat; drop in the tomatoes and boil 20 seconds. Drain and rinse under cold running water. Peel off the skins.

Spicy Hunan-Style Tofu with Chilies and Cumin

If you like it hot ("la"), this fragrant and fabulous tofu dish is for you.

SERVES 4

1 pound extra-firm tofu, rinsed and drained

2 tablespoons Shaoxing rice wine, dry sherry, sake, or dry white wine

2 tablespoons dark soy sauce

¼ teaspoon salt, plus additional, to taste

1½ tablespoons peanut oil

½ tablespoon toasted (dark) sesame oil

2 scallions, white and green parts
  separated, thinly sliced
2 to 3 fresh red chili peppers, seeded and
  finely chopped
4 large cloves garlic, finely chopped
1 tablespoon finely chopped fresh ginger
1½ to 2 teaspoons ground cumin
¼ teaspoon crushed red pepper flakes, or
  to taste
Salt and freshly ground black pepper, to
  taste
2 tablespoons finely chopped fresh
  cilantro, for garnish (optional)

Place the tofu on a deep-sided plate or shallow bowl. Top with a second plate and weight with a heavy can. Let stand for a minimum of 15 minutes (preferably 1 hour). Drain excess water. Cut crosswise into ⅓-inch-thick slices.

In a shallow dish large enough to hold the tofu slices in a single layer, combine the wine, soy sauce, and ¼ teaspoon salt. Add the tofu slices, turning to coat. Let stand at room temperature about 20 minutes, turning a few times. (Alternatively, cover and refrigerate up to 24 hours, turning once or twice.)

In a large nonstick skillet, heat the peanut oil over medium-high heat. Add the tofu, reserving marinade, and cook, turning often, until nicely browned, 3 to 4 minutes. Remove from the skillet and set briefly aside. Working quickly, add the sesame oil, white parts of the scallion, fresh chilies, garlic, ginger, cumin, red pepper flakes, salt, and pepper; cook, stirring constantly, 30 seconds. Reduce heat to medium, return the tofu, and add the reserved marinade; cook, turning often, 1 minute. Remove from the heat and sprinkle with the scallion greens and cilantro, if desired. Serve at once.

{PER SERVING} Calories 177 · Protein 11g · Total Fat 13g · Sat Fat 2g · Cholesterol 0mg · Carbohydrate 8g · Dietary Fiber 2g · Sodium 447mg

Baked Five-Spice Seasoned Tofu

Use this tasty seasoned tofu in stir-fries, salads, soups, sandwiches, or wherever baked or pressed five-spice tofu is called for in recipes. To reduce the salt, replace all or part of the vegetable broth with water.

MAKES 4 TO 6 SERVINGS

1 pound firm or extra-firm tofu, drained
1 cup low-sodium vegetable broth
¼ cup reduced-sodium soy sauce
2 tablespoons toasted (dark) sesame oil
½ teaspoon five-spice powder

Place the tofu on a deep-sided plate or shallow bowl. Top with a second plate and weight with a heavy can. Let stand for a minimum of 15 minutes (preferably 1 hour). Drain off the excess water. Cut horizontally in half, then cut crosswise into ½-inch-thick strips.

Meanwhile, preheat oven to 350F (175C). Lightly oil a 9-by-13-inch baking dish.

In a small bowl, whisk together the broth, soy sauce, sesame oil, and five-spice powder. Arrange the tofu slices in a single layer in the prepared baking dish and pour the broth mixture over top. Bake 15 minutes. Turn tofu over and bake an additional 15 minutes; repeat process until all of the liquid has been absorbed, about 1 hour total. Serve warm, chilled, or at room temperature. Completely cooled tofu can be covered and refrigerated, 5 to 7 days.

{PER SERVING} Calories 169 · Protein 13g · Total Fat 12g · Sat Fat 2g · Cholesterol 0mg · Carbohydrate 4g · Dietary Fiber 2g · Sodium 737mg

Kung Pao Tofu with Dried Chilies, Sichuan-Style

In Sichuan Province, kung pao tofu is typically made with dried red chili peppers, Sichuan peppercorns, and scallions—the peanuts, essential in Western-style variations, though delicious, are optional.

MAKES 4 SERVINGS

1 pound extra-firm tofu, drained

⅔ cup low-sodium vegetable broth

2 tablespoons reduced-sodium soy sauce

2 tablespoons Shaoxing rice wine, sake, dry sherry, or dry white wine

1 tablespoon brown sugar

½ tablespoon toasted (dark) sesame oil

½ tablespoon cornstarch

1 teaspoon Chinese black vinegar or balsamic vinegar

Salt, to taste

1½ tablespoons peanut oil

4 to 6 small dried red chilies, seeded, cut into small pieces, soaked in warm water to cover 5 minutes to soften, drained

6 to 8 Sichuan peppercorns, crushed

3 large cloves garlic, finely chopped

½ tablespoon chopped fresh ginger

4 scallions, white and green parts, cut into ½-inch lengths

¼ cup unsalted roasted peanuts (optional)

Place the tofu on a deep-sided plate or shallow bowl. Top with a second plate and weight with a heavy can. Let stand for a minimum of 15 minutes (preferably 1 hour). Drain excess water. Cut into ½-inch cubes.

In a small bowl, whisk together the broth, soy sauce, wine, sugar, sesame oil, cornstarch, vinegar, and salt until thoroughly blended; set aside.

In a wok or large nonstick skillet, heat 1 tablespoon of the peanut oil over medium-high heat. Add the tofu and cook, stirring often, until nicely browned, 6 to 8 minutes. Transfer tofu to a plate and set briefly aside. Add the remaining ½ tablespoon peanut oil, chilies, peppercorns, garlic, and ginger to the wok and cook, stirring constantly, 1 minute. Return the tofu, add the scallions, and stir in the broth mixture; bring to a brisk simmer. Reduce the heat to medium and stir in the peanuts, if using; cook, stirring, until thickened, 2 to 3 minutes. Serve at once.

{PER SERVING} (without peanuts) Calories 214 · Protein 13g · Total Fat 12g · Sat Fat 2g · Cholesterol 0mg · Carbohydrate 15g · Dietary Fiber 4g · Sodium 403mg

Cantonese-Style Tofu-Stuffed Asian Eggplant and Bell Peppers

This Cantonese specialty typically calls for deep-frying after the initial steaming. In this healthier but equally delicious version, the stuffed vegetables are broiled, instead, before being served up in a lively black bean–ginger sauce.

MAKES 3 MAIN DISH OR 4 TO 6 SIDE DISH SERVINGS

1 tablespoon peanut oil

3 dried shiitake mushrooms, soaked in hot water to cover 20 minutes, or until softened, rinsed, drained, stemmed, and chopped

2 large cloves garlic, finely chopped

8 ounces firm tofu, drained, chopped

2 scallions, white and green parts, thinly
sliced

¼ teaspoon salt, or to taste

Freshly ground black pepper, to taste

1 tablespoon plus 1 teaspoon toasted (dark)
sesame oil

1 long Chinese eggplant (about 8 ounces),
cut crosswise into 4 equal lengths

2 small red and/or green bell peppers
(about 4 ounces each), cut lengthwise in
half, ribbed and seeded

1 fresh green or red chili, seeded and finely
chopped

1 tablespoon salted (fermented) black
beans, rinsed and slightly crushed

1 tablespoon finely chopped fresh ginger

1 cup reduced-sodium vegetable broth

1 teaspoon reduced-sodium soy sauce

2 teaspoons cornstarch mixed with 2
teaspoons water

In a medium nonstick skillet, heat ½ tablespoon peanut oil over medium heat. Add the mushrooms and cook, stirring, until softened, 2 to 3 minutes. Add half the garlic and cook, stirring constantly, 1 minute. Add the tofu, scallions, salt, and pepper and cook, stirring, until heated through, about 2 minutes. Remove from heat and stir in ½ tablespoon sesame oil. Using a fork, mash the mixture until well combined. Set aside to cool about 10 minutes.

Make a slit down the long side of each piece of eggplant, not cutting all the way through. Fill the eggplant and bell peppers with the tofu stuffing.

Place a steaming basket in a medium stockpot set over about 1½ inches of water. Working in batches, as needed, place the stuffed vegetables in the steaming basket; bring to a boil over high heat. Reduce the heat to medium, cover, and steam until the vegetables are tender and the stuffing is cooked through, about 10 minutes. Carefully transfer the stuffed vegetables to a large, ungreased, rimmed baking sheet. Brush with 1 teaspoon sesame oil and set aside.

Preheat the oven to broil. Set oven rack 6 to 8 inches from heat source.

Meanwhile, in a small saucepan, heat the remaining ½ tablespoon peanut oil over medium heat. Add the chili, black beans, ginger, and remaining garlic; cook, stirring, 1 minute, or until softened and fragrant. Add the broth and soy sauce and bring to a brisk simmer over medium-high heat. Reduce the heat to medium-low and add the remaining ½ tablespoon sesame oil and the cornstarch mixture. Cook, stirring constantly, until thickened, about 2 minutes. Remove from heat, cover, and keep warm.

Place stuffed vegetables under the broiler. Broil until the tops are lightly browned, about 5 minutes, turning the baking sheet a few times to promote even browning. To serve, cut the stuffed peppers crosswise in half. Ladle equal amounts of the black bean–ginger sauce in deep-welled serving plates and top with equal amounts of the stuffed vegetables. Serve at once.

{PER SERVING} Calories 265 · Protein 13g · Total Fat 17g · Sat Fat 3g · Cholesterol 0mg · Carbohydrate 19g · Dietary Fiber 7g · Sodium 430mg

Barbecued Tofu with Hoisin Sauce

Even tofu naysayers typically enjoy these tasty grilled morsels. In a pinch, whip up Quick Spicy Hoisin Sauce (page 140), or use prepared hoisin sauce.

MAKES 4 SERVINGS

- 1 pound extra-firm tofu, drained and rinsed
- ½ recipe Hoisin Sauce (recipe below), ½ cup Quick Spicy Hoisin Sauce (page 140), or ½ cup prepared hoisin sauce, plus additional, to serve
- Chopped scallion greens (optional)

Place the tofu on a deep-sided plate or shallow bowl. Top with a second plate and weight with a heavy can. Let stand for a minimum of 15 minutes (preferably 1 hour). Drain off the excess water. Slice the tofu lengthwise into 6 slices (about ½ inch in thickness), then cut in half crosswise, for a total of 12 pieces. Transfer to a shallow dish large enough to hold the tofu slices in a single layer. Brush the tops with half the hoisin sauce. Turn and brush with remaining sauce. Cover and marinate at room temperature 1 hour, or refrigerate overnight.

Prepare a medium-hot charcoal or gas grill, or preheat a broiler. Position an oiled grill rack or oven rack 4 to 6 inches from the heat source. If broiling, lightly oil a large baking sheet and set aside. Alternatively, place a nonstick stovetop grilling pan with grids over medium-high heat.

Grill or broil the tofu slices until nicely browned, 3 to 4 minutes per side. Transfer to a serving plate and sprinkle with the scallion greens, if using, and serve warm or at room temperature, with additional hoisin sauce passed separately.

{PER SERVING} Calories 139 · Protein 11g · Total Fat 7g · Sat Fat 1g · Cholesterol 0mg · Carbohydrate 11g · Dietary Fiber 2g · Sodium 705mg

HOISIN SAUCE

Feel free to adjust the degree of sweetness and/or heat in this ever-popular Chinese barbecue sauce. For a sweeter version, add additional molasses or brown sugar. For a milder version, use less chili paste, or omit altogether.

MAKES ABOUT 1 CUP

- ½ cup reduced-sodium soy sauce
- ½ cup mashed cooked sweet potato or canned pumpkin puree
- ¼ cup black bean sauce with garlic
- 2 to 3 tablespoons molasses
- 1 to 2 tablespoons dark brown sugar
- 2 teaspoons toasted (dark) sesame oil
- 2 teaspoons red wine vinegar
- 1 teaspoon Chinese chili paste, or to taste
- 1 to 2 tablespoons water, or as needed (optional)

Place all ingredients (except the water) in a food processor fitted with the knife blade, or a blender; process or blend until smooth and pureed. For a thinner sauce, add water as needed. Serve at room temperature. Sauce can be refrigerated, covered, up to 5 days.

{PER SERVING} (about 2 tablespoons, or ⅛ of recipe) Calories 53 · Protein 1g · Total Fat 2g · Sat Fat 0g · Cholesterol 0mg · Carbohydrate 9g · Dietary Fiber 1g · Sodium 697mg

Mushroom-Smothered Tofu

For mushroom lovers of all ages, this mildly spiced dish makes a delightful fall-weather meal served over brown rice and accompanied by a side dish of steamed fresh broccoli. Fresh enoki, or golden needle mushrooms, or cultivated white mushrooms can replace the oyster variety, if necessary.

MAKES 4 SERVINGS

16 ounces extra-firm tofu, drained

8 dried shiitake mushrooms, soaked in 1¼ cups hot water to cover 20 minutes, or until softened

Water or low-sodium vegetable broth, as needed

1½ tablespoons peanut oil

8 fresh oyster mushrooms, stems trimmed, cut into ½-inch-thick slices

4 scallions, white and green parts separated, thinly sliced

1 tablespoon chopped fresh ginger

2 large cloves garlic, finely chopped

2 tablespoons dark soy sauce

1 tablespoon Shaoxing rice wine, dry sherry, sake, or dry white wine

½ teaspoon sugar

1 tablespoon toasted (dark) sesame oil

Salt and freshly ground black pepper, to taste

Place the tofu on a deep-sided plate or shallow bowl. Top with a second plate and weight with a heavy can. Let stand for a minimum of 15 minutes (preferably 1 hour). Drain off the excess water. Cut tofu into 4 squares and then cut each square into 2 triangles. Turn each triangle on its longest side and cut into 3 thin triangles for a total of 24 thin triangles. Set aside.

Drain the shiitake mushrooms, reserving the soaking liquid. Strain the reserved soaking liquid through a coffee filter or paper towel to remove any grit; squeeze mushrooms over filter to extract excess liquid. Add water or vegetable broth, if necessary, to equal ½ cup. Rinse the mushrooms; remove and discard the stems. Cut the caps into ½-inch-thick slices.

In a large nonstick skillet, heat 1 tablespoon peanut oil over medium-high heat. Add the tofu and cook until browned on both sides, about 5 minutes. Remove from skillet and set briefly aside. Add the remaining ½ tablespoon peanut oil, shiitake mushrooms, oyster mushrooms, white parts of the scallions, ginger, and garlic; cook, stirring constantly, 2 minutes, or until softened and fragrant. Add the reserved mushroom soaking liquid, soy sauce, wine, and sugar and bring to a simmer. Reduce the heat to medium and add the reserved tofu, scallion greens, ½ tablespoon sesame oil, salt, and pepper; stir well to combine. Cook, stirring often, until mushrooms are tender and liquid is reduced by about half, 2 to 3 minutes. Stir in remaining ½ tablespoon sesame oil and serve at once.

{PER SERVING} Calories 212 · Protein 12g · Total Fat 14g · Sat Fat 2g · Cholesterol 0mg · Carbohydrate 13g · Dietary Fiber 3g · Sodium 314mg

Red Lentil and Tofu Curry

This tasty Tibetan-style curry is delicious over rice or boiled potatoes.

MAKES 4 SERVINGS

½ pound extra-firm tofu, rinsed and
    drained
2 tablespoons canola oil
1 small onion (about 4 ounces), chopped
3 large cloves garlic, finely chopped
1 tablespoon chopped fresh ginger
2 cups low-sodium vegetable broth
1 cup water
½ cup red lentils, rinsed and drained
1 teaspoon whole cumin seeds
1 teaspoon mild curry powder
¼ teaspoon salt, or to taste
¼ cup chopped fresh cilantro
Freshly ground black pepper, to taste

Place the tofu on a deep-sided plate or shallow bowl. Top with a second plate and weight with a heavy can. Let stand for a minimum of 15 minutes (preferably 1 hour). Drain excess water. Cut into ½-inch cubes and set aside.

In a large saucepan, heat 1 tablespoon oil over medium heat. Add the onion and cook, stirring, until softened, about 2 minutes. Add the garlic and ginger and cook, stirring constantly, 1 minute. Add the broth, water, and lentils and bring to a boil over high heat. Reduce heat to medium-low and simmer, partially covered, until lentils are just tender, 30 to 40 minutes, stirring occasionally.

In a wok or large nonstick skillet, heat the remaining 1 tablespoon oil over medium heat. Add the cumin and cook, stirring constantly, until fragrant, about 30 seconds. Add the tofu and cook, stirring occasionally, until lightly browned, 3 to 4 minutes.

Add curry powder and salt and cook, stirring often, 1 minute. Add the lentil mixture, cilantro, and pepper, stirring well to combine; bring to a brisk simmer over medium-high heat. Reduce the heat to medium and cook, uncovered, stirring occasionally, 5 to 10 minutes, until thickened. Serve warm.

{PER SERVING} Calories 228 · Protein 18g · Total Fat 10g · Sat Fat 1g · Cholesterol 0mg · Carbohydrate 20g · Dietary Fiber 10g · Sodium 801mg

Sichuan Pepper Tofu-Mushroom Patties

I like to serve these fragrant patties inside hamburger buns and top with spinach leaves, red onion, and sweet chili sauce.

MAKES 4 PATTIES

12 ounces firm tofu, drained
¼ pound sliced fresh cultivated white
    mushrooms
½ tablespoon toasted (dark) sesame oil
¼ teaspoon ground Sichuan peppercorns
Salt, to taste
1 cup all-purpose flour
1 tablespoon canola or peanut oil
Sichuan sauce, sweet chili sauce. or hoisin
    sauce, to serve

In a food processor fitted with a knife blade, process the tofu, mushrooms, sesame oil, pepper, and salt until just combined. Add the flour and process until thoroughly combined but still slightly chunky. Transfer to a flat work surface and divide the mixture into 4 portions. Shape into 4 ½-inch-thick patties.

In a large nonstick skillet, heat the canola oil over medium heat. Add the patties and cook until nicely browned, 3 to 4 minutes per side. Serve at once, with the sauce passed separately.

{PER SERVING} Calories 231 · Protein 11g · Total Fat 10g · Sat Fat 1g · Cholesterol 0mg · Carbohydrate 27g · Dietary Fiber 2g · Sodium 8mg

Sesame-Crusted Tofu with Spicy Pineapple Rice Noodles

From Yunnan Province, where pineapple rules, this refreshing yet spicy dish's heat can be toned down by halving the amount of crushed red pepper flakes, or omitting them entirely—it will still taste delicious.

MAKES 4 SERVINGS

16 ounces extra-firm tofu, drained

⅓ cup sesame seeds, preferably a mixture of white and black

1 tablespoon plus 1 teaspoon cornstarch

½ teaspoon salt

Freshly ground black pepper, to taste

3 tablespoons reduced-sodium soy sauce

1½ tablespoons canola oil

1 tablespoon finely chopped fresh ginger

2 large cloves garlic, finely chopped

½ teaspoon crushed red pepper flakes, or to taste

8 ounces fresh snow peas, trimmed and cut diagonally in half

¾ cup pineapple juice, preferably fresh

2 cups diced fresh pineapple

2 teaspoons toasted (dark) sesame oil

8 ounces thin dry rice noodles (vermicelli-style), cooked according to package directions until just al dente, drained, rinsed under cold running water, drained well

Place the tofu on a deep-sided plate or shallow bowl. Top with a second plate and weight with a heavy can. Let stand for a minimum of 15 minutes (preferably 1 hour). Drain off the excess water. Cut lengthwise into 8 thin slices.

In a shallow bowl, mix together the sesame seeds, 1 tablespoon cornstarch, ¼ teaspoon salt, and pepper; set aside. In a small bowl, whisk together the soy sauce and remaining 1 teaspoon cornstarch until thoroughly blended; set aside.

Pat the tofu slices dry with paper towel. Press both sides of the tofu slices into the sesame seed mixture. In a large nonstick skillet, heat 1 tablespoon canola oil over medium-high heat. Add the tofu and cook until golden brown, about 3 minutes per side. Transfer to a plate, cover, and keep warm.

Wipe out the skillet and heat the remaining ½ tablespoon canola oil over medium-high heat. Add the ginger, garlic, and red pepper flakes and cook, stirring, until fragrant, about 30 seconds. Add the snow peas and cook, stirring, 30 seconds. Add the pineapple juice and remaining ¼ teaspoon salt and bring to a boil; reduce the heat to medium and cook, stirring, 1 minute. Add the soy sauce mixture and cook, stirring, until the sauce is thickened, about 2 minutes. Reduce heat to medium-low and add the pineapple, sesame oil, and the noodles; cook, tossing and stirring constantly with a wide spatula, until heated through, about 2 minutes. To serve, divide the noodle mixture evenly among 4 serving plates. Top each with 2 slices of tofu and serve at once.

{PER SERVING} Calories 528 · Protein 14g · Total Fat 19g · Sat Fat 2g · Cholesterol 0mg · Carbohydrate 79g · Dietary Fiber 4g · Sodium 736mg

Glazed Tofu Steaks with Fresh Peanut Sauce

While these tofu steaks can be served with any of your favorite Asian-style sauces in lieu of the peanut sauce, they are quite tasty on their own.

MAKES 4 SERVINGS

16 ounces extra-firm tofu, drained
2 teaspoons toasted (dark) sesame oil
1 tablespoon canola or peanut oil
2 tablespoons reduced-sodium soy sauce
Fresh Peanut Sauce, below

Place the tofu on a deep-sided plate or shallow bowl. Top with a second plate and weight with a heavy can. Let stand for a minimum of 15 minutes (preferably 1 hour). Drain off the excess water. Slice the tofu lengthwise into quarters. Brush top and bottom sides evenly with the sesame oil.

In a large nonstick skillet, heat the canola oil over medium-high heat. Add the tofu and cook until nicely browned on both sides, about 8 minutes total, turning once halfway through cooking. Remove skillet from heat. Sprinkle tofu with the soy sauce and quickly return to medium-low heat; cook, turning often, until soy sauce has evaporated and tofu is glazed, 1 to 2 minutes. Serve at once, with the peanut sauce passed separately.

{PER SERVING} Calories 287 · Protein 15g · Total Fat 23g · Sat Fat 3g · Cholesterol 0mg · Carbohydrate 9g · Dietary Fiber 3g · Sodium 759mg

FRESH PEANUT SAUCE

This fragrant sauce is delicious tossed with countless steamed vegetables and noodles, as well.

MAKES ABOUT ¾ CUP

1 tablespoon peanut oil
½ cup raw peanuts
¼ cup reduced-sodium vegetable broth or water, plus additional, as needed
2 tablespoons plain rice vinegar
Juice of 1 lime (about 2 tablespoons)
1 tablespoon reduced-sodium soy sauce, plus additional, as needed
½ to 1 teaspoon Chinese chili paste
2 large cloves garlic, finely chopped
½ teaspoon salt, or to taste
¼ cup finely chopped fresh cilantro

In a small heavy bottomed skillet, heat the oil over medium-low heat. Add the peanuts and cook, stirring often, until fragrant and golden, 3 to 5 minutes. Transfer to a food processor fitted with the knife blade and pulse broth, vinegar, lime juice, soy sauce, chili paste, garlic, and salt until smooth but still slightly chunky.

Transfer the peanut mixture to a serving bowl and stir in the cilantro; add additional soy sauce, if necessary. For a thinner sauce, add additional broth or water as needed. Serve at room temperature. At this point, sauce can be covered and refrigerated up to 2 days before returning to room temperature and serving.

{PER SERVING} (per tablespoon, or ¹/₁₂ of recipe) Calories 49 · Protein 2g · Total Fat 4g · Sat Fat 1g · Cholesterol 0mg · Carbohydrate 2g · Dietary Fiber 1g · Sodium 150mg

Spinach-Stuffed Tofu in Shiitake Mushroom Sauce

If you are searching for a dinner party main dish that impresses without the stress, look no further—most of the cooking can be done 24 hours ahead of serving.

MAKES 4 SERVINGS

1 tablespoon peanut oil

3 teaspoons toasted (dark) sesame oil

16 ounces extra-firm tofu, drained, cut lengthwise into 4 rectangles

2 tablespoons canola oil

8 ounces fresh shiitake mushrooms, stemmed, thinly sliced

1 teaspoon finely chopped fresh ginger

¼ cup all-purpose flour

2 cups reduced-sodium vegetable broth

1 tablespoon Shaoxing rice wine, dry sherry, sake, or dry white wine

2 tablespoons finely chopped scallion greens

1 tablespoon plus 2 teaspoons reduced-sodium soy sauce

½ teaspoon plain rice vinegar

½ teaspoon salt, plus additional, to taste

Freshly ground black pepper, to taste

¼ cup finely chopped fresh spinach

¼ teaspoon five-spice powder

Preheat oven to 375F (190C). Lightly oil a baking dish large enough to hold the tofu pieces comfortably in a single layer.

In a small bowl, combine the peanut oil with 1 teaspoon of the sesame oil. Arrange tofu pieces in a single layer in the prepared baking dish and brush the tops with half the peanut–sesame oil mixture.

Bake 15 minutes and turn tofu pieces over; brush tops with remaining oil mixture. Bake an additional 15 minutes. Remove from oven (do not turn off oven if completing recipe) and let cool about 15 minutes. (At this point, completely cooled tofu can be refrigerated, covered, up to 1 day before returning to room temperature and continuing with the recipe.)

Meanwhile, in a medium deep-sided skillet, heat the canola oil over medium heat. Add the mushrooms and ginger and cook, stirring, until mushrooms are tender and have released their liquid, about 5 minutes. Add the flour and cook, stirring constantly, 2 minutes. Slowly add the broth, stirring constantly. Add the wine and increase the heat to medium-high; bring to a boil, stirring constantly. Boil until mixture begins to thicken, stirring constantly, about 3 minutes. Remove from heat and add the scallion greens, 1 tablespoon soy sauce, 1 teaspoon sesame oil, vinegar, salt, and pepper, stirring well to blend. Set aside. (At this point, completely cooled mixture can be refrigerated, covered, up to 1 day before returning to room temperature and continuing with the recipe.)

In a small bowl, combine the spinach, remaining 1 teaspoon sesame oil, five-spice powder, salt, and pepper. Using a thin, sharp knife, cut a slit along the side of each tofu piece. Standing each tofu piece slit side up in the baking dish, fill each slit with ½ teaspoon of remaining soy sauce. Using a table knife, carefully stuff equal portions of the spinach mixture into each slit. Place tofu pieces back in baking dish and spoon the mushroom sauce evenly over top. Bake an additional 25 to 30 minutes, or until sauce is thickened and bubbly. Serve at once.

{PER SERVING} Calories 283 · Protein 17g · Total Fat 19g · Sat Fat 2g · Cholesterol 0mg · Carbohydrate 13g · Dietary Fiber 4g · Sodium 789mg

Hunan-Style Braised Tofu Puffs over Rice

Swift, spicy, and superb describes this homey Hunan specialty. Tofu puffs—also known as bean kow or bean curd puffs— are golden squares of chewy, deep-fried bean curd that can be found in the refrigerated section of Asian markets, next to the regular tofu. Their super-absorbency makes them popular additions to stews and braised dishes.

MAKES 4 SERVINGS

1 tablespoon peanut oil

2 to 3 fresh red chili peppers, seeded and thinly sliced

3 large cloves garlic, finely chopped

1 tablespoon chopped fresh ginger

2 cups reduced-sodium vegetable broth

1 tablespoon dark soy sauce

1 tablespoon regular reduced-sodium soy sauce

½ tablespoon black bean paste with garlic

½ tablespoon Chinese chili paste, or to taste

2 (4-ounce) packages deep-fried tofu puffs, each piece halved

6 garlic chives, cut into 2-inch pieces, or 3 scallions, green parts only, halved lengthwise, cut into 2-inch pieces

1 tablespoon toasted (dark) sesame oil

1 teaspoon cornstarch mixed with 2 teaspoons water

3 cups hot cooked rice

In a wok or large nonstick skillet, heat the oil over medium-high heat. Add the peppers, garlic, and ginger and cook, stirring, 2 minutes. Add the broth, both soy sauces, black bean paste, chili paste, and tofu and bring to a boil. Reduce the heat to medium-low and simmer, covered, stirring occasionally, 5 to 7 minutes, or until tofu has absorbed about half of the liquid. Add the chives and sesame oil and cook, stirring, 30 seconds. Add the cornstarch mixture and cook, stirring, until thickened, 1 to 2 minutes. Serve at once, over the rice.

{PER SERVING} Calories 351 · Protein 15g · Total Fat 12g · Sat Fat 2g · Cholesterol 0mg · Carbohydrate 47g · Dietary Fiber 4g · Sodium 594mg

Steamed Silken Tofu with Scallions

This silky tofu dish is heavenly with a side of Stir-Fried Shiitake Mushrooms with Shallots in Garlic Sauce (page 165), steamed broccoli, and brown rice. Silken tofu has a higher moisture content than regular cake tofu; hence, its lovely, custard-like texture. If your steamer basket has a handle in the center, cut the tofu in half crosswise and place on aluminum foil in lieu of the plate.

MAKES 4 SERVINGS

1 (20-ounce) container silken firm tofu, drained

2 scallions, white and green parts, thinly sliced

2 tablespoons vegetarian oyster sauce or mushroom soy sauce

1 tablespoon dark soy sauce

1 tablespoon reduced-sodium regular soy sauce

1 teaspoon toasted (dark) sesame oil

In a medium stockpot, place a steamer basket over about 1½ inches of water. Place the tofu on a heat-proof plate and place on the steamer basket. Sprinkle the top of the tofu with half the scallions. Bring to a boil over high heat. Reduce the heat to medium, cover, and steam 15 minutes.

In a small bowl, combine the oyster sauce, soy sauces, and sesame oil. Set aside.

To serve, carefully remove plate with tofu from the steamer basket and drain off any accumulated water. Drizzle the tofu evenly with half the oyster sauce mixture. Garnish with the remaining scallions and serve at once, with the remaining sauce passed separately.

{PER SERVING} Calories 132 · Protein 12g · Total Fat 8g · Sat Fat 1g · Cholesterol 0mg · Carbohydrate 5g · Dietary Fiber 2g · Sodium 623mg

Braised Curried Tofu with Sweet Potatoes

Precooking the sweet potatoes ensures that this delicious and fragrant dish is ready in about 20 minutes.

MAKES 6 SERVINGS

2 tablespoons canola oil
1 pound extra-firm tofu, drained well, cut into ½-inch cubes
2 large cooked (baked or microwaved) sweet potatoes (about 8 ounces each), peeled, cut into ½-inch cubes
1 medium onion (about 6 ounces), thinly sliced into half-circles
1 tablespoon chopped fresh ginger
1 cup reduced-sodium vegetable broth
1 to 2 tablespoons reduced-sodium soy sauce
1 tablespoon mild curry powder
½ teaspoon salt
Freshly ground black pepper, to taste

In a large nonstick skillet with a lid, heat 1 tablespoon of the oil over medium-high heat. Add tofu and cook, stirring often, until lightly browned, about 5 minutes. Remove from skillet and set aside. Add sweet potatoes and cook, stirring often, until lightly browned, 2 to 3 minutes. Remove from skillet and set aside.

Add remaining 1 tablespoon oil, onion, and ginger to skillet; cook, stirring often, about 2 minutes, or until softened and fragrant. Add broth, soy sauce, curry powder, salt, and pepper and let come to a boil, stirring often. Reduce heat to medium-low and return the tofu and sweet potatoes to skillet, stirring to combine. Simmer, covered, 5 minutes, stirring occasionally. Uncover and simmer another few minutes, if necessary, stirring occasionally, until liquid is greatly reduced. Serve at once.

{PER SERVING} Calories 308 · Protein 15g · Total Fat 13g · Sat Fat 1g · Cholesterol 0mg · Carbohydrate 36g · Dietary Fiber 7g · Sodium 572mg

Sweet-and-Sour Tofu Balls

Serve these delectable little tofu balls over rice for supper, or alone as appetizers.

MAKES 4 MAIN DISH OR 6 TO 8 APPETIZER SERVINGS

3 tablespoons cornstarch, or more, if
  necessary
16 ounces extra-firm tofu, drained
4 to 6 scallions, white and green parts,
  chopped
¼ cup finely chopped fresh cilantro
2 tablespoons peanut butter
1 tablespoon Asian sesame paste or sesame
  tahini
1 to 2 teaspoons Chinese chili paste, or to
  taste (optional)
½ teaspoon salt, or to taste
Freshly ground black pepper, to taste
2 tablespoons peanut oil
Sweet-and-Sour Sauce, below

In a small bowl, place the cornstarch and set aside.

In a medium bowl, mash the tofu well with a fork (or use your fingers) and add the scallions, cilantro, peanut butter, sesame paste, chili paste (if using), salt, and pepper. Mix until thoroughly combined. (If desired, cover and chill in refrigerator about 30 minutes for easier handling.) Form into lightly packed 2-inch balls (about 24). (At this point, tofu balls can be refrigerated, covered, up to 24 hours before proceeding with the recipe.) Roll in the cornstarch, shaking off excess.

In a large skillet, heat the oil over medium heat. Add the tofu balls and cook until browned on all sides, turning often yet gently (they are fragile), 5 to 7 minutes. Remove skillet from heat and add the sweet-and-sour sauce. Return the skillet to the heat and cook over low heat, gently turning the tofu balls in the sauce, about 5 minutes, or until heated through. Serve warm.

{PER SERVING} Calories 361 · Protein 13g · Total Fat 20g · Sat Fat 3g · Cholesterol 0mg · Carbohydrate 38g · Dietary Fiber 4g · Sodium 501mg

SWEET-AND-SOUR SAUCE

This classic Chinese sauce can be used with countless tofu dishes and vegetables.

MAKES ABOUT 2 CUPS

1 cup water
1 medium green bell pepper (about
  6 ounces), cored, seeded, and chopped
½ small carrot (about 2 ounces), chopped
¼ cup ketchup
¼ cup distilled white vinegar
¼ cup sugar
2 tablespoons crushed canned pineapple
2 tablespoons cornstarch mixed with
  2 tablespoons water
½ tablespoon toasted (dark) sesame oil

In a small saucepan, combine water, pepper, carrot, ketchup, vinegar, sugar, and pineapple; bring to a boil over medium heat, stirring occasionally. Add the cornstarch mixture and cook, stirring constantly, until thickened, about 2 minutes. Remove from heat and add the oil, stirring until thoroughly blended. Serve warm. Completely cooled sauce can be stored, covered, in the refrigerator for several days before reheating over low heat.

{PER SERVING} (about ¼ cup, or ⅛ of recipe) Calories 58 · Protein 0g · Total Fat 1g · Sat Fat 0g · Cholesterol 0mg · Carbohydrate 13g · Dietary Fiber 1g · Sodium 92mg

Grilled Tofu and Vegetable Kebabs with Cilantro

Kebabs are popular street food all over China, especially in Xi'an, which has a huge Muslim quarter almost exclusively devoted to selling delicious ethnic food. Chunks of fresh pineapple and cherry tomatoes can replace 1 zucchini and 1 bell pepper, if desired. Bamboo skewers should be soaked in cold water for 30 minutes before grilling to prevent them from burning.

MAKES 4 SERVINGS

16 ounces extra-firm tofu, drained

3 tablespoons reduced-sodium soy sauce

2 tablespoons orange juice

1 tablespoon plain rice vinegar

2 tablespoons toasted (dark) sesame oil

1 teaspoon finely chopped fresh ginger

¼ teaspoon five-spice powder

2 tablespoons finely chopped cilantro

2 medium zucchini (about 6 ounces each), trimmed, each sliced into 8 pieces

2 medium red bell peppers (about 6 ounces each), cored, seeded, each cut into 8 chunks

8 large fresh shiitake mushrooms, stemmed, halved

4 jalapeño peppers, seeded, each cut into 4 pieces

4 to 8 sprigs cilantro, for garnish

Prepared hoisin sauce, Hoisin Sauce (page 116), Quick Spicy Hoisin Sauce (page 140), or Fresh Peanut Sauce (page 120), to serve

Place the tofu on a deep-sided plate or shallow bowl. Top with a second plate and weight with a heavy can. Let stand for a minimum of 15 minutes (preferably 1 hour). Drain off the excess water. Cut into 16 cubes.

In a medium bowl, combine the soy sauce, orange juice, vinegar, 1 tablespoon sesame oil, ginger, and five-spice powder. Stir in the chopped cilantro and add the tofu, tossing to coat. Cover and marinate in the refrigerator 15 minutes to 1 hour, or overnight, stirring a few times.

Remove the tofu, reserving marinade. Thread the tofu on 4 (12-inch) or 8 (6-inch) bamboo skewers, alternating pieces with zucchini, bell peppers, mushrooms, and jalapeños. Brush evenly with the remaining 1 tablespoon sesame oil.

Prepare a medium-hot charcoal or gas grill, or preheat a broiler. Position an oiled grill rack or oven rack 4 to 6 inches from the heat source. If broiling, lightly oil a large baking sheet and set aside. Alternatively, place a nonstick stovetop grilling pan with grids over medium-high heat.

Grill or broil the tofu kebabs until nicely browned, 8 to 10 minutes, turning frequently and basting with the reserved marinade. Transfer to a warmed serving platter and serve at once, garnished with fresh cilantro sprigs, with the hoisin sauce passed separately.

{PER SERVING} (without sauce) Calories 233 · Protein 13g · Total Fat 13g · Sat Fat 2g · Cholesterol 0mg · Carbohydrate 22g · Dietary Fiber 6g · Sodium 467mg

Tea-Marinated Lemon Tofu over Rice

This simple yet sophisticated recipe is steeped in inspiration from my beloved student Ada, who gave me the gifts of tea from her small hometown and love from her big heart. While I highly recommend using the specialty tea of Yuanling County (nestled in the northwestern region of Hunan Province) if you are lucky enough to find it, any good-quality tea can be used with success.

MAKES 4 SERVINGS

    1 pound firm or extra-firm tofu,
       drained
    Juice of 1 medium lemon (3 tablespoons)
    3 teaspoons black or green tea
       leaves
    3 large cloves garlic, finely chopped
    ½ teaspoon salt
    Freshly ground black pepper, to taste
    2 tablespoons vegetarian oyster sauce or
       mushroom soy sauce, plus additional,
       to serve
    1 tablespoon water
    1 teaspoon toasted (dark) sesame oil
    1 tablespoon peanut oil
    2 scallions, green parts only, thinly
       sliced
    3 cups hot cooked rice

Place the tofu on a deep-sided plate or shallow bowl. Top with a second plate and weight with a heavy can. Let stand for a minimum of 15 minutes (preferably 1 hour). Drain off the excess water. Cut into 1-inch cubes.

In a medium bowl, combine the tofu, 2 tablespoons lemon juice, 2 teaspoons tea leaves, garlic, salt, and pepper; toss until tofu has absorbed most of the lemon juice. Cover and marinate 30 minutes at room temperature, stirring a few times. Alternatively, refrigerate 1 hour or overnight.

In a small bowl, combine 1 tablespoon oyster sauce, water, and remaining 1 teaspoon tea leaves; microwave on high 10 seconds, or until a boil is reached. Cover and let steep 5 minutes. Strain the mixture into another small bowl and discard the leaves. Stir in ½ tablespoon lemon juice, ½ tablespoon oyster sauce, and sesame oil and set aside.

In a wok or large nonstick skillet, heat the peanut oil over medium-high heat. Add the tofu mixture (do not drain) and cook, tossing and stirring constantly, 2 minutes. Reduce the heat to medium-low and add the oyster sauce–tea mixture; cook, stirring constantly, 2 minutes. Add the remaining ½ tablespoon lemon juice, remaining ½ tablespoon oyster sauce, and the scallion greens and cook, stirring, 1 to 2 more minutes. Serve at once, over the rice, with additional oyster sauce passed separately.

{PER SERVING} Calories 323 · Protein 14g · Total Fat 10g · Sat Fat 2g · Cholesterol 0mg · Carbohydrate 45g · Dietary Fiber 2g · Sodium 592mg

Braised Tofu and Vegetable Hot Pot

Hot pot, also known as steam boat or fire pot, is a perennial favorite throughout China—I encountered vegetarian variations in Changsha, Beijing, Hong Kong, Shanghai, and Xi'an. Essentially, a large pot is place on a burner in the center of the table and everyone cooks their own food. A fondue pot with a burner, a saucepan placed on a portable burner, or an electric wok or frying pan are needed for the following recipe. Feel free to experiment with your favorite veggie combinations and dipping sauces. Most of all, have fun!

MAKES 4 SERVINGS

1 pound extra-firm tofu, drained

1 tablespoon peanut oil

3¼ cups water

2 tablespoons reduced-sodium soy sauce

1 tablespoon dark brown sugar

1 tablespoon toasted (dark) sesame oil

4 cups low-sodium vegetable broth

1 carrot, thinly sliced

1 stalk celery, thinly sliced

2 scallions, thinly sliced

1 tablespoon chopped fresh ginger

¼ teaspoon black peppercorns

4 small heads baby bok choy/Shanghai bok choy (about ½ pound), root ends trimmed about ⅛ inch, each cut lengthwise into quarters

½ pound fresh snow peas, trimmed

¼ pound fresh shiitake, cremini, or cultivated white mushrooms, stemmed and quartered

¼ pound fresh enoki (golden needle) mushrooms, separated into small clusters

Sherry-Ginger Dipping Sauce, below

½ pound dried rice noodles, flat (stir-fry or linguine-style) or thin (vermicelli-style), or dried cellophane noodles (mung bean threads)

Place the tofu on a deep-sided plate or shallow bowl. Top with a second plate and weight with a heavy can. Let stand for a minimum of 15 minutes (preferably 1 hour). Drain off the excess water. Cut into 1-inch cubes.

In a wok or large nonstick skillet, heat the peanut oil over medium-high heat. Add the tofu and cook, stirring, until browned on all sides, 5 to 7 minutes. Remove wok from heat. Add ¼ cup water, soy sauce, sugar, and sesame oil; cook over medium heat, stirring constantly, until tofu has absorbed most of the sauce, about 2 minutes. Transfer tofu to a serving plate; set aside.

In a medium stockpot, bring the broth, remaining 3 cups water, carrot, celery, scallions, ginger, and peppercorns to a boil over high heat. Reduce heat to medium and cook, uncovered, 10 minutes, stirring occasionally.

To serve, arrange the bok choy, snow peas, shiitakes, and enoki mushrooms on serving plates, along with the braised tofu. Place equal amounts (about ¼ cup) of the dipping sauce in each of 4 soup bowls. Transfer the boiling broth to a fondue pot or saucepan and place on a heating unit; adjust heat to maintain a simmer. Using chopsticks or a fork, direct each diner to add pieces of vegetables and tofu to the hot broth and cook them for about 2 minutes, or until vegetables are tender and tofu is heated through. Each diner removes his food with chopsticks or a slotted spoon, dips the pieces in the sauce in his bowl, and eats. When the vegetables and tofu are nearly finished, the noodles are added to the broth (return it to a boil), along with the remaining vegetables and tofu; they are cooked 3 to 4 minutes, or until noodles are al dente. The contents of the hot pot are divided equally among the bowls containing the remaining dipping sauce, and the soup is eaten.

{PER SERVING} (without sauce) Calories 463 · Protein 25g · Total Fat 13g · Sat Fat 2g · Cholesterol 0mg · Carbohydrate 66g · Dietary Fiber 9g · Sodium 889mg

SHERRY-GINGER DIPPING SAUCE

This dark, rich dipping sauce is one of my favorites.

MAKES ABOUT 1 CUP

⅓ cup reduced-sodium soy sauce

⅓ cup dry sherry

2 tablespoons dark brown sugar

2 teaspoons toasted (dark) sesame oil

4 scallions, green parts only, thinly sliced

1 tablespoon finely chopped fresh ginger

In a small bowl, combine all ingredients, stirring until the sugar is dissolved. Serve at room temperature.

{PER SERVING} (per tablespoon, or ¹⁄₁₆ of recipe) Calories 18 · Protein 0g · Total Fat 1g · Sat Fat 0g · Cholesterol 0mg · Carbohydrate 2g · Dietary Fiber 0g · Sodium 201mg

Caramelized Tofu with Walnuts

This exquisitely sweet northern-style tofu dish is delicious served with steamed fresh broccoli, brown rice, and a bowl of fresh mandarin oranges for dessert. Slivered almonds or chopped peanuts can replace the walnuts, if desired.

MAKES 4 SERVINGS

16 ounces extra-firm tofu, drained

2 tablespoons peanut or canola oil

4 large cloves garlic, finely chopped

1 cup water

6 tablespoons light brown sugar

¼ cup chopped walnuts

Salt and freshly ground black pepper, to
taste

Place the tofu on a deep-sided plate or shallow bowl. Top with a second plate and weight with a heavy can. Let stand for a minimum of 15 minutes (preferably 1 hour). Drain off the excess water. Cut into 1-inch cubes.

In a wok or large nonstick skillet, heat the oil over medium-high heat. Add the tofu and cook, stirring, until golden brown, 6 to 8 minutes. Add the garlic and cook, stirring constantly, 30 seconds. Add water and brown sugar and let come to a simmer, stirring constantly until reduced and caramelized, 5 to 8 minutes. Remove from heat and add the chopped walnuts, salt, and pepper, stirring well to combine. Serve at once.

{PER SERVING} Calories 275 · Protein 11g · Total Fat 17g · Sat Fat 2g · Cholesterol 0mg · Carbohydrate 24g · Dietary Fiber 2g · Sodium 17mg

Tofu and Mixed Vegetable Stir-Fry

Serve this classic stir-fry over brown rice for the quintessential wholesome Chinese vegan meal, or splurge and present it over the Crispy Noodle Pancake (page 17). All of the ingredients can typically be found in well-stocked Western supermarkets—if vegetarian oyster sauce or mushroom soy sauce is unavailable, substitute with 1 tablespoon of black bean sauce and use an additional ½ tablespoon of reduced-sodium soy sauce in the recipe. For a milder dish, use half the amount of crushed red pepper flakes, or omit altogether.

MAKES 4 SERVINGS

1 pound firm or extra-firm tofu, drained

1 cup reduced-sodium vegetable broth

2 tablespoons reduced-sodium soy sauce

2 tablespoons vegetarian oyster sauce or
mushroom soy sauce

1½ tablespoons cornstarch

1 tablespoon plain rice vinegar

½ tablespoon toasted (dark) sesame oil

1 teaspoon sugar

½ teaspoon crushed red pepper flakes, or
to taste

Freshly ground black pepper, to taste

1½ tablespoons peanut oil or canola oil

1 small onion (about 4 ounces), sliced into
thin half-rounds

1 small red bell pepper (about 4 ounces),
thinly sliced

½ tablespoon finely chopped fresh ginger

2 cloves garlic, finely chopped

4 ounces fresh shiitake or cultivated white
mushrooms, stemmed and thinly sliced

4 ounces fresh broccoli florets, cut into
bite-size pieces

½ cup shredded carrot

4 ounces fresh snow peas, trimmed

1 (8-ounce) can sliced water chestnuts,
drained

¼ cup chopped fresh cilantro (optional)

Place the tofu on a deep-sided plate or shallow bowl. Top with a second plate and weight with a heavy can. Let stand for a minimum of 15 minutes (preferably 1 hour). Drain excess water. Cut into ½-inch cubes.

In a small bowl, whisk together the broth, soy sauce, oyster sauce, cornstarch, vinegar, sesame oil, sugar, red pepper flakes, and pepper until thoroughly blended; set aside.

In a wok or large nonstick skillet, heat 1 tablespoon peanut oil over medium-high heat. Add the tofu and cook, stirring often, until nicely browned,

6 to 8 minutes. Transfer tofu to a plate and set briefly aside. Add remaining ½ tablespoon peanut oil, onion, bell pepper, ginger, and garlic to the wok; cook, stirring constantly, 1 minute. Add the mushrooms, broccoli, and carrot and cook, stirring constantly, 2 minutes. Add the snow peas and water chestnuts and cook, stirring constantly, 1 minute. Return the tofu, stir in the broth mixture, and let come to a brisk simmer, stirring. Reduce the heat to medium and cook, stirring, until thickened, 2 to 3 minutes. Remove from heat and stir in the cilantro, if using. Serve at once.

{PER SERVING} Calories 268 · Protein 16g · Total Fat 13g · Sat Fat 2g · Cholesterol 0mg · Carbohydrate 27g · Dietary Fiber 6g · Sodium 771mg

Quick Tofu and Mixed Vegetables in a White Sauce

Frozen stir-fry vegetables make quick work of this delicious dish, which can be stretched further if served over rice.

MAKES 4 SERVINGS

1 pound firm or extra-firm tofu, drained

1 tablespoon peanut oil

1 tablespoon chopped fresh ginger

2 large cloves garlic, finely chopped

¼ teaspoon crushed red pepper flakes, or
to taste (optional)

Salt and freshly ground black pepper,
to taste

12 ounces frozen stir-fry vegetables,
slightly undercooked according to
package directions, drained well

Basic Chinese White Sauce, below

Place the tofu on a deep-sided plate or shallow bowl. Top with a second plate and weight with a heavy can. Let stand for a minimum of 15 minutes (preferably 1 hour). Drain excess water. Cut into 1-inch cubes.

In a wok or large nonstick skillet, heat the oil over medium heat. Add the tofu and cook, stirring often, until just beginning to brown, 3 to 4 minutes. Add the ginger, garlic, red pepper flakes (if using), salt, and pepper; cook, stirring constantly, until tofu is lightly browned, 2 to 3 minutes. Add the vegetables and toss well to combine. Reduce the heat to medium-low and add the white sauce; cook, stirring, until heated through, 1 to 2 minutes. Serve at once.

{PER SERVING} Calories 215 · Protein 15g · Total Fat 9g · Sat Fat 1g · Cholesterol 0mg · Carbohydrate 20g · Dietary Fiber 4g · Sodium 296mg

BASIC CHINESE WHITE SAUCE

Use this basic, or master, white sauce to dress up countless vegetable and tofu dishes. Seasonings such as ground ginger, garlic powder, and cayenne pepper can be added according to the other ingredients in the recipe. For best results, use shortly after preparing.

MAKES ABOUT 1 CUP

- ¾ cup low-sodium vegetable broth
- 2½ tablespoons Shaoxing rice wine, dry sherry, sake, or dry white wine
- 1 tablespoon reduced-sodium soy sauce
- 1 tablespoon sugar
- 2 teaspoons cornstarch mixed with 4 teaspoons water

In a small saucepan, bring the broth, wine, soy sauce, and sugar to a boil over medium-high heat. Stir in the cornstarch mixture and reduce heat to medium. Cook, stirring constantly, until thickened, about 3 minutes. Use as directed in recipe.

{PER SERVING} (about ¼ cup, or ¼ of recipe) Calories 41 · Protein 2g · Total Fat 0g · Sat Fat 0g · Cholesterol 0mg · Carbohydrate 6g · Dietary Fiber 1g · Sodium 247mg

· SEITAN DISHES ·

Beijing Mock Duck

Mock duck, with its distinctive flavor and artificial plucked duck texture, is actually a type of wheat gluten, or seitan. It is available in Asian markets and some well-stocked supermarkets in canned or frozen form. Ready in minutes, this tasty dish will soon be filed under your easy dinner party recipes.

MAKES 4 TO 6 SERVINGS

- ½ cup duck sauce (plum sauce)
- ½ tablespoon toasted (dark) sesame oil
- ¼ teaspoon five-spice powder
- 1 tablespoon peanut oil
- 1 tablespoon chopped fresh ginger
- 3 large cloves garlic, finely chopped
- 2 (10-ounce) cans vegetarian mock duck, rinsed, drained, patted dry with paper towels, cut into thin slices

About 24 (7-inch) prepared fresh or thawed
 frozen Chinese pancakes, or 2 recipes
 Classic Chinese Pancakes (page 15),
 warmed
Prepared hoisin sauce or Hoisin Sauce
 (page 116), to serve
4 scallions, thinly sliced, to serve
1 large cucumber (about 12 ounces),
 unpeeled, sliced into thin sticks, to serve

In a small bowl, combine the duck sauce, sesame oil, and five-spice powder; set aside.

In a wok or large nonstick skillet, heat the peanut oil over medium-high heat. Add the ginger and garlic and cook, stirring constantly, 30 seconds. Add the mock duck and cook, stirring constantly, 2 minutes. Reduce the heat to medium and add the duck sauce mixture; cook, stirring, until hot and bubbly, about 2 minutes. Transfer to a serving bowl.

To serve, spread a warm pancake thinly with hoisin sauce; add scallions, cucumber, and mock duck mixture. Roll up and serve at once.

{PER SERVING} Calories 356 · Protein 22g · Total Fat 11g · Sat Fat 2g · Cholesterol 0mg · Carbohydrate 45g · Dietary Fiber 1g · Sodium 281mg

Crispy Seitan with Peanuts and Scallions

Seitan is processed wheat gluten that is higher in protein and has a chewier, meatier texture than tofu. This dish is delicious served with steamed broccoli and brown rice.

MAKES 4 SERVINGS

¼ cup Shaoxing rice wine, dry sherry, sake,
 or dry white wine
¼ cup water
1 tablespoon hoisin sauce
1 tablespoon light brown sugar
1 tablespoon plain rice vinegar
½ tablespoon toasted (dark) sesame oil
1 teaspoon cornstarch
¼ teaspoon salt
Freshly ground black pepper, to taste
1 tablespoon peanut oil
1 pound seitan, drained, patted dry with
 paper towels, cut into bite-size pieces
¼ cup chopped unsalted peanuts
1 tablespoon chopped fresh ginger
4 scallions, white and green parts, thinly
 sliced
¼ cup chopped fresh cilantro

In a small bowl, whisk together the wine, water, hoisin, sugar, vinegar, sesame oil, cornstarch, salt, and pepper until blended; set aside.

In a wok or large nonstick skillet, heat the peanut oil over medium-high heat. Add seitan and cook, stirring frequently, until lightly browned, 4 to 5 minutes. Add the peanuts and ginger and cook, stirring constantly, until nuts are lightly browned, 1 to 2 minutes. Reduce the heat to medium and add the hoisin sauce mixture and scallions; cook, stirring, until the sauce is thickened, about 2 minutes. Stir in the cilantro and serve warm.

{PER SERVING} Calories 376 · Protein 24g · Total Fat 19g · Sat Fat 3g · Cholesterol 0mg · Carbohydrate 30g · Dietary Fiber 1g · Sodium 211mg

Seitan and Vegetable Lettuce Wraps

These flavorful lettuce wraps also make a great appetizer or snack. Extra-firm tofu can replace the seitan, if desired.

MAKES 4 MAIN DISH OR 8 APPETIZER SERVINGS

4 tablespoons reduced-sodium soy sauce

2 tablespoons water

1 tablespoon Shaoxing rice wine, dry sherry, sake, or dry white wine

1 teaspoon sugar

1 teaspoon cornstarch

½ to 1 teaspoon Chinese chili paste, or to taste

¼ teaspoon salt, or to taste

Freshly ground black pepper, to taste

1 tablespoon toasted (dark) sesame oil

½ tablespoon peanut oil

¾ pound seitan, drained, patted dry with paper towels, cut into ½-inch cubes

1 medium red bell pepper (about 6 ounces), chopped

3 scallions, white and green parts separated, chopped

1 stalk celery, chopped

2 cloves garlic, finely chopped

1 teaspoon finely chopped fresh ginger

1 (8-ounce) can water chestnuts, rinsed, drained, and chopped

1 head iceberg lettuce or romaine lettuce leaves, washed, dried, leaves separated, large outer leaves cut lengthwise in half

Prepared hoisin sauce, Hoisin Sauce (page 116), or Quick Spicy Hoisin Sauce (page 140), to serve

In a small bowl, mix together the soy sauce, water, wine, sugar, cornstarch, chili paste, salt, and black pepper until well blended; set aside.

In a large nonstick skillet, heat ½ tablespoon sesame oil and the peanut oil over medium-high heat. Add the seitan, bell pepper, white parts of the scallions, and celery; cook, stirring, 3 minutes. Add the garlic and ginger and cook, stirring constantly, 2 minutes. Add the water chestnuts and green parts of the scallions and cook, stirring constantly, 30 seconds. Reduce the heat to medium and add the reserved soy sauce mixture. Cook, stirring, until heated through and thickened, 2 to 3 minutes. Remove from heat and stir in the remaining ½ tablespoon sesame oil; let cool a few minutes.

To serve, place 1 to 2 heaping teaspoons of the seitan and vegetable mixture into the middle of a lettuce leaf. Top with hoisin sauce. Fold into a packet or roll up. Serve slightly warm or at room temperature.

{PER SERVING} (without sauce) Calories 285 · Protein 19g · Total Fat 12g · Sat Fat 2g · Cholesterol 0mg · Carbohydrate 30g · Dietary Fiber 2g · Sodium 757mg

Sichuan-Style Mapo Seitan

This spicy seitan variation of Sichuan's famous mapo doufu is a favorite of mine—serve over hot cooked rice for a hearty and homey meal. Feel free to tone down the heat by using a smaller amount of crushed red pepper flakes and omitting the Chinese hot oil altogether. Try to use soft silken tofu instead of the regular soft variety, as the former holds its shape better in this dish. Hot bean sauce, also known as hot bean paste or chili bean sauce/paste, is a fermented paste that combines hot chilies with broad beans and/or soybeans and other seasonings; if you can't locate it, black bean sauce can be substituted for a less spicy alternative. Moreover, if fermented black beans are unavailable, replace with black bean sauce.

MAKES 6 SERVINGS

½ to 1 teaspoon Sichuan peppercorns

6 ounces seitan, drained, patted dry with
   paper towels, cut into ½-inch cubes

1 tablespoon plus 2 teaspoons cornstarch

¼ cup water

3 tablespoons peanut oil

3 large cloves garlic, finely chopped

1 tablespoon chopped fresh ginger

½ cup chopped scallion greens, plus
   additional, for garnish

3 tablespoons hot bean sauce or paste

1 tablespoon salted (fermented) black
   beans, rinsed and chopped

½ teaspoon crushed red pepper flakes, or
   to taste

1 cup low-sodium vegetable broth

1 tablespoon Shaoxing rice wine, dry
   sherry, sake, or dry white wine

2 teaspoons reduced-sodium soy sauce

2 teaspoons sugar

1 teaspoon toasted (dark) sesame oil

1 teaspoon Chinese hot oil, or to taste
   (optional)

16 ounces soft tofu, drained, cut into
   ½-inch cubes

In a small heavy-bottomed skillet over medium-low heat, cook the Sichuan peppercorns, stirring and shaking the pan occasionally, until fragrant and toasted, about 3 minutes. Transfer to a mortar and pestle; lightly crush and set aside.

In a small mixing bowl, toss the seitan with 2 teaspoons of the cornstarch until evenly coated; set aside. In another small bowl, mix the remaining 1 tablespoon cornstarch with the water until blended; set aside.

In a wok or large nonstick skillet, heat the peanut oil over medium-high heat. Add the seitan and cook, stirring and turning often, until lightly browned on all sides, about 5 minutes. With a slotted spoon, transfer seitan to a holding plate. Add the garlic and ginger and cook, stirring constantly, 1 minute. Reduce the heat to medium-low and add the scallion greens and hot bean sauce; cook, stirring, until fragrant, about 15 seconds. Add black beans and red pepper flakes and cook, stirring, 15 seconds. Add a pinch of the crushed Sichuan peppercorns and stir quickly to combine. Add broth, wine, soy sauce, sugar, sesame oil, and hot oil (if using); bring to a simmer over medium-high heat. Reduce the heat to medium-low, add the tofu, and cook, stirring gently so that the tofu holds together, 3 minutes. Return seitan to skillet and stir gently to combine. Add cornstarch mixture and cook, stirring gently, until thickened, 2 to 3 minutes. Serve at once, sprinkled evenly with remaining crushed peppercorns and garnished with scallion greens.

{PER SERVING} Calories 240 · Protein 15g · Total Fat 14g · Sat Fat 2g · Cholesterol 0mg · Carbohydrate 16g · Dietary Fiber 2g · Sodium 171mg

Pineapple Sweet-and-Sour Seitan with Bell Peppers

Ideal for entertaining, this colorful and mildly spiced dish is one that guests of all ages typically enjoy. Serve over couscous or orzo pasta in lieu of rice, if desired.

MAKES 6 SERVINGS

3 tablespoons all-purpose flour

2 tablespoons cornstarch

1 pound seitan, drained, patted dry with paper towels, and cut into bite-size chunks or strips

4 tablespoons canola oil

Salt and freshly ground black pepper, to taste

1 medium green bell pepper (about 6 ounces), cut into bite-size chunks

1 medium red bell pepper (about 6 ounces), cut into bite-size chunks

1 medium onion (about 6 ounces), cut into bite-size wedges

1 cup cubed fresh or canned pineapple

¾ cup prepared sweet-and-sour sauce or Sweet-and-Sour Sauce (page 124)

¼ cup reduced-sodium soy sauce

4 ½ cups hot cooked white or brown rice

Line a baking sheet with a few layers of paper towels and set aside.

In a medium bowl, mix together flour and cornstarch. Roll seitan in flour mixture until well coated.

In a large nonstick skillet, heat 3½ tablespoons of the oil over medium-high heat. Add seitan and cook, turning with a spatula every few minutes, until nicely browned on all sides, about 5 minutes.

Transfer to prepared baking sheet and season with salt and pepper.

Add remaining oil, bell peppers, and onion to the skillet; continue cooking over medium-high heat, stirring often, until lightly browned, about 5 minutes. Reduce heat to medium-low and add the pineapple, sweet-and-sour sauce, and soy sauce; cook, stirring occasionally, 3 minutes, or until heated through. Add the seitan and cook, stirring occasionally, until heated through, 1 to 2 minutes. Serve hot, over the rice.

{PER SERVING} Calories 464 · Protein 18g · Total Fat 11g · Sat Fat 1g · Cholesterol 0mg · Carbohydrate 62g · Dietary Fiber 5g · Sodium 416mg

Curried Seitan with Potatoes and Onions

This homey dish is nice served with pita bread to sop up the delicious sauce.

MAKES 4 TO 6 SERVINGS

2 tablespoons peanut oil

1 pound seitan, drained, patted dry with paper towels, and cut into bite-size pieces

2 medium onions (about 6 ounces each), sliced into thin half-moons

4 large cloves garlic, finely chopped

4 medium boiling potatoes (about 4 ounces each), peeled and cut into 1-inch cubes

1 cup water or low-sodium vegetable broth, plus additional, as needed

2 tablespoons reduced-sodium soy sauce

1 tablespoon mild curry powder

1 tablespoon sugar

1 teaspoon salt

Freshly ground black pepper, to taste

1 tablespoon cornstarch mixed with
    1 tablespoon water

In a wok or large nonstick skillet with a lid, heat 1 tablespoon oil over medium-high heat. Add the seitan and cook, stirring often, until lightly browned, 4 to 5 minutes. Remove seitan from skillet and transfer to a holding plate. Add remaining 1 tablespoon of oil and onions to the skillet; cook, stirring constantly, 2 minutes. Add the garlic and cook, stirring constantly, 30 seconds. Return the seitan to the skillet and add the potatoes, water, soy sauce, curry powder, sugar, salt, and pepper; bring to a boil, stirring. Reduce heat to medium, cover, and simmer 20 minutes, stirring occasionally, or until potatoes are tender, adding water as needed. Reduce the heat to medium-low and stir in cornstarch mixture; cook, stirring often, until thickened, 1 to 2 minutes. Serve at once.

{PER SERVING} Calories 419 · Protein 25g · Total Fat 16g · Sat Fat 2g · Cholesterol 0mg · Carbohydrate 50g · Dietary Fiber 4g · Sodium 849mg

Sesame Seitan with Snow Peas in Apricot Sauce

Here is a pleasant, mild-tasting dish that will please most palates. Well-drained and cubed tofu can replace the seitan, if desired. Serve on a bed of rice or cellophane noodles, if desired.

MAKES 4 TO 6 SERVINGS

1 tablespoon canola oil

1 pound seitan, drained, patted dry with
    paper towels, and cut into bite-size
    cubes or strips

1 tablespoon sesame seeds

3 cloves garlic, finely chopped

½ teaspoon finely chopped fresh ginger

½ cup duck sauce

⅓ cup sliced dried apricots

2 tablespoons water

1 tablespoon reduced-sodium soy sauce

½ to 1 teaspoon extra-hot Chinese mustard

Salt and freshly ground black pepper,
    to taste

12 ounces snow peas, trimmed

½ tablespoon toasted (dark) sesame oil

In a wok or large nonstick skillet, heat the oil over medium-high heat. Add seitan and cook, stirring and turning frequently, until beginning to brown, 2 to 3 minutes. Add sesame seeds, garlic, and ginger and cook, stirring and turning constantly, 2 minutes. Reduce heat to medium and stir in the duck sauce, apricots, water, soy sauce, mustard, salt, and pepper. Quickly add the snow peas and cook, stirring often, until snow peas are crisp-tender, 4 to 5 minutes, adding the sesame oil the last minute or so of cooking. Serve warm.

{PER SERVING} Calories 421 · Protein 25g · Total Fat 20g · Sat Fat 3g · Cholesterol 0mg · Carbohydrate 42g · Dietary Fiber 3g · Sodium 178mg

Silk Road Eggplant and Tofu Pita Pockets

Along the Silk Road, the Uyghur cuisine in north-western China has a decidedly Middle Eastern accent, where spices such as cumin, and flatbreads such as pita, figure prominently. If using Chinese eggplant, salting is not necessary.

MAKES 4 SERVINGS

8 ounces extra-firm tofu, drained

1 pound of eggplant (about 1 large Western eggplant or 2 medium Chinese eggplants), unpeeled, cut into ½-inch dice, placed in a colander, sprinkled with salt, and drained 30 minutes (salting is optional)

2 tablespoons olive oil

½ medium red onion (about 3 ounces), thinly sliced into half rounds

4 large fresh shiitake mushrooms, stemmed and thinly sliced

1 tablespoon Xinjiang spice mix (below), or to taste

2 large cloves garlic, finely chopped

½ teaspoon salt, or to taste

¼ cup water or broth

½ teaspoon Chinese chili paste, or to taste (optional)

2 to 3 tablespoons sweet chili sauce

1 tablespoon reduced-sodium soy sauce (optional)

½ tablespoon toasted (dark) sesame oil

1 cup chopped fresh cilantro

4 (6-inch) pita breads, preferably whole wheat

Chopped scallion greens and/or fresh cilantro sprigs, to serve

Place the tofu on a deep-sided plate or shallow bowl. Top with a second plate and weight with a heavy can. Let stand for a minimum of 15 minutes (preferably 1 hour). Drain off the excess water. Cut into 1-inch cubes.

Rinse the drained eggplant under cold running water. Dry between paper towels.

In a wok or large nonstick skillet, heat 1 tablespoon olive oil over medium-high heat. Add the tofu and cook, stirring, until lightly browned, about 5 minutes. Remove from wok and set briefly aside. Add remaining 1 tablespoon olive oil, eggplant, onion, and mushrooms and cook, stirring, until softened, about 3 minutes. Return the tofu, and add the spice mix, garlic, and salt and cook, stirring, until eggplant is tender and tofu is nicely browned, 2 to 3 minutes. Stir in the water and chili paste, if using, and reduce the heat to medium; cook, covered, stirring a few times, until eggplant is very tender, about 3 minutes. Stir in the sweet chili sauce, soy sauce (if using), and sesame oil. Remove from heat and toss with the chopped cilantro.

To serve, stuff each pita half with equal portions of the eggplant-tofu mixture and serve at once, with the garnishes passed separately.

{PER SERVING} Calories 332 · Protein 12g · Total Fat 13g · Sat Fat 2g · Cholesterol 0mg · Carbohydrate 45g · Dietary Fiber 5g · Sodium 602mg

XINJIANG SPICE MIX

Use this exotic Silk Road spice mix as a rub for grilled tofu, portobello mushrooms, and eggplant; and add to countless stir-fries, sauces, soups, and stews.

MAKES ABOUT ⅓ CUP

¼ cup whole cumin seed

1 tablespoon whole Sichuan peppercorns

2 tablespoons whole black peppercorns

1 tablespoon crushed red pepper flakes

1 tablespoon ground ginger

1 tablespoon garlic powder

½ tablespoon chili powder

½ tablespoon salt

In a small heavy-bottomed skillet over medium heat, cook the cumin seeds, stirring constantly, until fragrant and lightly toasted, about 2 minutes. Transfer to a spice grinder or small food processor fitted with the knife blade.

In the same skillet, over medium-low heat, cook the Sichuan peppercorns, stirring and shaking the pan occasionally, until fragrant and toasted, about 3 minutes. Add to the spice grinder and let contents cool to room temperature. Add the black peppercorns and red pepper flakes to the spice grinder; process until finely ground. Transfer to a small bowl and add the remaining ingredients, mixing well to thoroughly blend. Cover tightly and store at room temperature up to 6 months, or longer if refrigerated.

{PER SERVING} (per tablespoon) Calories 30 · Protein 1g · Total Fat 1g · Sat Fat 0g · Cholesterol 0mg · Carbohydrate 5g · Dietary Fiber 1g · Sodium 549mg

Chinese Yam Cakes with Cilantro and Black Bean Sauce

The long white Chinese yam is popular throughout Asia, where its viscous texture is savored. Unlike other yams or sweet potatoes, it can be enjoyed raw. A combination of equal parts russet potato and Daikon radish, white turnip, or jicama can be substituted, if necessary; in this instance, add 1 tablespoon, or more, of water when mixing to moisten.

MAKES 4 TO 6 SERVINGS (12 SMALL CAKES)

2 dried shiitake mushrooms, soaked in hot water to cover 20 minutes, or until softened, rinsed, drained, stemmed, and chopped

14 ounces Chinese yam, peeled and grated (see Cook' s Tip, page 138)

1 cup all-purpose flour

1 large bunch cilantro with stems, chopped

2 tablespoons toasted sesame seeds

½ teaspoon salt

Freshly ground black pepper, to taste

3 tablespoons peanut or canola oil

2 tablespoons black bean sauce with garlic, plus additional, to serve

Fresh cilantro leaves, for garnish

Squeeze the chopped mushrooms dry between paper towels. Transfer to a large bowl and add the yam, flour, cilantro, sesame seeds, salt, and pepper; mix well to thoroughly combine. Divide evenly into 12 portions and shape into flat cakes about ½ inch in thickness.

In a 12-inch nonstick skillet, heat the oil over medium heat. Add the yam cakes and cook until nicely browned, about 3 minutes per side. Transfer cakes to paper towels to drain. Place cakes on a warmed serving platter and brush the tops evenly with the black bean sauce. Garnish with the cilantro leaves and serve at once, with additional black bean sauce passed separately.

{PER SERVING} Calories 281 · Protein 6g · Total Fat 13g · Sat Fat 2g · Cholesterol 0mg · Carbohydrate 36g · Dietary Fiber 3g · Sodium 373mg

The skin and sticky coating of Chinese yam may cause an allergic reaction in the form of itching and/or a rash in some people. As a precaution, wear plastic or latex gloves when peeling the skin, and then rinse the flesh under cold running water before handling without gloves. If grating in a food processor, take care not to overprocess, as the yam will become too gluey and runny.

Yunnan-Style Fava Beans with Chilies, Garlic, and Star Anise

China is the world's largest producer of fava beans, or broad beans, yet most Westerners have never come across a fava bean in a typical Chinese restaurant. This spicy and colorful dish comes from the Bai people, one of Yunnan Province's many ethnic minorities. Fresh or frozen shelled soybeans, or edamames, can stand in for the favas; however, simmer them for about half the amount of time. For an even heartier meal, serve over brown rice.

MAKES 6 SERVINGS

2 pounds unshelled fava beans
   (broad beans), shelled (about 2 cups),
   or 1 pound fresh or frozen
   shelled soybeans, thawed (about
   2 cups)
1 tablespoon peanut oil
1 to 2 fresh red chili peppers, seeded and
   thinly sliced
6 cloves garlic, thinly sliced
½ teaspoon star anise pieces
1 cup low-sodium vegetable broth
½ teaspoon salt, or to taste

1 teaspoon toasted (dark) sesame oil
2 teaspoons cornstarch blended with
   2 tablespoons water

If using fava beans: In a medium stockpot filled with boiling salted water, cook the fava beans 2 minutes. Drain in a colander and rinse immediately under cold running water to stop the cooking. To remove the outer skins, pinch each bean on the side opposite where it was attached to the pod; the bean should easily slip from the skin. Remove and discard the outer skins. Set the beans aside.

In a wok or large nonstick skillet with a lid, heat the peanut oil over medium-high heat. Add the chilies and garlic and cook, stirring, 30 seconds. Add the fava beans and star anise and cook, stirring, 1 minute. Add the broth and salt and bring to a boil; reduce heat to medium-low and simmer, covered, until beans are tender, about 15 minutes for fava beans and about 7 minutes for soybeans, stirring occasionally. Stir in the sesame oil and add the cornstarch mixture; cook, stirring, until liquid is thickened, about 2 minutes. Serve at once.

{PER SERVING} Calories 217 • Protein 15g • Total Fat 4g • Sat Fat 1g • Cholesterol 0mg • Carbohydrate 32g • Dietary Fiber 13g • Sodium 272mg

Five-Spice Vegetable Stir-Fry with Almonds

Chinese five-spice powder is an exotic blend of spices that typically includes cinnamon, cloves, star anise, fennel seed, and Sichuan peppercorns. Chopped walnuts or cashews can replace the almonds, if desired.

MAKES 6 SERVINGS

½ cup reduced-sodium vegetable broth

2 tablespoons reduced-sodium soy sauce

1 tablespoon rice vinegar

1 tablespoon toasted (dark) sesame oil

½ tablespoon cornstarch

1 teaspoon five-spice powder

¼ cup slivered almonds

1 tablespoon canola oil

4 large cloves garlic, finely chopped

1 cup chopped onion

1 medium red bell pepper (about 6 ounces),
    sliced

1 cup shredded carrots

2 stalks celery, sliced

1 (15-ounce) can straw mushroom pieces,
    rinsed and drained

½ (15-ounce) can cut baby corn, rinsed and
    drained

2 scallions, white and green parts, thinly
    sliced

Salt and freshly ground black pepper,
    to taste

4½ cups hot cooked white or brown rice

In a small bowl, whisk together the broth, soy sauce, vinegar, sesame oil, cornstarch, and five-spice powder until thoroughly blended. Set aside.

Place a wok or large nonstick skillet over medium-high heat for 1 minute. Add the almonds and cook, stirring constantly, until fragrant and lightly toasted, 1 to 2 minutes. Immediately transfer almonds to a holding plate and set aside. Add the canola oil to the wok and heat over medium-high heat 30 seconds. Add the garlic and onion and cook, stirring constantly, 30 seconds. Add the bell pepper, carrots, and celery and cook, stirring constantly, until softened, about 3 minutes. Add the mushrooms and corn and cook, stirring constantly, until heated through, about 1 minute. Reduce the heat to medium and stir in the reserved broth mixture. Cook, stirring constantly, until thickened, 2 to 3 minutes. Remove wok from heat and add the reserved almonds, scallions, salt, and pepper, tossing well to combine. Serve at once, over rice.

{PER SERVING} Calories 308 · Protein 8g · Total Fat 8g · Sat Fat 1g · Cholesterol 0mg · Carbohydrate 52g · Dietary Fiber 3g · Sodium 322mg

Sichuan-Grilled Portobello Mushroom Burgers with Spicy Hoisin Sauce

Serve these juicy mushroom burgers with Chinese Potato Salad (page 58), Shredded Cabbage, Apple, and Raisin Salad (page 56), and grilled or steamed corn on the cob, brushed with some Quick Spicy Hoisin Sauce, below, at your next summer cook-out.

MAKES 4 SERVINGS

2 tablespoons reduced-sodium soy sauce

2 teaspoons peanut or canola oil

1 teaspoon toasted (dark) sesame oil

1 large clove garlic, finely chopped

½ teaspoon ground Sichuan peppercorns or
    crushed red pepper flakes

Freshly ground black pepper, to taste

4 extra-large (about 3 ounces each)
    portobello mushroom caps

½ recipe Quick Spicy Hoisin Sauce, below,
    or prepared hoisin sauce, plus
    additional, if desired

4 large Kaiser rolls, preferably whole
    wheat, split

Iceburg or other lettuce leaves, sliced tomato,
and sliced red onion, for topping (optional)

Prepare a medium-hot charcoal or gas grill, or heat a nonstick grill pan over medium-high heat.

In a small bowl, whisk together the soy sauce, peanut oil, sesame oil, garlic, Sichuan peppercorns, and pepper until thoroughly blended. Place mushrooms in a large resealable plastic bag and add the soy sauce mixture. Close bag securely and shake to thoroughly coat the mushrooms. Marinate at room temperature 15 minutes, or refrigerate up to 8 hours, turning occasionally.

Remove mushrooms from marinade, reserving any remaining marinade. Place mushrooms, gill sides down, on the grill; grill 3 minutes, brushing with any remaining marinade. Turn over and grill 3 to 4 more minutes, rotating each mushroom a half turn after 2 minutes, or until bottoms are nicely browned. As they are grilling, fill each mushroom cavity with equal amounts (about 1¼ tablespoons) of the Quick Spicy Hoisin Sauce, below.

Place a filled mushroom, gill side up, on the bottom half of each roll. Top with lettuce, tomato, and/or onion, if using. Close each roll and serve at once, with additional Quick Spicy Hoisin Sauce passed separately, if desired.

{PER SERVING} (without sauce) Calories 170 · Protein 6g · Total Fat 6g · Sat Fat 1g · Cholesterol 0mg · Carbohydrate 24g · Dietary Fiber 3g · Sodium 500mg

QUICK SPICY HOISIN SAUCE

You can use this lively sauce just about everywhere hoisin is called for in this book.

MAKES ABOUT ⅔ CUP

4 tablespoons hoisin sauce

4 tablespoons mild chili sauce (American-style) or tomato ketchup

1 tablespoon reduced-sodium soy sauce

1 to 2 teaspoons Chinese chili paste

1 teaspoon toasted (dark) sesame oil

½ to 1 teaspoon Chinese hot oil

In a small bowl, mix together all ingredients until thoroughly blended. Use as directed in recipe, or cover and refrigerate up to 2 weeks.

{PER SERVING} (per tablespoon, or ⅒ of recipe) Calories 22 · Protein 0g · Total Fat 1g · Sat Fat 0g · Cholesterol 0mg · Carbohydrate 3g · Dietary Fiber 0g · Sodium 165mg

Konjac with Broccoli Slaw and Bean Sprouts

Konjac, also known as moyu or konnyaku, is a gray to white colored, gelatinous mass that is made from the starchy corms of the konjac plant, which grows in southern China. Consisting mostly of water and soluble fiber, it has almost no calories or taste, yet possesses a chewy, bouncy texture that absorbs the flavors in which it is cooked. It is available in some Asian markets in the refrigerated section, next to the regular tofu, or behind the deli counter. The use of preshredded broccoli stems or slaw makes quick work of this tasty and unusual dish.

MAKES 4 SERVINGS

1 pound gray or white konjac, moyu, or
konnyaku, rinsed and drained, and cut
into 1-inch cubes

2 tablespoons reduced-sodium soy sauce,
   plus additional, to taste

1 tablespoon peanut oil

1 tablespoon toasted (dark) sesame oil

¼ teaspoon crushed red pepper flakes, or
   more, to taste

Salt, to taste

4 to 6 large cloves garlic, finely chopped

Freshly ground black pepper, to taste

2 cups broccoli slaw

1 cup mung bean sprouts

2 scallions, green parts only, thinly sliced

Bring a large pot of water to a boil over high heat. Add the konjac and boil 2 to 3 minutes. Drain in a colander and leave to cool and dry out, about 20 minutes. Pat dry with paper towels.

Place a wok or large nonstick skillet over medium-high heat. When droplets of water sizzle on surface, carefully add the konjac and toss a few times (konjac will squeak and may sputter). Add the soy sauce, ½ tablespoon peanut oil, ½ tablespoon sesame oil, red pepper, and salt; cook, tossing and stirring constantly, until konjac is lightly browned, about 3 minutes. Add the remaining ½ tablespoon peanut oil and ½ tablespoon sesame oil, garlic, and black pepper; cook, stirring, 30 seconds. Add the broccoli slaw and cook, stirring, 1 minute. Add the bean sprouts and scallion greens and cook, stirring, 1 minute. Serve at once, with additional soy sauce passed separately.

{PER SERVING} Calories 149 · Protein 6g · Total Fat 7g · Sat Fat 1g · Cholesterol 0mg · Carbohydrate 18g · Dietary Fiber 3g · Sodium 338mg

Shanghai-Style Mi Dou Fu with Black Bean Sauce and Scallions

Shanghainese savory dishes are typically characterized by their sweetness—this superb one is no exception. Smoother and more gelatinous than regular tofu, mi dou fu is made from rice instead of soybeans. It is available in some Asian markets in the refrigerated section, next to the regular tofu, or behind the deli counter. Medium-firm tofu, cut into triangles and blanched in boiling water 1 minute, drained well, can stand in for the mi dou fu, if necessary. Though optional, the yellow buds of the flowering Chinese chive lend a subtle hint of garlic as well as a sophisticated, festive touch.

MAKES 4 TO 6 SERVINGS

12 ounces mi dou fu (rice tofu), drained,
   as needed

1 tablespoon peanut oil

6 to 8 scallions, cut into 2-inch lengths

1 tablespoon finely chopped fresh ginger

1 tablespoon rinsed and drained
   fermented black beans, left whole
   (optional)

2 large cloves garlic, finely chopped

2 tablespoons black bean sauce

2 tablespoons Shaoxing rice wine,
   dry sherry, sake, or dry white wine

2 tablespoons sugar

1 tablespoon black vinegar or balsamic
   vinegar

1 tablespoon reduced-sodium soy sauce

½ teaspoon toasted (dark) sesame oil

Chinese flowering chive buds, for garnish
   (optional)

Cut mi dou fu into 4 squares and then cut each square into 2 triangles. Turn each triangle on its longest side and cut into 3 thin triangles for a total of 24 thin triangles. Set aside.

In a wok or large nonstick skillet, heat peanut oil over medium-high heat. Add the scallions, ginger, fermented black beans (if using), and garlic; cook, stirring constantly, until fragrant and softened, about 2 minutes. Reduce the heat to medium and add the black bean sauce, wine, sugar, vinegar, soy sauce, and sesame oil; cook, stirring, 1 minute. Add the mi dou fu and cook, turning and stirring often, until mi dou fu is heated through and sauce is bubbly, about 3 minutes. Serve at once, garnished with the flowering chive buds, if using.

{PER SERVING} Calories 387 · Protein 1g · Total Fat 5g · Sat Fat 1g · Cholesterol 0mg · Carbohydrate 84g · Dietary Fiber 1g · Sodium 258mg

Moo Shu Vegetables with Tofu

Fresh or frozen Chinese pancakes, similar to crepes, are available at Asian markets and specialty stores. See Classic Chinese Pancakes (page 15) to prepare your own. In a pinch, snack-size flour tortillas can be substituted.

4 SERVINGS

1 tablespoon toasted (dark) sesame oil
1 tablespoon finely chopped fresh ginger
2 large cloves garlic, finely chopped
1 (12-ounce) bag broccoli slaw
2 cups shredded cabbage
6 to 8 scallions, white and green parts, thinly sliced

2 tablespoons reduced-sodium soy sauce
1 tablespoon rice vinegar
4 ounces extra-firm tofu, drained and finely diced (about 1 cup)
¼ cup prepared hoisin sauce or Hoisin Sauce (page 116), plus additional, to serve
8 (7-inch) fresh or thawed frozen Chinese pancakes or Classic Chinese Pancakes (page 15), warmed
Plum sauce or duck sauce, to serve (optional)

In a large wok or nonstick skillet, heat the oil over medium heat. Add ginger and garlic and cook, stirring, until softened and fragrant, about 1 minute. Add broccoli slaw, cabbage, half the scallions, soy sauce, and vinegar; stir well to combine. Cover and cook, stirring once or twice, until the vegetables are crisp-tender, 3 to 4 minutes. Add the tofu and hoisin; cook, uncovered, stirring often, until vegetables are tender but not mushy, 2 to 3 minutes. Stir in the remaining scallions and remove from heat. To serve, spoon a bit of additional hoisin sauce or plum sauce onto each pancake. Place about ½ cup vegetable mixture in the center of each pancake. Roll up, burrito-style, and serve at once.

{PER SERVING} (per 2 filled pancakes) Calories 299 · Protein 11g · Total Fat 8g · Sat Fat 1g · Cholesterol 0mg · Carbohydrate 45g · Dietary Fiber 4g · Sodium 837mg

{COOK'S TIP}

To heat fresh or thawed frozen Chinese pancakes, preheat oven to 325F (165C) degrees. Wrap pancakes tightly in foil and place in oven about 8 minutes, or until warm. Unwrap just before using.

Vegetable Rolls with Garlic–Black Bean Sauce

Jicama is a crisp tuber known in China as sweet turnip or bang kuang. It has a texture similar to water chestnuts, which can be substituted in the recipe. Cellophane noodles or rice vermicelli, cooked and drained according to package directions, and then cut into 3-inch lengths, can replace the shredded tofu, if desired.

MAKES 12 ROLLS

1 (8-ounce) package shredded tofu or bean curd strands
1 tablespoon peanut oil
3 cups shredded Napa or green cabbage
2 cups shredded carrots
2 cups shredded jicama
4 ounces fresh shiitake mushrooms, stemmed, thinly sliced
1 tablespoon chopped fresh ginger
3 tablespoons vegetarian oyster sauce or mushroom soy sauce
1 tablespoon reduced-sodium soy sauce
Freshly ground black pepper, to taste
12 large butter lettuce leaves or spinach leaves
12 (7-inch) fresh or thawed frozen Chinese pancakes or Classic Chinese Pancakes (page 15), or flour tortillas
24 large fresh basil leaves
Garlic–Black Bean Sauce, below

In a medium stockpot, cook the shredded tofu in boiling salted water until separated and al dente, 5 to 9 minutes, depending on freshness, stirring occasionally. Drain in a colander and rinse under cold running water. Drain well and pat dry with paper towel. Set aside.

In a wok or large nonstick skillet, heat the peanut oil over medium-high heat. Add the cabbage, carrots, jicama, mushrooms, and ginger; cook, stirring constantly, until cabbage is wilted, about 5 minutes. Add the oyster sauce, soy sauce, and pepper, stirring well to combine. Remove from heat and let cool to room temperature.

To make the rolls, place 1 lettuce leaf on each pancake. Divide shredded tofu evenly between 12 lettuce leaves and top with 2 basil leaves. Spoon about ¼ cup of the vegetable mixture on top. Fold in sides of pancake, then roll up burrito-style, enclosing the filling completely. (At this point, vegetable rolls can be covered with plastic wrap and refrigerated up to 12 hours before returning to room temperature and serving.) Serve with Garlic–Black Bean Sauce.

{PER SERVING} (per roll, without sauce) Calories 141 · Protein 5g · Total Fat 4g · Sat Fat 1g · Cholesterol 0mg · Carbohydrate 22g · Dietary Fiber 4g · Sodium 339mg

GARLIC–BLACK BEAN SAUCE

This versatile sauce goes well with countless spring rolls, wontons, dumplings, and tofu. Black bean sauce with garlic is available in Asian markets; regular black bean sauce, found in most major supermarkets, can be substituted.

MAKES ABOUT 1¼ CUPS

1 cup water
6 tablespoons black bean sauce with garlic
¼ cup sugar
2 teaspoons Chinese chili paste
2 large cloves garlic

In a small saucepan, combine all ingredients; bring to a simmer over medium-high heat, stirring occasionally. Reduce the heat to medium and simmer

3 minutes, stirring occasionally. Remove from heat and let cool to room temperature. (Completely cooled sauce can be refrigerated, covered, up to 3 days before returning to room temperature and using.)

{PER SERVING} **(per tablespoon, or $\frac{1}{20}$ of recipe) Calories 16 · Protein 0g · Total Fat 0g · Sat Fat 0g · Cholesterol 0mg · Carbohydrate 3g · Dietary Fiber 0g · Sodium 56mg**

CHAPTER SEVEN

Vegetable Side Dishes

In traditional Chinese cuisine—theoretically speaking, that is—steamed rice is the core dish and all other dishes are side dishes. As a boon to vegetarians, on a typical Chinese table, most of these side dishes showcase vegetables, which are economical and lend both healthfulness and eye-catching appeal to the meal. While it goes without saying that I'm into vegetables, living in China introduced me to a whole new world of veggie possibilities. Familiar Western standbys such as asparagus, cauliflower, corn, eggplant, green beans, and potatoes are taken to other levels with unique blends of herbs, spices, and seasonings, and unexpected cooking and preparation methods, as well. For example, lettuce and cucumbers are served stir-fried or braised more often than raw, and bamboo shoots and water chestnuts are typically prepared in their fresh, versus canned, state. Then there are the vegetables I'd never even heard of or seen before coming to China: celtuce (this is not a typo), long beans (also known as "snake" beans), lotus root, and fuzzy melon, to name a few. Most exciting of all, the Chinese make cooking vegetables a breeze. Whether you're new to Chinese cooking or just looking for a quick recipe, the majority of the following recipes are ready in minutes. Many can be made with ingredients that are available at most local supermarkets, while others will most definitely require a trip to your local Asian market—trust me, the journey will be worth it!

Bamboo Shoots with Mushrooms

If preparing this tasty dish with fresh bamboo shoots, select the more tender and highly prized winter bamboo shoots for best results. See the Cook's Tip (page 35) for safe handling of fresh bamboo shoots, which can contain small amounts of hydrogen cyanide.

MAKES 4 SERVINGS

1 tablespoon peanut oil

½ pound fresh shiitake mushrooms, stemmed and thinly sliced

2 large cloves garlic, finely chopped

2 pounds fresh winter bamboo shoots, prepared and precooked (see Cook's Tip, page 35), drained and coarsely chopped, or 1 (16-ounce) can bamboo shoots, drained, blanched 1 minute in boiling water, drained, and coarsely chopped

¼ cup low-sodium vegetable broth

1 teaspoon sugar

Salt and freshly ground black pepper, to taste

In a wok or large nonstick skillet, heat the peanut oil over medium-high heat. Add the mushrooms and garlic and cook, stirring, until softened, about 2 minutes. Add the remaining ingredients and cook, stirring, until bamboo shoots are heated through and liquid is reduced, 1 to 2 minutes. Serve at once.

{PER SERVING} Calories 73 · Protein 4g · Total Fat 4g · Sat Fat 1g · Cholesterol 0mg · Carbohydrate 8g · Dietary Fiber 3g · Sodium 38mg

Grilled Baby Bok Choy with Orange Sauce

Baby bok choy, or Shanghai bok choy, available in Asian markets and some well-stocked supermarkets, is smaller and tenderer than mature bok choy. To sop up all the delicious orange sauce, I like to serve the grilled bok choy on a bed of rice or couscous.

MAKES 4 SERVINGS

Juice of 1 medium orange (about ⅓ cup)

2 tablespoons reduced-sodium soy sauce

1½ tablespoons toasted (dark) sesame oil

½ tablespoon light brown sugar

Pinch cayenne red pepper, or to taste (optional)

8 very small heads baby bok choy (about 2 ounces each), root ends trimmed about ⅛ inch

Salt and freshly ground black pepper, to taste

In a small bowl, whisk together the orange juice, soy sauce, ½ tablespoon sesame oil, sugar, and cayenne, if using. Let stand a few minutes to allow the sugar to dissolve. Whisk again and set aside.

Place a stovetop grilling pan with grids over medium-high heat. Brush the bok choy with remaining 1 tablespoon sesame oil, and season with salt and black pepper. Grill until browned and tender, 2 to 3 minutes per side. Transfer to a warmed serving platter (or individual serving plates); drizzle evenly with the orange sauce. Serve warm.

{PER SERVING} Calories 80 · Protein 2g · Total Fat 5g · Sat Fat 1g · Cholesterol 0mg · Carbohydrate 7g · Dietary Fiber 1g · Sodium 375mg

Grilled Sesame Asparagus

These juicy and flavorful asparagus are always a treat on the outdoor grill. For a more intense taste sensation, roast the asparagus as directed in the Cook's Tip, below.

MAKES 4 SERVINGS

1¼ pounds medium-thick asparagus, tough ends trimmed

3 tablespoons reduced-sodium soy sauce

1½ tablespoons toasted (dark) sesame oil

1 teaspoon toasted sesame seeds

Prepare a medium charcoal or gas grill. Or preheat a broiler or place a stovetop grilling pan with grids over medium heat.

In a shallow container large enough to hold the asparagus in a single layer, whisk together the soy sauce, sesame oil, and sesame seeds. Add the asparagus and turn to thoroughly coat. Let stand 10 minutes at room temperature, turning a few times.

Remove the asparagus from the marinade, reserving marinade. If grilling, arrange the asparagus in a single layer on a vegetable grid. If broiling, arrange in a single layer on a baking sheet with sides. Position the charcoal grill rack or oven rack 6 to 8 inches from the heat source. If using a stovetop grill pan, arrange the asparagus in a single layer in the pan; cook in two batches to avoid overcrowding.

Grill or broil asparagus until nicely browned but not charred, turning frequently, 7 to 10 minutes. Transfer to a serving platter and drizzle with the reserved marinade. Serve warm or at room temperature.

{PER SERVING} Calories 71 · Protein 2g · Total Fat 6g · Sat Fat 1g · Cholesterol 0mg · Carbohydrate 4g · Dietary Fiber 1g · Sodium 451mg

{COOK'S TIP}

To make Roasted Sesame Asparagus, preheat the oven to 425F (220C). Marinate the asparagus as directed in the recipe. Transfer the asparagus to a baking sheet with sides and place in the oven for 10 to 15 minutes, or until the asparagus are browned and tender, turning once or twice. Serve as otherwise directed.

Asparagus and Mushrooms with Black Bean Sauce

When one of my most playful students, Kathy, submitted the inspiration for this recipe, I told her she was psychic—how else could she have known that asparagus and mushrooms are, in my mind, a match made in heaven? Shaoxing rice wine is available in Asian markets and some well-stocked supermarkets. Dry sherry, sake, or dry white wine can be substituted, if necessary.

MAKES 4 TO 6 SERVINGS

1 pound medium-thick asparagus, trimmed, cut into 2-inch lengths

1 tablespoon peanut oil

2 large cloves garlic, finely chopped

¼ pound fresh shiitake, cremini, or cultivated white mushrooms, stemmed and sliced

3 tablespoons black bean paste

1 tablespoon reduced-sodium soy sauce

1 tablespoon Shaoxing rice wine, sake, dry sherry or dry white wine

In a large pot of boiling salted water, blanch the asparagus until barely softened, about 2 minutes.

Drain, rinse under cold running water, and drain again. Set aside.

In a wok or large nonstick skillet, heat the oil over medium-high heat. Add the garlic and cook, stirring constantly, 30 seconds. Add the asparagus and mushrooms and cook, stirring constantly, until asparagus is crisp-tender and mushrooms have begun to release their liquid, 2 to 3 minutes. Reduce heat to medium-low and add the remaining ingredients; cook, stirring constantly, until heated through and slightly thickened, 1 to 2 minutes. Serve at once.

{PER SERVING} Calories 69 · Protein 3g · Total Fat 4g · Sat Fat 1g · Cholesterol 0mg · Carbohydrate 7g · Dietary Fiber 2g · Sodium 293mg

Steamed Broccoli with Brown Sauce

You can dress up frozen broccoli, cooked according to package directions, with this delicious brown sauce any time of the year. For a nutritious meal, serve over brown rice and sprinkle with chopped peanuts.

MAKES 4 TO 6 SERVINGS

> ½ teaspoon salt
> 1¼ pounds fresh broccoli florets
> 1 teaspoon toasted (dark) sesame oil
> Freshly ground black pepper, to taste
> Basic Chinese Brown Sauce, below

In a large nonstick skillet, bring about ¼ inch water to a boil over high heat; add salt and broccoli florets. Cover, reduce heat to medium, and steam until broccoli is crisp-tender, 4 to 5 minutes. Drain and transfer to a serving bowl. Add sesame oil and season with pepper; toss well to combine. Add Brown Sauce, tossing to combine. Serve at once.

{PER SERVING} Calories 79 · Protein 7g · Total Fat 2g · Sat Fat 0g · Cholesterol 0mg · Carbohydrate 12g · Dietary Fiber 5g · Sodium 570mg

BASIC CHINESE BROWN SAUCE

Brown sauce is a staple of Chinese cuisine, enhancing the flavor of numerous vegetable and tofu dishes. For best results, use shortly after preparing.

MAKES ABOUT 1 CUP

> 1 cup reduced-sodium vegetable broth
> 1 tablespoon reduced-sodium soy sauce
> 1 tablespoon cornstarch
> 1 large clove garlic, finely chopped
> ¼ teaspoon ground ginger
> ⅛ teaspoon crushed red pepper flakes, or
>   to taste
> 1 tablespoon molasses or dark brown sugar
> Salt and freshly ground black pepper,
>   to taste

In a small saucepan, whisk together the broth, soy sauce, cornstarch, garlic, ginger, and red pepper flakes until thoroughly blended. Bring to a simmer over medium heat, stirring often; cook, stirring constantly, until thickened. Reduce heat to low, stir in the molasses, and season with salt and black pepper. Use as directed in recipe.

{PER SERVING} (about ¼ cup, or ¼ of recipe) Calories 28 · Protein 3g · Total Fat 0g · Sat Fat 0g · Cholesterol 0mg · Carbohydrate 4g · Dietary Fiber 1g · Sodium 280mg

Yunnan-Style Crispy Red Beans with Mint

This tasty and unusual dish is a Yunnanese specialty. Red beans, also known as adzuki beans, are available in Asian markets in dried and canned form; red kidney beans or pinto beans can replace them in a pinch. Serve with brown rice and fresh pineapple for a refreshing, complete-protein meal.

MAKES 4 TO 6 SERVINGS

- 3 tablespoons all-purpose flour, plus additional, if necessary
- ¼ teaspoon salt, plus additional, to taste
- Pinch cayenne pepper, or to taste
- 1 (16-ounce) can red beans (adzuki), rinsed, drained, patted dry with paper towels
- ¼ cup peanut oil
- ½ cup coarsely chopped fresh mint, stems included
- Freshly ground black pepper, to taste

In a small bowl, combine the flour, salt, and cayenne. Working with a few tablespoons at a time, add the beans and stir to coat. Transfer to a plate, leaving excess flour mixture in the bowl. Repeat until all beans are coated with flour mixture, adding additional flour, if necessary.

Line a baking sheet with paper towels and set aside. In a wok or deep-sided skillet, heat the oil over medium-high heat until a bean placed in the oil sizzles. Add the remaining beans and cook until crispy and golden, about 3 minutes, stirring gently. Using a slotted spoon, return the beans to the plate and add the mint; cook, stirring, 30 seconds. Return the beans to the wok and cook, stirring, until combined with the mint, about 30 seconds. Transfer beans and mint to the prepared baking sheet to

briefly drain. Serve at once, seasoned with additional salt and black pepper, as needed.

{PER SERVING} Calories 256 · Protein 8g · Total Fat 14g · Sat Fat 2g · Cholesterol 0mg · Carbohydrate 27g · Dietary Fiber 6g · Sodium 144mg

Stir-Fried Baby Bok Choy with Garlic and Ginger

Baby bok choy, also known as Shanghai bok choy, has a sweeter flavor than the adult variety.

MAKES 4 SERVINGS

- 1 tablespoon reduced-sodium soy sauce
- ½ tablespoon cornstarch
- 1½ tablespoons peanut or canola oil
- 4 cloves garlic, thinly sliced
- 1 tablespoon chopped fresh ginger
- 4 heads small baby bok choy (about 1¼ pounds), root ends trimmed about ⅛ inch, halved lengthwise
- ⅓ cup low-sodium vegetable broth
- ¼ teaspoon salt, or to taste
- Freshly ground black pepper, to taste
- ½ tablespoon toasted (dark) sesame oil

In a small bowl, mix together the soy sauce and cornstarch; set aside.

In a wok or large nonstick skillet, heat the oil over medium-high heat. Add the garlic and ginger and cook, stirring constantly, 15 seconds. Add the bok choy and cook, stirring and turning constantly, until leaves are limp and bright green, about 2 minutes. Reduce the heat to medium and add the broth, salt, and pepper; cover and cook until bok choy is crisp-tender, 2 to 3 minutes, stirring a few times. Stir in the cornstarch mixture and sesame oil and cook, stirring constantly, until thickened, 1 to 2 minutes. Serve at once.

{PER SERVING} Calories 94 · Protein 4g · Total Fat 7g · Sat Fat 1g · Cholesterol 0mg · Carbohydrate 6g · Dietary Fiber 2g · Sodium 419mg

Hunan-Style Cauliflower with Chili Peppers and Garlic

Cauliflower dishes are a specialty of Hunan Province, where it grows in abundance. Broccoli can be prepared in the same fashion, if desired.

MAKES 4 SERVINGS

1½ tablespoons peanut oil
4 to 6 large cloves garlic, slivered
¼ teaspoon crushed red pepper flakes, or
    to taste
¼ teaspoon coarse salt, plus additional,
    to taste
4 cups cauliflower florets (from about 1
    medium head), cut into bite-size pieces
1 to 2 small fresh red chili peppers, seeded
    and thinly sliced
1 tablespoon reduced-sodium soy sauce, or
    to taste
Freshly ground black pepper, to taste

In a small heavy-bottomed saucepan, heat the oil over medium-low heat. Add the garlic, red pepper flakes, and salt; cook, stirring often, until garlic is lightly browned and tender, about 5 minutes. Set aside.

Meanwhile, in a large pot of boiling salted water, cook the cauliflower and chili until cauliflower is crisp-tender, 2 to 3 minutes. Drain well and transfer to a serving bowl. Add the garlic mixture, soy sauce, additional salt, if necessary, and pepper; toss well to thoroughly combine. Serve warm or at room temperature.

{PER SERVING} 81 Calories · Protein 3g · Total Fat 5g · Sat Fat 1g · Cholesterol 0mg · Carbohydrate 8g · Dietary Fiber 3g · Sodium 299mg

Celtuce and Mushroom Stir-Fry

Also known as asparagus lettuce, celtuce is grown primarily for its stems, which lend a crunchy, slightly nutty flavor to raw and cooked dishes.

MAKES 4 SERVINGS

2 teaspoons peanut oil
1 pound celtuce, peeled, thinly sliced
    crosswise
½ pound fresh shiitake mushrooms,
    stemmed and thinly sliced
½ cup low-sodium vegetable broth
2 tablespoons reduced-sodium soy sauce
1 teaspoon toasted (dark) sesame oil
Salt and freshly ground black pepper,
    to taste

In a wok or large nonstick skillet, heat the peanut oil over medium-high heat. Add the celtuce and mushrooms and cook, stirring, until softened, about 2 minutes. Add the remaining ingredients and cook, stirring, until vegetables are tender and liquid is greatly reduced, about 3 minutes. Serve at once.

{PER SERVING} Calories 69 · Protein 4g · Total Fat 4g · Sat Fat 1g · Cholesterol 0mg · Carbohydrate 6g · Dietary Fiber 2g · Sodium 368mg

Stir-Fried Bok Choy and Shiitake Mushrooms

This quick and easy stir-fry makes an excellent supper served over brown rice, sprinkled with chopped peanuts.

MAKES 4 SERVINGS

1 tablespoon peanut oil

3 large cloves garlic, finely chopped

¼ teaspoon crushed red pepper flakes, or to taste (optional)

1 (2-pound) bok choy, tough base trimmed, thinly sliced crosswise

8 ounces fresh shiitake mushrooms, stemmed and sliced

2 tablespoons vegetarian oyster sauce or mushroom soy sauce

1 tablespoon toasted (dark) sesame oil

Salt and freshly ground black pepper, to taste

In a wok or large nonstick skillet, heat the peanut oil over medium-high heat. Add the garlic and red pepper flakes (if using), and cook, stirring constantly, 30 seconds. Add the bok choy and mushrooms and cook, stirring constantly, until just tender, 4 to 5 minutes. Add the oyster sauce, sesame oil, salt, and black pepper and cook, stirring constantly, 30 seconds. Remove from heat and serve at once.

{PER SERVING} Calories 112 · Protein 5g · Total Fat 8g · Sat Fat 1g · Cholesterol 0mg · Carbohydrate 9g · Dietary Fiber 3g · Sodium 450mg

Yunnan-Style Braised Eggplant

You can make this tasty dish using regular eggplant; in this instance, salting the eggplant for 30 minutes in a colander to draw out the bitter juices is recommended before cooking.

MAKES 4 SERVINGS

2 medium-long Asian eggplants (about 8 ounces each), peeled, quartered lengthwise, cut into 3-inch lengths, or 2 medium regular eggplants (about 8 ounces each), peeled, quartered lengthwise, cut into 3-inch lengths, set in a colander, and lightly salted to drain 30 minutes (salting is recommended)

¼ cup cornstarch, or more, as needed

2½ tablespoons peanut oil

3 large cloves garlic, finely chopped

1 tablespoon chopped fresh ginger

1 cup low-sodium vegetable broth

1 tablespoon reduced-sodium soy sauce

1 teaspoon tomato paste

1 teaspoon sugar

Salt and freshly ground black pepper, to taste

If using salted regular eggplant, rinse the drained eggplant under cold running water. Dry between paper towels.

Place the cornstarch in a deep-welled plate or bowl. Roll each piece of eggplant lightly in the cornstarch, shaking off any excess; set aside.

In a large nonstick skillet with a lid, heat 2 tablespoons of the oil over medium heat. Add the eggplant and cook, stirring occasionally, until just softened, 4 to 5 minutes. Add the remaining ½ tablespoon of oil, garlic, and ginger; cook, stirring often, until fragrant and eggplant is lightly browned, about 3 minutes. Add the remaining ingredients, stirring well to combine; bring to a brisk simmer over medium-high heat, stirring occasionally. Reduce the heat, cover, and simmer gently, stirring occasionally, until eggplant is tender and liquid is thickened and reduced, about 5 minutes. Serve warm.

{PER SERVING} Calories 153 · Protein 4g · Total Fat 9g · Sat Fat 2g · Cholesterol 0mg · Carbohydrate 16g · Dietary Fiber 3g · Sodium 294mg

Chinese Broccoli with Vegetarian Oyster Sauce

Chinese broccoli has a bittersweet flavor that goes well with vegetarian oyster sauce, which is typically made with mushrooms and available at most well-stocked Asian markets. Regular broccoli or broccolini can be substituted for the Chinese broccoli, if necessary.

MAKES 4 SERVINGS

½ cup water
2 tablespoons vegetarian oyster sauce or
    mushroom soy sauce
1 tablespoon Shaoxing rice wine, dry
    sherry, sake, or dry white wine
1 teaspoon cornstarch
1 tablespoon peanut oil
1 tablespoon finely chopped fresh ginger
1 pound Chinese broccoli (gai lan), tough
    ends trimmed, leaves and stalks cut into
    1-inch pieces

1 tablespoon reduced-sodium soy sauce, or
    to taste
½ teaspoon sugar
Freshly ground black pepper, to taste
½ tablespoon toasted (dark) sesame oil

In a small bowl, combine ¼ cup water, oyster sauce, rice wine, and cornstarch; set aside.

In a wok or large nonstick skillet with a lid, heat the peanut oil over medium-high heat. Add the ginger and cook, stirring, 1 minute. Reduce the heat to medium and add the broccoli, remaining ¼ cup water, soy sauce, sugar, and pepper; toss well to combine. Cook, covered, until broccoli stalks are crisp-tender, about 5 minutes, stirring a few times. Add the oyster sauce mixture and cook, stirring, until thickened, 2 to 3 minutes. Add the sesame oil and stir well to combine. Serve at once.

{PER SERVING} Calories 94 · Protein 4g · Total Fat 6g · Sat Fat 1g · Cholesterol 0mg · Carbohydrate 9g · Dietary Fiber 4g · Sodium 481mg

Hunan-Style Hot-and-Sour Chinese Cabbage

Regular green cabbage can easily stand in for the Napa variety, if desired. Serve over rice and garnish with peanuts for a satisfying meal.

MAKES 4 SERVINGS

1 small long Napa cabbage (about 1 pound), cored, leaves separated

1 tablespoon peanut oil

1 to 2 fresh red chili peppers, seeded, if desired, chopped

1 tablespoon chopped fresh ginger

2 large cloves garlic, finely chopped

2 tablespoons reduced-sodium soy sauce

2 tablespoons black vinegar or balsamic vinegar

2 tablespoons sugar

1 tablespoon Shaoxing rice wine, dry sherry, sake, or dry white wine

1 teaspoon cornstarch mixed with 1 teaspoon water

½ teaspoon salt

¼ teaspoon crushed red pepper flakes, or to taste

Freshly ground black pepper, to taste

1 teaspoon toasted (dark) sesame oil

Cut the cabbage leaves lengthwise in half, then quarter each half crosswise. In a wok or large nonstick skillet, heat the peanut oil over medium-high heat. Add the chili, ginger, and garlic and cook, stirring constantly, 30 seconds. Add the cabbage and cook, stirring constantly, until just softened, 1 to 2 minutes. Reduce the heat to medium and add the soy sauce, vinegar, sugar, wine, cornstarch mixture, salt, red pepper, and black pepper; cook, stirring often, until cabbage is tender but not shriveled and liquid is slightly thickened, about 2 minutes. Remove from heat and add the sesame oil, stirring well to thoroughly combine. Serve warm.

{PER SERVING} Calories 100 · Protein 2g · Total Fat 5g · Sat Fat 1g · Cholesterol 0mg · Carbohydrate 13g · Dietary Fiber 1g · Sodium 585mg

Glazed Five-Spice Carrots

Chinese five-spice powder takes glazed carrots to a whole new level—sublime!

MAKES 4 SERVINGS

1 tablespoon canola oil

½ to ¾ teaspoon five-spice powder

1 pound fresh carrots (6 to 8 medium), sliced diagonally into ½-inch-thick pieces

¾ cup water

2 tablespoons reduced-sodium soy sauce

2 tablespoons dark brown sugar

Salt and freshly ground black pepper, to taste

½ tablespoon toasted (dark) sesame oil

In a large nonstick skillet, heat the canola oil over medium heat. Add the five-spice powder and stir 15 seconds. Add the carrots, water, soy sauce, and sugar and bring to a boil over high heat. Reduce the heat to medium-low, cover, and simmer until carrots are fork-tender, 5 to 8 minutes. Uncover, season with salt and pepper, and raise the heat to medium-high. Cook, stirring often, until the liquid has largely evaporated, 7 to 9 minutes, adding the sesame oil the last minute or so of cooking. Serve hot.

{PER SERVING} Calories 103 · Protein 2g · Total Fat 5g · Sat Fat 1g · Cholesterol 0mg · Carbohydrate 13g · Dietary Fiber 3g · Sodium 335mg

Roasted Carrots with Sesame and Ginger

Whole peeled baby carrots can be substituted for the carrot sticks in this simply delicious recipe.

MAKES 4 TO 6 SERVINGS

> 3 tablespoons reduced-sodium soy sauce
> 3 tablespoons plain rice vinegar
> 1 tablespoon finely chopped fresh ginger
> 1 tablespoon toasted (dark) sesame oil
> 1 tablespoon brown sugar
> 2 large cloves garlic, finely chopped
> Freshly ground black pepper, to taste
> 6 large carrots, about 3 ounces each,
>   halved, cut lengthwise into sticks

In a small bowl, combine the soy sauce, rice vinegar, ginger, sesame oil, sugar, garlic, and pepper, stirring until the sugar is dissolved. Transfer to a resealable plastic bag and add the carrots; seal and turn to coat. Let marinate at room temperature 30 minutes, or refrigerate up to 24 hours.

Preheat the oven to 425F (220C) degrees. Lightly oil a baking sheet with sides. Remove the carrots from the marinade (reserving ¼ cup of the marinade) and arrange in a single layer on the prepared baking sheet. Bake in the center of the oven 20 to 25 minutes, or until tender and browned, tossing halfway through cooking with 2 tablespoons reserved marinade. Transfer to a serving bowl, toss with remaining 2 tablespoons reserved marinade, and serve warm.

{PER SERVING} Calories 104 · Protein 2g · Total Fat 4g · Sat Fat 1g · Cholesterol 0mg · Carbohydrate 17g · Dietary Fiber 4g · Sodium 492mg

Stir-Fried Chestnuts and Chinese Cabbage

The Chinese love tree-born chestnuts. This tasty side dish makes an inviting addition to any winter holiday table.

MAKES 6 TO 8 SERVINGS

> 2 tablespoons peanut oil
> 1 tablespoon chopped fresh ginger
> 2 large cloves garlic, finely chopped
> 1 pound Napa cabbage, quartered
>   lengthwise, cored, sliced diagonally into
>   ¼-inch-wide strips
> 2 cups rinsed and drained canned whole
>   chestnuts (about 10 ounces), halved
> 1 tablespoon reduced-sodium soy sauce
> ½ tablespoon toasted (dark) sesame oil
> ½ teaspoon sugar
> ¼ teaspoon salt
> Freshly ground black pepper, to taste

In a wok or large nonstick skillet, heat the peanut oil over medium-high heat. Add the ginger and garlic and cook, stirring constantly, 30 seconds, or until fragrant. Add the cabbage and cook, tossing and stirring constantly, until just beginning to wilt, about 2 minutes. Reduce the heat to medium-low and add the remaining ingredients, stirring well to combine. Cook, covered, until cabbage is tender, about 3 minutes, stirring a few times. Serve at once.

{PER SERVING} Calories 318 · Protein 2g · Total Fat 24g · Sat Fat 4g · Cholesterol 0mg · Carbohydrate 26g · Dietary Fiber 2g · Sodium 204mg

Cauliflower with Water Chestnuts and Shiitake Mushrooms

Broccoli can replace the cauliflower, if desired.

MAKES 4 SERVINGS

- 6 dried shiitake mushrooms, soaked in 1¼ cups hot water 20 minutes, or until softened
- 2 tablespoons cornstarch
- 2 tablespoons reduced-sodium soy sauce
- 2 tablespoons Shaoxing rice wine, dry sherry, sake, or dry white wine
- 2 tablespoons water
- Salt and freshly ground black pepper, to taste
- 1½ tablespoons peanut or canola oil
- 1 small cauliflower (about 1 pound), washed and trimmed, separated into small florets
- ¼ cup drained and sliced canned water chestnuts
- 2 large cloves garlic, finely chopped
- ¼ cup chopped walnuts (optional)

Drain the mushrooms, reserving the soaking liquid. Strain the soaking liquid through a coffee filter or paper towel to remove any grit. Rinse the mushrooms; remove and discard the stems. Thinly slice the caps; set aside. In a small bowl, stir the cornstarch, soy sauce, wine, water, salt, and pepper until well blended; set aside.

In a wok or large nonstick skillet, heat the oil over medium-high heat. Add the cauliflower and mushrooms and cook, stirring constantly, until softened, 2 to 3 minutes. Add the water chestnuts and garlic and cook, stirring constantly, 2 minutes. Add the reserved soaking liquid and bring to a boil.

Stir in the cornstarch mixture and walnuts (if using); reduce the heat to medium. Cook, stirring constantly, until thickened, 2 to 3 minutes. Serve at once.

{PER SERVING} Calories 126 · Protein 3g · Total Fat 5g · Sat Fat 1g · Cholesterol 0mg · Carbohydrate 16g · Dietary Fiber 4g · Sodium 336mg

Stir-Fried Flowering Chinese Chives

The key to this simple yet delicious side dish is not to overcook the chives, also known as flowering garlic chives or flowering leeks. Toss with plain, cooked rice noodles and sprinkle with chopped roasted peanuts for an outstanding main meal. If flowering Chinese chives are unavailable, substitute with Chinese garlic chives or the green parts of scallions, sliced lengthwise in half before cutting into 2-inch pieces.

MAKES 4 SIDE DISH SERVINGS

- 2 tablespoons reduced-sodium soy sauce
- 2 tablespoons water
- ½ teaspoon sugar
- 1 tablespoon peanut oil
- 2 bunches flowering Chinese chives (about 8 ounces), cut diagonally into 2-inch pieces (include buds)
- 1 teaspoon cornstarch mixed with 4 teaspoons water
- Salt and freshly ground black pepper, to taste

In a small bowl, combine the soy sauce, water, and sugar. In a wok or large nonstick skillet, heat the oil over medium-high heat. Add the chives and cook, stirring constantly, 1 minute, or until bright green. Add the soy sauce mixture and cook, stirring constantly, 30 seconds. Reduce the heat to medium and add the cornstarch mixture; cook, stirring constantly, until thickened, about 30 seconds. Remove from heat, season with salt and pepper, and serve at once.

{PER SERVING} Calories 57 · Protein 2g · Total Fat 4g · Sat Fat 1g · Cholesterol 0mg · Carbohydrate 6g · Dietary Fiber 2g · Sodium 309mg

Stir-Fried Yellow Corn with Pine Nuts

This northern-style dish is immensely popular in Hunan, where corn in all forms is eaten with relish. Chopped celtuce, carrot, or green bell pepper can replace the celery, if desired.

MAKES 6 SERVINGS

 1 tablespoon peanut oil
 3 cups frozen yellow corn kernels, thawed
 2 tablespoons finely chopped celery
 2 tablespoons pine nuts
 ½ teaspoon finely chopped fresh ginger
 ¼ teaspoon salt, or to taste
 1 tablespoon water, plus additional, as needed
 2 scallions, green parts only, thinly sliced
 Freshly ground black pepper, to taste

In a wok or large nonstick skillet, heat the oil over medium heat. Add the corn, celery, pine nuts, ginger, and salt; cook, stirring constantly, until corn is tender and pine nuts are fragrant, 4 to 5 minutes, adding water as needed to keep the mixture from becoming too dry. Stir in the scallions and remove from heat. Season with pepper and serve warm.

{PER SERVING} Calories 112 · Protein 3g · Total Fat 5g · Sat Fat 1g · Cholesterol 0mg · Carbohydrate 18g · Dietary Fiber 2g · Sodium 95mg

Spicy Corn with Hoisin and Cilantro

Here is a wonderful way to dress up plain frozen corn.

MAKES 6 SERVINGS

 3 cups frozen yellow corn
 ¼ cup chopped fresh cilantro
 1½ tablespoons canola oil
 1 tablespoon hoisin sauce
 ¼ to ½ teaspoon Chinese chili paste
 Salt and freshly ground black pepper, to taste

Cook the corn according to package directions; drain and transfer to a medium bowl. Add the remaining ingredients, tossing well to thoroughly combine. Serve warm or at room temperature.

{PER SERVING} Calories 108 · Protein 3g · Total Fat 4g · Sat Fat 0g · Cholesterol 0mg · Carbohydrate 18g · Dietary Fiber 2g · Sodium 46mg

Hunan-Style Pan-Fried Cucumber with Basil

This swift and simple recipe elevates the ordinary cucumber to the extraordinary. Cilantro can replace the basil, if desired.

MAKES 4 SERVINGS

1 tablespoon peanut oil

2 small cucumbers (about 8 ounces each), halved lengthwise, seeded, cut crosswise into ¼-inch-thick slices

2 large cloves garlic, finely chopped

1 tablespoon reduced-sodium soy sauce

1 teaspoon plain rice vinegar

1 teaspoon toasted (dark) sesame oil

½ to 1 teaspoon Chinese chili paste

Salt and freshly ground black pepper, to taste

¼ cup chopped fresh basil

In a large nonstick skillet, heat peanut oil over medium-high heat. Add the cucumber and cook, stirring constantly, 2 minutes. Continue to cook, stirring every 30 seconds or so, until lightly browned on all sides, 5 to 7 minutes. Add the garlic and cook, stirring constantly, 1 minute. Remove the skillet from the heat and stir in the soy sauce, vinegar, sesame oil, chili paste, salt, and pepper. Return to heat and cook, stirring constantly, 1 minute. Remove from heat and stir in the basil. Serve warm.

{PER SERVING} Calories 61 · Protein 1g · Total Fat 5g · Sat Fat 1g · Cholesterol 0mg · Carbohydrate 4g · Dietary Fiber 1g · Sodium 153mg

Hunan-Style Stir-Fried Daikon Radish

These crunchy, slivered radishes are wonderful on their own, or tossed with thin Asian noodles. Cold leftovers make a delicious topping for veggie burgers. For a milder dish, omit the chili pepper.

MAKES 6 SERVINGS

1 pound daikon radish, peeled and shredded

½ teaspoon salt

2 tablespoons water

¾ teaspoon cornstarch

1½ tablespoons peanut oil

1 fresh red chili pepper, seeded and finely chopped

2 scallions, green parts only, thinly sliced

1 tablespoon reduced-sodium soy sauce

2 teaspoons plain rice vinegar

1 teaspoon toasted (dark) sesame oil

Place the radish in a colander set over a deep-welled plate and sprinkle with salt; toss to combine. Let stand 15 minutes. Squeeze radish dry between paper towels and set aside.

In a small container, mix together the water and cornstarch until thoroughly blended. Set aside.

In a wok or large nonstick skillet, heat the peanut oil over medium-high heat. Add chili and cook, stirring constantly, 10 seconds. Add the radish and cook, stirring constantly, 1 minute. Add the scallions, soy sauce, and vinegar; cook, stirring constantly, 1 to 2 minutes, or until radish is crisp-tender. Reduce the heat to medium-low and add the cornstarch mixture and sesame oil; cook, stirring constantly, until thickened and glossy, 1 to 2 minutes. Serve at once.

{PER SERVING} Calories 56 · Protein 1g · Total Fat 4g · Sat Fat 1g · Cholesterol 0mg · Carbohydrate 4g · Dietary Fiber 1g · Sodium 292mg

Hunan-Style Eggplant

Here is one of my favorite ways to prepare eggplant. If you use the less seedy Asian variety, salting the eggplant is never necessary. Sprinkle with the optional peanuts and serve over brown rice for a delicious and nutritious meal.

MAKES 6 SERVINGS

3 medium Asian eggplants (about 8 ounces each), unpeeled, cut into 1-inch chunks, or 2 medium regular eggplants, about 12 ounces each, unpeeled, cut into 1-inch chunks, set in a colander and lightly salted to drain 30 minutes (salting is optional)

2 tablespoons peanut oil

4 large cloves garlic, finely chopped

1 tablespoon finely chopped fresh ginger

½ cup low-sodium vegetable broth

2 tablespoons reduced-sodium soy sauce

1 tablespoon Chinese chili paste, or to taste

1 tablespoon plain rice vinegar

2 teaspoons sugar

4 scallions, green parts only, thinly sliced

¼ cup chopped roasted peanuts (optional)

½ tablespoon toasted (dark) sesame oil

If using salted regular eggplant, rinse the drained eggplant under cold running water. Dry between paper towels.

In a wok or large nonstick skillet, heat peanut oil over medium-high heat. Add eggplant and cook, stirring and tossing constantly, until softened, about 4 minutes. Add garlic and ginger and cook, stirring constantly, 2 minutes. Add broth, soy sauce, chili paste, vinegar, and sugar; cook, stirring constantly, until eggplant is tender and has absorbed most of the liquid, about 2 minutes. Reduce heat to medium and add the scallion greens, peanuts (if using), and sesame oil; cook, stirring, 1 minute. Serve warm or at room temperature.

{PER SERVING} Calories 95 · Protein 3g · Total Fat 6g · Sat Fat 1g · Cholesterol 0mg · Carbohydrate 10g · Dietary Fiber 3g · Sodium 249mg

Spicy Hoisin-Glazed Green Beans

This spicy yet sweet green bean dish is delicious— if you prefer a milder version, use less chili paste, or omit altogether.

MAKES 4 SERVINGS

1 tablespoon peanut oil

3 large cloves garlic

1 pound green beans, trimmed

3 tablespoons hoisin sauce

1½ tablespoons reduced-sodium soy sauce

1 to 2 teaspoons Chinese chili paste, or to taste

1 teaspoon toasted (dark) sesame oil

Salt, to taste

In a wok or large nonstick skillet with a lid, heat the peanut oil over medium-high heat. Add the garlic and cook, stirring constantly, 15 seconds. Add the green beans and cook, stirring constantly, 2 minutes, or until softened. Reduce the heat to medium and add the remaining ingredients; cook, covered, stirring a few times, until beans are crisp-tender, about 3 minutes. Serve at once.

{PER SERVING} Calories 109 · Protein 3g · Total Fat 5g · Sat Fat 1g · Cholesterol 0mg · Carbohydrate 15g · Dietary Fiber 4g · Sodium 427mg

Microwaved Sichuan Green Beans

This is a great buffet dish, as it can be served warm or at room temperature. For added crunch and protein, toss with slivered almonds just before serving.

MAKES 6 SERVINGS

2 scallions, white and green parts, finely chopped

4 large cloves garlic, finely chopped

1 tablespoon finely chopped fresh ginger

1 tablespoon peanut oil

¼ teaspoon crushed red pepper flakes, or to taste

2 tablespoons reduced-sodium soy sauce

1 tablespoon plain rice vinegar

1 pound fresh green beans, trimmed

½ tablespoon toasted (dark) sesame oil

Freshly ground black pepper, to taste

In a 2½-quart microwave-safe casserole, combine scallions, garlic, ginger, peanut oil, and red pepper flakes. Cook, uncovered, on high, for 3 minutes. Stir in 1 tablespoon soy sauce and the vinegar. Add green beans, tossing and turning with a spatula to thoroughly combine. Cook, uncovered, on high until tender and shriveled, 12 to 15 minutes, stirring and turning every 3 minutes. Add the remaining 1 tablespoon soy sauce, sesame oil, and pepper, tossing well to combine. Serve warm or at room temperature.

{PER SERVING} Calories 63 · Protein 2g · Total Fat 4 · Sat Fat 1g · Cholesterol 0mg · Carbohydrate 7g · Dietary Fiber 3g · Sodium 206mg

Roasted Sesame Green Beans

Roasting green beans concentrates their natural sugars and renders them irresistible. Chinese long beans and medium-thick asparagus can be prepared in a similar fashion.

MAKES 4 SERVINGS

3 cloves garlic, finely chopped

1 teaspoon finely chopped fresh ginger

1 teaspoon light brown sugar

½ teaspoon toasted (dark) sesame oil

¼ teaspoon crushed red pepper flakes (optional)

Freshly ground black pepper, to taste

1 pound fresh green beans, trimmed

1 tablespoon canola oil

½ teaspoon coarse salt

1 tablespoon sesame seeds

Preheat oven to 425F (220C). Adjust oven rack to middle position. Line a baking sheet with aluminum foil. In a small container, combine the garlic, ginger, sugar, sesame oil, red pepper flakes (if using), and pepper; set aside.

Spread the beans on the prepared baking sheet and drizzle with the canola oil. Using your hands, toss to evenly coat. Sprinkle the beans with the coarse salt and toss to coat; redistribute in an even layer. Bake 10 minutes. Remove baking sheet from oven. Sprinkle the beans with the garlic-ginger mixture. Using tongs, toss to evenly coat; redistribute in an even layer. Bake an additional 10 minutes, or until beans are wrinkled and browned in spots, sprinkling evenly with the sesame seeds the last few minutes of cooking. Serve warm.

{PER SERVING} Calories 91 · Protein 3g · Total Fat 5g · Sat Fat 1g · Cholesterol 0mg · Carbohydrate 11g · Dietary Fiber 4g · Sodium 243mg

Hunan-Style Baked Sweet Potato "French Fries" with Chili Sauce

Though traditionally made with deep-fried white potatoes, these sweet potatoes are no less scrumptious and a lot healthier baked in the oven, before being coated in a devilishly hot chili sauce. Russet potatoes can replace one or both of the sweet potatoes, if desired.

MAKES 4 SERVINGS

3 tablespoons cornstarch

½ teaspoon salt

⅛ teaspoon ground black pepper

2 large sweet potatoes (about 8 ounces each), peeled, cut into thin French fry–like fingers

2 tablespoons tomato ketchup

2 teaspoons Chinese chili paste, or to taste

2 teaspoons reduced-sodium soy sauce

2 teaspoons distilled white vinegar

2 teaspoons sugar

1 teaspoon toasted (dark) sesame oil

1 tablespoon peanut oil

½ tablespoon Chinese hot oil, or to taste

2 scallions, mostly green parts, thinly sliced

Preheat oven to 425F (220C). Lightly oil a large baking sheet and set aside.

In a large bowl, combine the cornstarch with the salt and pepper. Add the potatoes, tossing well to thoroughly coat. Shake off excess cornstarch and arrange in a single layer on the prepared baking sheet. Bake in the center of the oven until tender through the center, about 20 minutes, turning halfway through cooking. Remove from oven and set aside to cool slightly (at this point, potatoes can be left at room temperature up to 1 hour before continuing with the recipe).

In a small bowl, combine the ketchup, chili paste, soy sauce, vinegar, sugar, and sesame oil. In a large nonstick skillet, heat the peanut oil and hot oil over medium-high heat. Add the potatoes and cook, tossing and stirring often, until nicely browned, about 5 minutes. Reduce the heat to medium and add the ketchup mixture; cook, tossing and stirring often, until potatoes are coated and sauce is heated through, about 2 minutes. Transfer to a warmed serving plate and serve at once, garnished with the scallions.

{PER SERVING} Calories 170 · Protein 3g · Total Fat 6g · Sat Fat 1g · Cholesterol 0mg · Carbohydrate 27g · Dietary Fiber 2g · Sodium 465mg

Microwaved Kohlrabi with Snow Peas and Ginger

The turniplike kohlrabi is one of the most popular vegetables in Chinese cuisine.

MAKES 4 SERVINGS

- 1 (8-ounce) kohlrabi, peeled, sliced into thin French fry–like strips
- 1 teaspoon finely chopped fresh ginger
- 1 tablespoon peanut or canola oil
- 3 ounces fresh snow peas, trimmed
- ½ small red bell pepper (about 2 ounces), cut into thin strips
- 2 scallions, white and green parts, thinly sliced
- 1 tablespoon reduced-sodium soy sauce
- 1 tablespoon Chinese black vinegar or balsamic vinegar
- Salt and freshly ground black pepper, to taste
- ½ tablespoon toasted (dark) sesame oil

In a 1½-quart microwave-safe dish with a lid, combine kohlrabi, ginger, and peanut oil. Cover and microwave on high 2 minutes; stir. Re-cover and microwave on high 1 minute. Add remaining ingredients except the sesame oil and toss well to thoroughly combine. Cover and microwave on high 2 minutes; stir. Re-cover and microwave 1 minute, or until vegetables are crisp-tender, microwaving, covered, in 30-second intervals. Add the sesame oil, stirring well to thoroughly combine. Serve warm or at room temperature.

{PER SERVING} Calories 80 · Protein 2g · Total Fat 5g · Sat Fat 1g · Cholesterol 0mg · Carbohydrate 8g · Dietary Fiber 2g · Sodium 164mg

Stir-Fried Lettuce

Here is a delicious Chinese New Year side dish, as lettuce is considered to be a lucky food.

MAKES 4 TO 6 SERVINGS

- 2 teaspoons reduced-sodium soy sauce
- 1½ teaspoons Shaoxing rice wine, dry sherry, sake, or dry white wine
- 1½ teaspoons toasted (dark) sesame oil
- 1 teaspoon sugar
- 1 tablespoon peanut oil
- ½ tablespoon chopped fresh ginger
- 2 cloves garlic, finely chopped
- ¼ teaspoon crushed red pepper flakes, or to taste (optional)
- 1 head iceberg lettuce, washed, drained, leaves separated, cut crosswise into 1-inch-wide pieces
- ½ teaspoon coarse salt
- Freshly ground black pepper, to taste

In a small bowl, combine the soy sauce, rice wine, ½ teaspoon sesame oil, and sugar; set aside. In a wok or large nonstick skillet, heat the peanut oil over medium-high heat. Add the ginger, garlic, and red pepper flakes, if using; cook, stirring constantly, 15 seconds, or until fragrant. Add the lettuce and salt and cook, tossing and stirring constantly, until lettuce is beginning to wilt, about 1 minute. Add the reserved soy sauce mixture and pepper; cook, tossing and stirring constantly, until the lettuce is wilted and dark green but not shriveled, 1 to 2 minutes. Remove from the heat and add the remaining 1 teaspoon sesame oil, tossing well to thoroughly combine. Serve at once.

{PER SERVING} Calories 73 · Protein 2g · Total Fat 5g · Sat Fat 1g · Cholesterol 0mg · Carbohydrate 5g · Dietary Fiber 2g · Sodium 348mg

Chinese Long Beans in Scallion-Ginger Sauce

I love the nutty flavor of Chinese long beans, often called "snake" beans after the benign garden variety they closely resemble.

MAKES 4 SERVINGS

- ¾ pound Chinese long beans, trimmed, cut into 2-inch lengths
- 1 tablespoon peanut oil
- 4 scallions, white and green parts, finely chopped
- 1 tablespoon finely chopped fresh ginger
- 3 large cloves garlic, finely chopped
- ¼ teaspoon crushed red pepper flakes, or to taste (optional)
- ½ cup low-sodium vegetable broth
- 1 tablespoon brown sugar
- Salt and freshly ground black pepper, to taste
- 1 tablespoon toasted (dark) sesame oil
- 1 to 2 tablespoons toasted sesame seeds (optional)

In a large pot of boiling salted water, blanch long beans for 1 to 2 minutes, or until slightly tender. Drain in a colander and rinse under cold running water. Set aside.

In a wok or large nonstick skillet, heat peanut oil over medium-high heat. Add scallions, ginger, garlic, and red pepper flakes, if using; cook, stirring constantly, 1 minute. Add long beans and cook, stirring, 1 minute. Add broth, brown sugar, salt, and pepper; cook, stirring, until liquid is reduced by half, 4 to 5 minutes. Remove from heat and add the sesame oil and sesame seeds, if using; toss well to combine. Serve at once.

{PER SERVING} Calories 117 · Protein 4g · Total Fat 7g · Sat Fat 1g · Cholesterol 0mg · Carbohydrate 12g · Dietary Fiber 4g · Sodium 282mg

Stir-Fried Spinach with Garlic

Serve this classic Chinese spinach dish on a bed of brown rice sprinkled with chopped peanuts for a delicious meal.

MAKES 4 SERVINGS

- 1 tablespoon peanut oil
- 4 large cloves garlic, finely chopped
- ¼ to ½ teaspoon coarse salt
- ¼ teaspoon Chinese chili paste, or to taste
- 1 (10-ounce) bag baby spinach
- ½ teaspoon toasted (dark) sesame oil
- ¼ teaspoon sugar
- Freshly ground black pepper, or to taste

In a wok or large nonstick skillet with a lid, heat the peanut oil over medium-high heat. Add the garlic, salt, and chili paste; cook, stirring constantly, 15 seconds. Add the spinach and toss with a spatula until beginning to wilt, 1 to 2 minutes. Cover, remove from heat, and let stand 2 minutes. Add the sesame oil, sugar, and pepper and toss well to combine. Serve at once.

{PER SERVING} Calories 55 · Protein 2g · Total Fat 4g · Sat Fat 1g · Cholesterol 0mg · Carbohydrate 3g · Dietary Fiber 2g · Sodium 307mg

Braised Stuffed Bitter Melon

In Chinese medicine, bitter melon actually sweetens health and promotes longevity. In the following recipe, stuffed with a savory shiitake mushroom and tofu stuffing, it's simply delicious. Serve on a bed of brown rice for a complete meal.

MAKES 4 SERVINGS

1 pound bitter melon (1 large or 2 small), cut crosswise into 1-inch-thick pieces

3 dried Shiitake mushrooms, soaked in hot water to cover 20 minutes, or until softened, rinsed and drained

6 ounces firm tofu, drained and mashed

2 scallions, green parts only, finely chopped

2 tablespoons finely chopped fresh cilantro

1½ tablespoons cornstarch

2 teaspoons reduced-sodium soy sauce

1 teaspoon Shaoxing rice wine, dry sherry, sake, or dry white wine

1 teaspoon toasted (dark) sesame oil

½ teaspoon salt, plus additional, to taste

Freshly ground black pepper, to taste

2 tablespoons peanut oil

1 fresh red chili pepper, seeded and thinly sliced

1 teaspoon fermented (salted) black beans, rinsed and chopped

2 large cloves garlic, finely chopped

1 cup reduced-sodium vegetable broth

2 tablespoons vegetarian oyster sauce or mushroom soy sauce

1 teaspoon sugar

1 tablespoon water

In a large saucepan, cook the bitter melon in boiling salted water 2 minutes; drain and let cool.

Stem the mushrooms; finely chop 2 and thinly slice 1. Place chopped mushrooms in a small bowl and set the sliced one aside. Add the tofu, scallion greens, cilantro, ½ tablespoon cornstarch, 1 teaspoon soy sauce, wine, ½ teaspoon sesame oil, salt, and pepper to the bowl; mix well to thoroughly combine. Let stand 15 minutes to marinate at room temperature.

In a small skillet, heat ½ tablespoon peanut oil over medium heat. Add the chili pepper, black beans, and garlic; cook, stirring, until fragrant and softened, 2 to 3 minutes. Add the broth, oyster sauce, remaining 1 teaspoon soy sauce, sugar, salt, and black pepper; bring to a boil over medium-high heat. Remove from heat and set aside. In a small container, mix the remaining 1 tablespoon of cornstarch with the water until well blended; set aside.

Using a small spoon, carve out the seeds and some soft flesh in the middle of each melon slice.

Stuff each melon slice with equal amounts of the tofu mixture, forming a small dome on top.

In a large nonstick skillet with a lid, heat the remaining 1½ tablespoons of peanut oil over medium heat. Add the stuffed melon and cook 3 minutes, without stirring or turning, or until lightly browned on the underside. Add the reserved broth mixture and sliced mushroom and bring to a simmer; reduce the heat to medium-low and cook, covered, until melon and mushroom slices are tender, stirring the melon slices gently in the sauce occasionally, 5 to 10 minutes. Stir in the cornstarch mixture and remaining ½ teaspoon of sesame oil; cook, uncovered, stirring gently, until mixture is thickened, 2 to 3 minutes. Spoon some sauce over the stuffed melon. Serve at once.

{PER SERVING} Calories 175 · Protein 9g · Total Fat 10g · Sat Fat 2g · Cholesterol 0mg · Carbohydrate 14g · Dietary Fiber 4g · Sodium 806mg

Stir-Fried Chinese Okra with Chilies and Ginger

Chinese okra, also known as silk squash, is considerably longer than the Western-style variety. Serve over rice and garnish with chopped peanuts for a complete meal.

MAKES 4 SERVINGS

1½ tablespoons peanut oil
2 Chinese okras (about 10 ounces each), rough ridges peeled, cut into ⅜-inch-thick rounds
1 teaspoon finely chopped fresh ginger
2 to 3 fresh green or red chili peppers, seeded and thinly sliced
2 large cloves garlic, finely chopped
Salt, to taste
2 to 4 tablespoons water, as needed
1 tablespoon reduced-sodium soy sauce
½ tablespoon toasted (dark) sesame oil

In a wok or large nonstick skillet, heat the peanut oil over medium-high heat. Add the okra and ginger and cook, stirring, 3 minutes, or until okra is softened. Reduce the heat to medium and add the chilies, garlic, and salt; cook, stirring constantly, until okra is tender, about 3 minutes, adding water as needed, to prevent sticking. Add the soy sauce and sesame oil and cook, stirring, 1 minute, or until liquid is slightly reduced. Serve warm.

{PER SERVING} Calories 111 · Protein 3g · Total Fat 7g · Sat Fat 1g · Cholesterol 0mg · Carbohydrate 11g · Dietary Fiber 3g · Sodium 160mg

Stir-Fried Shiitake Mushrooms with Shallots in Garlic Sauce

Serve these juicy morsels on their own as an appetizer, or atop a bed of baby spinach as a warm salad. Oyster or cremini mushrooms can replace half of the shiitake variety, if desired.

MAKES 4 SERVINGS

1 tablespoon peanut oil
1 pound fresh shiitake mushrooms, stemmed, left whole if medium, halved or quartered if large
½ cup chopped shallots or red onion
6 large cloves garlic, finely chopped
2 tablespoons water or broth, plus additional, if necessary
2 tablespoons reduced-sodium soy sauce
1 teaspoon light brown sugar
Salt and freshly ground black pepper, to taste

In a large nonstick skillet, heat the oil over medium-high heat. Add the mushrooms and shallots and cook, stirring constantly, until mushrooms are softened, about 3 minutes. Add garlic and cook, stirring constantly, until mushrooms have released their liquid, about 2 minutes, adding water, if necessary, to prevent sticking. Reduce the heat to medium and add the soy sauce, sugar, salt, and pepper; cook, stirring constantly, 1 minute, or until liquid is slightly reduced. Serve warm.

{PER SERVING} Calories 87 · Protein 4g · Total Fat 4g · Sat Fat 1g · Cholesterol 0mg · Carbohydrate 12g · Dietary Fiber 2g · Sodium 308mg

Stir-Fried Fuzzy Melon with Mushrooms and Peas

Fuzzy melon, also known as hairy gourd, is a mild, refreshing squash covered with fuzz. Two medium zucchini, peeled or unpeeled, can stand in for the melon, if desired. Wood ear mushrooms have a unique jellylike texture that becomes slightly crunchy when cooked; cloud ear mushrooms, or black fungus, are interchangeable.

MAKES 4 SERVINGS

 1 tablespoon peanut oil

 2 large cloves garlic, finely chopped

 1 teaspoon finely chopped fresh ginger

 1 large fuzzy melon (about 1 pound), peeled, center core of seeds removed, thinly sliced

 ½ cup dried shredded wood ear mushrooms, soaked in hot water to cover 20 minutes, or until softened, rinsed and drained

 ½ cup frozen peas, thawed

 ¼ cup low-sodium vegetable broth

 1 tablespoon reduced-sodium soy sauce

 Salt and freshly ground black pepper, to taste

 1 teaspoon toasted (dark) sesame oil

In a wok or large nonstick skillet with a lid, heat the peanut oil over medium-high heat. Add the garlic and ginger and cook, stirring, 30 seconds, or until fragrant. Add the melon and mushrooms and cook, stirring, 2 minutes. Add the peas, broth, soy sauce, salt, and pepper and let come to a simmer; reduce heat to medium-low, cover, and simmer 2 to 3 minutes, or until vegetables are tender. Add the sesame oil, stirring well to combine. Serve warm.

{PER SERVING} Calories 79 · Protein 3g · Total Fat 5g · Sat Fat 1g · Cholesterol 0mg · Carbohydrate 7g · Dietary Fiber 3g · Sodium 206mg

Hunan-Style Sesame New Potatoes with Cumin and Chili Sauce

The largest community of Uyghurs in China outside Xinjiang Province is in south-central Hunan. Their influence upon the local cuisine is apparent in these cumin-scented potatoes, one of my favorite Chinese potato dishes, but one that's not for those with tender palates. If desired, reduce the amount of hot oil and chili paste by up to one-half.

MAKES 5 TO 6 SERVINGS

 1¼ pounds small new potatoes, unpeeled, left whole

 1 tablespoon toasted (dark) sesame oil

 1 tablespoon Chinese hot oil

 2 teaspoons whole cumin seed

 1 to 2 teaspoons sesame seeds

 ½ teaspoon coarse salt

 ¼ cup tomato ketchup

 1 tablespoon Chinese chili paste

 1 tablespoon reduced-sodium soy sauce

 1 tablespoon sugar

 1 tablespoon cider vinegar

 2 to 3 scallions, green parts only, thinly sliced

In a medium stockpot, bring the potatoes and enough salted water to cover to a boil over high heat. Reduce the heat slightly and boil until tender but not mushy, 10 to 15 minutes, depending on size. Drain and let cool slightly. (At this point, potatoes can be held up to 1 hour at room temperature before proceeding; alternatively, completely cooled potatoes can be refrigerated up to 12 hours before returning to room temperature and continuing with the recipe.)

In a wok or large nonstick skillet, heat both oils over medium-high heat. Add the potatoes, cumin, sesame seeds, and salt; cook, stirring constantly, 2 minutes. Reduce the heat to medium and add the ketchup, chili paste, soy sauce, sugar, and vinegar. Cook, stirring, until heated through, about 2 minutes. Add the scallion greens and cook, stirring, 30 seconds. Serve warm.

{PER SERVING} Calories 150 · Protein 3g · Total Fat 6g · Sat Fat 1g · Cholesterol 0mg · Carbohydrate 23g · Dietary Fiber 2g · Sodium 459mg

Hunan-Style Braised Sweet-and-Sour Pumpkin

Pumpkin is a popular vegetable throughout China, the world's largest producer of North America's beloved gourd. For a purely sweet-and-sour dish, omit the chili pepper.

MAKES 5 TO 6 SERVINGS

2 tablespoons reduced-sodium soy sauce
1 tablespoon vegetarian oyster sauce or mushroom soy sauce
1 tablespoon Chinese black vinegar or balsamic vinegar
1 tablespoon light brown sugar
1 tablespoon toasted (dark) sesame oil
1 tablespoon peanut oil

3 scallions, white and green parts separated, thinly sliced
6 cloves garlic, finely chopped
1¼ pounds cubed pumpkin or butternut squash (about 5 cups)
1 to 2 fresh red chilies, seeded and thinly sliced
¼ cup reduced-sodium vegetable broth, plus additional, as needed
Salt and freshly ground black pepper, to taste

In a small bowl, mix together the soy sauce, oyster sauce, vinegar, brown sugar, and sesame oil; set aside.

In a wok or large nonstick skillet with a lid, heat the peanut oil over medium-high heat. Add the white parts of the scallions and garlic and cook, stirring constantly, 1 minute. Add the pumpkin and chili and cook, stirring constantly, 1 minute. Add the broth, salt, and pepper; cover and reduce the heat to medium-low. Cook, stirring a few times, until pumpkin is fork-tender, 12 to 15 minutes, adding additional broth as needed to prevent sticking. Uncover and add the soy sauce mixture; cook, stirring, 2 minutes. Add the scallion greens and toss well to combine. Serve at once.

{PER SERVING} Calories 113 · Protein 3g · Total Fat 6g · Sat Fat 1g · Cholesterol 0mg · Carbohydrate 15g · Dietary Fiber 3g · Sodium 521mg

Northern-Style Chinese Stir-Fried Potatoes

In northern China's Inner Mongolia and Shanxi provinces, the potato is important not only as a staple food, but also as a source of income.

MAKES 4 TO 6 SERVINGS

1 pound small red potatoes, unpeeled, thinly sliced

1 tablespoon reduced-sodium soy sauce

1 teaspoon light brown sugar

1 teaspoon all-purpose flour

3 tablespoons peanut oil

1 cup low-sodium vegetable broth

1 teaspoon granulated sugar

¼ teaspoon salt, or to taste

Freshly ground black pepper, to taste

In a large bowl, combine potatoes, soy sauce, brown sugar, flour, and 1 tablespoon of peanut oil; stir to coat evenly. Cover and refrigerate 1 hour.

In a wok or large nonstick skillet with a lid, heat remaining 2 tablespoons of oil over medium-high heat. Add potato mixture and cook, tossing and stirring constantly, 3 minutes. Add broth, sugar, salt, and pepper, stirring well to combine. Reduce the heat to medium, cover, and cook until the potatoes are tender and have absorbed most of the liquid, about 10 minutes, stirring a few times. Serve at once.

{PER SERVING} Calories 182 · Protein 5g · Total Fat 10g · Sat Fat 2g · Cholesterol 0mg · Carbohydrate 19g · Dietary Fiber 2g · Sodium 418mg

Yunnan-Style Mashed Potatoes

Known as "old lady's potatoes" in China, these homey yet feisty potatoes get their kick from Asian chili powder, which, unlike Western-style varieties, is made entirely from dried chilies. For a more staid variation, use less chili powder or omit entirely and replace with a little paprika.

MAKES 4 SERVINGS

1 pound medium boiling potatoes (about 4), peeled and quartered

2 tablespoons peanut oil

4 scallions, white and green parts, thinly sliced

1 to 2 teaspoons Asian chili powder, or to taste

½ teaspoon coarse salt, plus additional, to serve

Freshly ground black pepper, to taste

In a large saucepan, bring the potatoes and salted water to cover to a boil over high heat. Reduce the heat slightly and boil until potatoes are tender but not mushy, 15 to 20 minutes. Drain and let cool slightly. When cool enough to handle, transfer potatoes to a cutting board and coarsely chop. (At this point, potatoes can be held at room temperature up to 30 minutes before continuing with the recipe.)

In a wok or large nonstick skillet, heat the peanut oil over medium-high heat. Add the scallions and chili powder and cook, stirring constantly, 1 minute. Add the potatoes and salt and stir well to thoroughly combine. With the back of a spatula or large wooden spoon, spread and flatten the potato mixture along the bottom, cutting with the edge of the spatula or spoon, and cook without stirring 1 minute. Stir and repeat a few times, or until potatoes are mashed but still chunky. Season with additional salt, if desired, and pepper. Serve at once.

{PER SERVING} Calories 139 · Protein 2g · Total Fat 7g · Sat Fat 1g · Cholesterol 0mg · Carbohydrate 18g · Dietary Fiber 3g · Sodium 262mg

Braised Chinese Spinach with Vegetarian Oyster Sauce

Swiss chard or regular spinach can replace the Chinese spinach, if desired. In this instance, tear the leaves into bite-size pieces.

MAKES 4 SERVINGS

1 tablespoon peanut oil

2 large cloves garlic, finely chopped

1 pound Chinese spinach, tough ends trimmed, leaves picked and left whole, stems cut into bite-size pieces

2 tablespoons vegetarian oyster sauce or mushroom soy sauce

2 teaspoons sugar

Salt and freshly ground black pepper, to taste

2 teaspoons cornstarch mixed with 2 tablespoons water

In a wok or large nonstick skillet, heat the oil over medium heat. Add the garlic and cook, stirring constantly, 1 minute. Add the spinach and toss until leaves are wilted, 1 to 2 minutes. Add oyster sauce, sugar, salt, and pepper and toss to combine. Cook, covered, until stems are tender, 1 to 2 minutes. Reduce the heat to medium-low and add the cornstarch mixture; cook, stirring, until thickened, 1 to 2 minutes. Serve at once.

{PER SERVING} Calories 75 · Protein 4g · Total Fat 4g · Sat Fat 1g · Cholesterol 0mg · Carbohydrate 9g · Dietary Fiber 3g · Sodium 390mg

Shanghai-Style Sugar Snap Peas

Shanghainese savory dishes have a penchant for sweetness—the following recipe is almost better than dessert. Snow peas can replace the sugar snap variety, if desired; in this instance, reduce the initial cooking time by about 1 minute.

MAKES 4 TO 6 SERVINGS

1 tablespoon peanut oil

1 pound sugar snap peas, trimmed

1 large clove garlic, finely chopped

2 tablespoons reduced-sodium soy sauce

1 tablespoon plain rice vinegar

1 tablespoon water

1 tablespoon brown sugar

½ tablespoon toasted (dark) sesame oil

Salt and freshly ground black pepper, to taste

Toasted sesame seeds (optional)

In a wok or large nonstick skillet, heat the peanut oil over medium-high heat. Add the snap peas and cook, stirring, until just softened, about 2 minutes. Add the garlic and cook, stirring constantly, 30 seconds. Reduce the heat to medium and add the remaining ingredients except the optional sesame seeds; cook, stirring, about 2 minutes, or until snap peas are crisp-tender and liquid is slightly reduced. Serve at once, sprinkled with the toasted sesame seeds, if using.

{PER SERVING} Calories 99 · Protein 3g · Total Fat 5g · Sat Fat 1g · Cholesterol 0mg · Carbohydrate 13g · Dietary Fiber 4g · Sodium 308mg

Hunan-Style Taro with Chilies and Fermented Black Beans

Taro root is a popular side dish in Hunan. Peel the taro with a vegetable peeler under running water to avoid any skin sensitivity to its sticky juices. Duo jiao, a fiery Hunan pepper sauce consisting of chopped red chilies pickled in brine, has a distinctive salty and sour taste; it is available in Asian markets. Chinese chili paste, a milder hot sauce flavored with garlic, can be substituted; in this instance, add it to the wok along with the sesame oil.

MAKES 4 TO 6 SERVINGS

1¼ pounds taro root, peeled, cut into
    ½-inch pieces
1 tablespoon peanut oil
1 to 2 teaspoons Hunan pepper sauce (duo
    jiao)
1 teaspoon rinsed and drained fermented
    black beans, crushed
2 cloves garlic, finely chopped
¼ cup low-sodium vegetable broth
½ tablespoon toasted (dark) sesame oil
Salt and freshly ground black pepper, to taste

Bring a large saucepan filled with water to a boil over high heat. Add the taro and reduce the heat to medium-high; cook until just tender, about 15 minutes. Drain and set aside.

In a wok or large nonstick skillet, heat the peanut oil over medium-high heat. Add the hot pepper sauce, black beans, and garlic and cook, stirring constantly, until fragrant, about 1 minute. Reduce the heat to medium and add the taro, broth, sesame oil, salt, and pepper; cook, stirring constantly, until taro has absorbed the broth, about 3 minutes. Serve warm.

{PER SERVING} Calories 173 · Protein 3g · Total Fat 5g · Sat Fat 1g · Cholesterol 0mg · Carbohydrate 31g · Dietary Fiber 5g · Sodium 55mg

Stir-Fried Zucchini with Shiitakes and Tomato, Shanghai-Style

This flavorful, mildly spiced side dish is always a hit with company.

MAKES 4 SERVINGS

½ cup reduced-sodium vegetable broth
3 tablespoons ketchup
2 teaspoons reduced-sodium soy sauce
2 teaspoons Chinese black vinegar or
    balsamic vinegar
1 teaspoon Shaoxing rice wine, dry sherry,
    sake, or dry white wine
1 teaspoon cornstarch
¼ teaspoon sugar
⅛ teaspoon salt, plus additional, to taste
1 tablespoon peanut oil
3 cloves garlic, finely chopped
½ tablespoon finely chopped fresh ginger
1 cup sliced fresh shiitake mushroom caps
1 small onion (about 4 ounces), coarsely
    chopped
1 pound zucchini (about 2 medium), sliced
    crosswise into ½-inch-thick pieces
1 large tomato (about 8 ounces), peeled,
    seeded, and chopped (see Cook's Tip,
    page 112)
2 scallions, thinly sliced
½ tablespoon toasted (dark) sesame oil
Freshly ground black pepper, to taste

In a small bowl, combine broth, ketchup, soy sauce, vinegar, wine, cornstarch, sugar, and salt in a small bowl; set aside.

In a wok or large nonstick skillet with a lid, heat peanut oil over medium-high heat. Add garlic and ginger and cook, stirring constantly, 30 seconds, or until fragrant. Add mushrooms and onion and cook, stirring, 1 minute. Add zucchini and tomato and cook, stirring, 1 minute. Add broth mixture and bring to a brisk simmer, stirring; reduce the heat to medium-low and simmer, covered, stirring occasionally, until zucchini is tender and liquid is thickened and reduced, about 10 minutes. Add the scallions, sesame oil, and pepper; cook, stirring, 1 minute. Season with additional salt and pepper, as needed. Serve at once.

{PER SERVING} Calories 119 · Protein 5g · Total Fat 6g · Sat Fat 1g · Cholesterol 0mg · Carbohydrate 15g · Dietary Fiber 4g · Sodium 377mg

CHAPTER EIGHT

Desserts and Other Sweets

In the Western world, desserts tend to carry a ton of weight, either as decadent concoctions representing the chef's grand finale or sweet rewards for cleaning the dinner plate. Not so in China. Rather than indulging in a fancy dessert after the evening meal, the Chinese prefer to eat fruit, usually in its fresh and natural state. It's not that the Chinese don't have a sweet tooth—far from it. In fact, to many Western palates, some of the traditional Chinese desserts that do exist are overly sweet. However, the Chinese normally prefer to indulge their cravings for sweets between meals, especially when entertaining company or celebrating special occasions and festivals. That desserts don't figure more prominently in Chinese cuisine is largely a practical matter, as well. For one, most households lack ovens and, until recently, even refrigerators. For another, the quick turnover in most Chinese restaurants is largely dependent upon a repertoire of quick-cooking, stir-fried dishes—the lengthy preparation of complicated desserts would invariably tie up the kitchen. Instead, households and restaurants alike prefer to leave the job of elaborate desserts and pastries to bakeries, of which there are many. Of course, you can always follow Chinese tradition and conclude your evening meal with a piece of fruit. Or, you can occasionally break with tradition and indulge in the following delicious desserts with no regrets—it's all good!

Sweet Rice Sesame-Peanut Dumplings with Coconut

Soft and chewy on the outside, sweet and crunchy on the inside, these delightful dumplings are best served shortly after steaming. For easy entertaining, the raw dumplings can be refrigerated up to 24 hours before steaming and rolling in the coconut. Make sure you purchase glutinous rice flour, also known as sweet rice flour, and not regular rice flour; the former is made from short-grain sticky rice, which creates the essential chewiness of the dumplings.

MAKES 12 DUMPLINGS

- ¼ cup chopped unsalted roasted peanuts
- 3 tablespoons dark brown sugar
- 2 tablespoons toasted sesame seeds
- 3 cups glutinous rice flour
- ⅔ cup boiling water
- ½ cup plus 2 tablespoons cold water (10 tablespoons)
- ½ cup shredded sweetened coconut, or more, as needed
- 6 candied cherries or citron, halved (optional)

In a small bowl, combine the peanuts, sugar, and sesame seeds; set aside. In a medium bowl, combine the rice flour and boiling water, mixing until thoroughly combined. Add the cold water and mix until the dough forms a ball. Turn the dough out onto a lightly floured work surface and knead until smooth, about 5 minutes. Cover with a damp towel and let rest 10 minutes.

Shape the dough into a long cylinder and cut into 12 equal pieces. Cover with the damp towel.

Roll each piece of dough into a 3½-inch circle, recovering as you finish to prevent from drying out. Place 2 teaspoons of the peanut-sesame mixture in the center of each circle; wrap up to form a smooth ball, pinching the edges of the dough together to seal. Re-cover with the damp towel. (At this point, the prepared dumplings can be covered in plastic wrap and refrigerated up to 24 hours before continuing with the recipe. For best results, store seam sides up, to prevent leakage of filling.)

Place a steaming basket in a medium stockpot set over about 1½ inches of water. Line the basket with aluminum foil and spray lightly with cooking oil. Working in batches, if necessary, place the dumplings in a single layer in the steaming basket, away from the edge, leaving about ½-inch space between each dumpling. Bring to boil over high heat; reduce heat to medium, cover tightly, and steam 10 minutes (add a few extra minutes if refrigerated). Remove pot from the heat and leave partially covered for 5 minutes.

Place the coconut in a small bowl. Working with one at time, using oiled tongs (dumplings will be sticky), remove a dumpling from the steaming basket and immediately roll in the coconut. Garnish each with half a candied cherry, if using. Serve at once, or return to the steamer basket (off the heat), cover, and hold up to 1 hour.

{PER SERVING} (per dumpling, or ½₂ of recipe) Calories 181 · Protein 3g · Total Fat 3g · Sat Fat 1g · Cholesterol 0mg · Carbohydrate 35g · Dietary Fiber 1g · Sodium 8mg

Stuffed Apples with Sticky Rice and Dried Fruits

Without the sauce, this wholesome and delicious dessert can also double as breakfast—yum!

MAKES 4 SERVINGS

About ¼ cup glutinous (sticky) rice

4 medium apples, preferably Fuji or other sweet, crisp variety (about 6 ounces each)

6 tablespoons dark brown sugar

4 pitted dried red dates (jujubes), chopped

4 walnuts, chopped

2 tablespoons raisins

¼ teaspoon ground cinnamon

1 cup apple juice

2 tablespoons cornstarch mixed with 2 tablespoons water

Chopped crystallized ginger (optional)

Bring a large saucepan filled halfway with water to a boil over high heat. Add the rice, reduce the heat slightly, and boil about 12 minutes, stirring occasionally, or until rice is tender but still chewy. Drain in a colander and let cool to room temperature (you will need ½ cup).

Meanwhile, slice off the tops of the apples about a quarter of the way from the top; reserve the tops. Using a melon baller, scoop out the core of each apple to remove all of the seeds. Scoop out about half of the remaining flesh and reserve. Finely chop the reserved flesh and transfer to a medium bowl; add ½ cup rice (reserve any extra for another use), 4 tablespoons sugar, dates, walnuts, raisins, and cinnamon, mixing to thoroughly combine. Fill the apples with equal amounts of the rice mixture. Replace the tops and fasten with toothpicks.

Place the apples in a steaming basket set over about 2 inches of water; bring to a boil over high heat. Reduce the heat to medium, cover, and steam about 15 minutes, or until apples are fork-tender but not mushy. Carefully remove apples from steaming basket and transfer to individual serving bowls or deep-welled plates. (At this point, apples can be served warm or at room temperature, without the sauce, if desired. Alternatively, completely cooled apples can be covered and refrigerated up to 2 days before serving chilled or returning to room temperature, without sauce. If serving with sauce, proceed with recipe while apples are still warm.)

Meanwhile, in a small saucepan, bring apple juice and remaining 2 tablespoons sugar to a boil over high heat. Reduce the heat to low and add the cornstarch mixture; cook, stirring constantly, until thickened, about 3 minutes. To serve, remove toothpick and pour equal amounts of the sauce over the apples and sprinkle with the crystallized ginger, if using. Serve at once.

{PER SERVING} Calories 248 · Protein 2g · Total Fat 3g · Sat Fat 0g · Cholesterol 0mg · Carbohydrate 56g · Dietary Fiber 5g · Sodium 4mg

Green Apples Steamed with Sweet Red Bean Paste

The Chinese have instinctively always known what recent studies have confirmed—an apple a day really does keep the doctor away, sustaining and protecting the body from head to toe, inside and out. China produces approximately one-third of all the apples on the planet—typically eaten out of hand as snacks, on special occasions they are plated and dressed up as desserts. Feel free to experiment with your favorite fillings.

MAKES 4 SERVINGS

>   6 tablespoons prepared sweet red bean (adzuki) paste or Sweet Red Bean Paste (page 182)
>   2 tablespoons finely chopped crystallized ginger
>   4 large Granny Smith apples (7 to 8 ounces each), unpeeled

In a small bowl, combine the red bean paste and ginger; set aside.

Slice off the tops of the apples about a quarter of the way from the top. Using a melon baller, scoop out the core of the apple to remove all of the seeds and create a cavity for the bean paste mixture. Fill the cored apples with equal amounts (about 2½ tablespoons) of the bean paste mixture. Replace the apple tops to cover; secure each with a toothpick.

Place the apples in a steaming basket set over about 2 inches of water; bring to a boil over medium-high heat. Reduce the heat to medium, cover, and steam about 15 minutes, or until fork-tender but not mushy. Carefully remove from steaming basket and transfer to individual serving plates or bowls. Remove toothpicks and serve warm or at room temperature. Alternatively, refrigerate completely cooled apples up to 2 days and serve chilled, or return to room temperature.

{PER SERVING} Calories 168 · Protein 3g · Total Fat 0g · Sat Fat 0g · Cholesterol 0mg · Carbohydrate 36g · Dietary Fiber 4g · Sodium 9mg

Coconut Jam

Kaya is a coconut jam highly popular in Singapore, Malaysia, and the tropical Chinese island of Hainan. Typically made with eggs, this scrumptious vegan variation uses canned pumpkin puree instead. Spread on breads (peanut butter and coconut jam sandwiches are yummy), stir into plain soy yogurt, or spoon over nondairy ice cream for a delightful taste sensation. Pandan leaves are available in Asian markets; if you can't locate them, omit from the recipe and stir in $\frac{1}{16}$ teaspoon of pandan essence or pure vanilla extract along with the other ingredients.

MAKES ABOUT 1½ CUPS

>   1 (15-ounce) can pumpkin puree (1¾ cups)
>   ¾ cup cream of coconut, such as Coco Lopez
>   ½ cup packed dark brown sugar
>   2 pandan leaves, tied in a knot

In a medium saucepan, combine all ingredients; bring to a simmer over medium heat, stirring occasionally. Reduce the heat to between low and medium-low and cook, stirring often, until mixture is thickened and smooth, 45 minutes to 1 hour. Remove and discard pandan leaves. Let cool to room temperature before serving. Mixture can be refrigerated, tightly covered, up to 2 weeks. Serve chilled or return to room temperature.

{PER SERVING} (per tablespoon, or ½₄ of recipe) Calories 60 · Protein 0g · Total Fat 1g · Sat Fat 0g · Cholesterol 0mg · Carbohydrate 13g · Dietary Fiber 1g · Sodium 3mg

Banana-Tofu Pudding

This protein-packed, calcium-rich dessert makes a wonderful after-school snack.

MAKES 6 SERVINGS

12 ounces soft tofu, drained

1 large ripe banana, quartered

½ cup cream of coconut, such as Coco Lopez

14 pitted dried red dates (jujubes), soaked in hot water to cover 30 minutes, or until very soft, drained

2 tablespoons dark brown sugar

¼ teaspoon ground ginger

¼ teaspoon ground cinnamon

Place tofu, banana, cream of coconut, 8 dates, sugar, ginger, and cinnamon in a food processor fitted with the knife blade, or a blender. Process or blend until smooth. Transfer to 6 small bowls and refrigerate, uncovered, 1 hour. Alternatively, cover and refrigerate up to 24 hours. Serve chilled, garnished with a date.

{PER SERVING} Calories 174 · Protein 5g · Total Fat 6g · Sat Fat 0g · Cholesterol 0mg · Carbohydrate 27g · Dietary Fiber 2g · Sodium 13mg

Caramel Bananas

The Chinese are crazy about caramel—so am I. For a fabulous taste sensation, serve with vanilla soy ice cream.

MAKES 6 LARGE OR 12 SMALL SERVINGS

½ cup packed dark brown sugar

½ cup granulated white sugar

⅓ cup light corn syrup

⅓ cup water

¼ teaspoon salt

6 ripe yet firm medium bananas, peeled and quartered crosswise

Chopped crystallized ginger or chopped roasted peanuts, for garnish (optional)

In a small heavy-bottomed, deep-sided skillet (about 7 inches in diameter), combine the sugars, corn syrup, water, and salt. Bring to a boil over medium heat, stirring occasionally until the sugar is dissolved. Boil without stirring until reduced to 1 cup, 4 to 5 minutes. Remove from heat. Let cool to room temperature. (At this point, mixture can be refrigerated, covered, several days before returning to room temperature and proceeding with the recipe. If using as a dip, keep chilled, as mixture will be thicker.)

To serve individually: Divide bananas equally among 6 serving bowls or deep-welled serving plates and top with equal amounts of the caramel. Sprinkle with the ginger or peanuts, if using. Serve at once.

To serve as a dip: In a small bowl, add the chilled caramel and place in the center of a serving platter. Surround with the bananas and serve at once, with the optional garnishes offered separately.

{PER SERVING} Calories 318 · Protein 1g · Total Fat 1g · Sat Fat 0g · Cholesterol 0mg · Carbohydrate 82g · Dietary Fiber 3g · Sodium 103mg

{VARIATION}

To make Caramel Apples, replace the bananas with 6 medium or 4 large Fuji or other crisp red apples, unpeeled, cut into eighths. Prepare as directed in the recipe.

Garnish with toasted sesame seeds, or other suggested garnishes, if desired. If serving as a dip, rub the cut apple sections with fresh lemon juice to prevent discoloration before serving, if desired.

Chinese Five-Spice Fruit Salad

Much of the fruit I consumed in China, especially the peaches, seemed sweeter and juicier than the fruit I remembered eating back home— perhaps it was my mind playing tricks on my senses, intensifying the familiar to help me feel at home. In any case, the fruit was fabulous—feel free to substitute with your favorites.

MAKES 4 TO 6 SERVINGS

3 tablespoons sugar
¼ teaspoon almond extract
¼ teaspoon five-spice powder
1 banana, peeled and sliced
1 cup mango slices, fresh or canned
2 kiwifruit, peeled and thinly sliced
1 large peach, peeled and thinly sliced
4 large strawberries, hulled and halved
½ tablespoon cider vinegar

Mix together the sugar and almond extract. Stir in the five-spice powder. Set aside.

In a large bowl, combine the fruit and sprinkle with the vinegar; toss gently. Sprinkle with half the sugar mixture and toss gently. Sprinkle with remaining sugar mixture and toss gently. Cover and refrigerate a minimum of 1 hour or overnight and serve chilled, tossing gently before serving.

{PER SERVING} Calories 171 · Protein 2g · Total Fat 1g · Sat Fat 0g · Cholesterol 0mg · Carbohydrate 43g · Dietary Fiber 7g · Sodium 5mg

Chocolate-Noodle Cookies

I am not quite sure how authentically Chinese these crunchy no-bake refrigerator cookies are, but they're definitely delicious with a cup of hot coffee or tea.

MAKES ABOUT 2 DOZEN COOKIES

8 ounces bittersweet baking chocolate
⅔ cup light coconut milk
1 cup crisp chow mein noodles
¼ cup sweetened shredded coconut (optional)

Line 1 large or 2 medium baking sheets with parchment or waxed paper and set aside.

Place the chocolate in the top of a double boiler set over barely simmering water. Heat, stirring occasionally, until completely melted. Stir in the coconut milk until thoroughly blended. Stir in the chow mein noodles until well combined. Drop by the heaping teaspoonfuls onto the prepared baking sheet. Sprinkle evenly with the shredded coconut, if using. Refrigerate 30 minutes, or until set. Serve chilled. Cookies can be stored, covered, in refrigerator up to 5 days.

{PER SERVING} (per cookie) Calories 68 · Protein 1g · Total Fat 7g · Sat Fat 4g · Cholesterol 0mg · Carbohydrate 4g · Dietary Fiber 2g · Sodium 12mg

Chinese Fruit and Nut Balls

These delectable little balls are a must with a cup of Chinese tea. Feel free to vary the mix of fruit, so long as dates predominate—try to select a moist, sweet variety, such as deglet noor or Medjool.

MAKES 64 TINY BALLS

About ½ cup confectioner's sugar (optional)
¼ cup cake flour
1 tablespoon sugar
¾ teaspoon baking powder
⅛ teaspoon salt
1 cup finely chopped walnuts
¾ cup finely chopped pitted brown dates
2 tablespoons finely chopped dried
    pineapple
1 tablespoon finely chopped candied orange
    peel
1 tablespoon finely chopped crystallized
    ginger
¼ cup water

Preheat oven to 350F (175C). Line an 8-inch-square baking dish with parchment or wax paper and set aside. Place the confectioner's sugar, if using, in a small bowl and set aside.

In a medium bowl, using a wire whisk, mix together the flour, sugar, baking powder, and salt until thoroughly blended. Add the walnuts, dates, pineapple, orange peel, and ginger, stirring well to combine. Slowly add the water, mixing until a soft dough is formed. Spread the dough evenly in the prepared baking dish. Bake in the center of the oven until firm, 20 to 25 minutes.

While still warm, cut the baked dough into 1-inch squares. While still warm, remove the squares and, using your hands, roll into balls; let cool to room temperature. Working in batches, roll the cooled balls in the confectioner's sugar, if using. Serve at room temperature. Completely cooled balls can be stored in an airtight container up to 1 week, or refrigerated up to 2 weeks.

{PER SERVING} (per 4 balls, or 1/16 of recipe) Calories 85 · Protein 2g · Total Fat 5g · Sat Fat 0g · Cholesterol 0mg · Carbohydrate 10g · Dietary Fiber 1g · Sodium 36mg

Chocolate-Ginger Litchis

Whole peeled, canned litchis make quick work of this elegant dessert, ideal for stress-free entertaining, as it can be prepared 24 hours ahead of serving.

MAKES 6 TO 8 SERVINGS (18 TO 24 PIECES)

1 (20-ounce) can whole peeled seedless
    litchis, drained
2 ounces crystallized ginger or candied
    cherries, slivered
6 ounces bittersweet chocolate, broken into
    small pieces
1 tablespoon vegetable shortening

Arrange litchis, round sides up, between several layers of paper towels. Let stand at room temperature about 1 hour, or until dry. Line a baking sheet with wax paper and set aside.

Stuff equal amounts of the ginger inside the cavity of each litchi.

In the top of a double-boiler set over simmering water, combine the chocolate and shortening. Cook, stirring constantly, until chocolate is melted. Remove top of double boiler from the heat and set aside to cool slightly, about 5 minutes.

Working in batches, carefully dip litchis, stuffed sides up, in the melted chocolate. Carefully lift the litchis out of the chocolate and place on the prepared baking sheet. When finished, drizzle litchis evenly with any remaining chocolate. Refrigerate, uncovered, until chocolate coating is chilled and set, about 1 hour. If not serving immediately, cover loosely with plastic wrap and store in the refrigerator up to 24 hours. Serve chilled.

{PER SERVING} (⅙ of recipe) Calories 274 · Protein 3g · Total Fat 18g · Sat Fat 10g · Cholesterol 0mg · Carbohydrate 27g · Dietary Fiber 5g · Sodium 11mg

Watermelon Bowl with 12 Fruits

Inspired by the offertory gifts of melons, mangoes, and apples at the Pentecost Sunday Mass in Changsha's Roman Catholic Church on June 12, 2011, this celebratory salad contains 9 more fruits, for a grand total of no less than 12. Each fruit represents, in my mind, the 12 fruits of the Holy Spirit—love, joy, peace, patience, kindness, goodness, forbearance, gentleness, faith, modesty, self-control, and purity—which I witnessed everywhere I went in China. Feel free to use whatever fresh fruits are in season for the filling—but in keeping with the "spirit" of the salad, try to use 12!

MAKES 12 SERVINGS

2 cups water

1 cup rock sugar (yellow or clear) or ¾ cup granulated sugar

¼ cup mango juice, fresh or canned, or apple juice

1 large oblong-shaped seedless watermelon (8 to 10 pounds)

1 cup cubed or balled cantaloupe

1 cup cubed or balled honeydew melon

1 cup mandarin orange segments (from about 2 oranges)

1 cup cubed pineapple

1 cup cubed mango

1 cup cubed papaya

1 cup cubed dragon fruit

1 cup fresh or canned peeled seedless litchi or longan halves

1 banana, peeled and thinly sliced

1 kiwifruit, peeled, quartered, and thinly sliced

1 apple, cored and chopped

In a medium saucepan, bring the water, rock sugar, and mango juice to a gentle boil over medium heat, stirring to dissolve the sugar. Boil gently until reduced to about 1½ cups, 12 to 15 minutes, stirring occasionally. Remove from heat and let cool to room temperature.

With a large, sharp knife, remove the top ¼ section of the watermelon. With a melon baller, scoop flesh from inside of watermelon, leaving about ½ inch of flesh inside the shell of the watermelon. Place 1 cup of the watermelon flesh in a large bowl and add the 11 other fruits. Reserve the remaining watermelon flesh for another use (if necessary, add more to fill up watermelon "bowl").

Add the cooled sugar syrup to the 12 fruits, tossing gently yet thoroughly to combine. Transfer to the prepared watermelon shell. Cover with plastic wrap and refrigerate a minimum of 1 hour, or overnight, and serve chilled.

{PER SERVING} Calories 130 · Protein 1g · Total Fat 1g · Sat Fat 0g · Cholesterol 0mg · Carbohydrate 33g · Dietary Fiber 2g · Sodium 5mg

Hainan-Style Sweet Mung Bean Soup

Grown in China for more than 5,000 years, mung beans are valued in Chinese medicine for their cleansing and detoxifying properties. Sweet mung bean soup is especially popular during the hot summer months, when it is consumed to prevent heat-related illnesses. On the tropical island of Hainan, this cooling and refreshing version is often prepared with the addition of coconut milk. Pandan leaves are available in Asian markets; if you can't locate them, omit from the recipe and stir in $\frac{1}{16}$ teaspoon of pandan essence or pure vanilla extract along with the coconut milk and sugar.

MAKES 4 TO 6 SERVINGS

6 cups water, plus additional, as needed
1 cup dried mung beans, rinsed and picked over, soaked overnight in water to cover by several inches, drained
2 pandan leaves, tied in a knot
1 cup unsweetened light or regular coconut milk
$\frac{2}{3}$ cup packed light brown sugar, or to taste

In a large stockpot, bring the water, mung beans, and pandan leaves to a boil over high heat. Reduce the heat to medium-low and simmer, partially covered, until beans have split open and are tender, about 45 minutes, stirring occasionally and adding water, if necessary. Add the coconut milk and sugar and cook, stirring, 5 minutes. For a thicker soup, simmer, uncovered, stirring occasionally, until desired consistency is achieved. Serve warm or at room temperature. Alternatively, completely cooled soup can be refrigerated, covered, up to 5 days and served chilled.

{PER SERVING} Calories 252 · Protein 10g · Total Fat 4g · Sat Fat 3g · Cholesterol 0mg · Carbohydrate 47g · Dietary Fiber 6g · Sodium 31mg

Green Tea Soy Ice Cream with Sweet Red Bean Paste

While vanilla soy ice cream is equally delicious here, the green tea variety provides a picture-perfect contrast to the red-hued topping. In a pinch, canned sweet red bean paste, available in Asian markets and some well-stocked supermarkets, can be used in lieu of a homemade batch, below.

MAKES 4 SERVINGS

1 pint green tea soy ice cream
$\frac{1}{2}$ cup Sweet Red Bean Paste, below, or prepared canned sweet red bean paste
Chopped crystallized ginger, for garnish (optional)
Chopped roasted peanuts, for garnish (optional)

Place $\frac{1}{2}$ cup soy ice cream in each of 4 small serving bowls. Top with 2 tablespoons Sweet Red Bean Paste. Sprinkle with the optional garnishes, if using. Serve at once.

{PER SERVING} Calories 203 · Protein 5g · Total Fat 4g · Sat Fat 1g · Cholesterol 0mg · Carbohydrate 38g · Dietary Fiber 2g · Sodium 63mg

SWEET RED BEAN PASTE

Use this recipe wherever sweet red bean paste is called for in this book. Though optional, the peanut oil lends it a smoother consistency and glossier sheen. For a less sweet paste, reduce the sugar by up to one-half.

MAKES ABOUT 2 CUPS

> 1 cup dried red beans (adzuki), picked over, rinsed, and drained
> 6 cups water, plus additional, as needed
> 1 cup granulated sugar, or less, to taste
> 1 to 2 tablespoons peanut or canola oil (optional)
> Pinch salt

Place the beans in a medium stockpot and cover with water; bring to a boil over high heat. Drain in a colander, discarding the water. Rinse, drain again, and return the beans to the pot; add the 6 cups of water and bring to a boil over high heat. Reduce the heat to medium, cover, and simmer until the beans are soft and tender and most of the water has been absorbed, 1 to 1½ hours, stirring occasionally and adding water as needed to prevent scorching.

Reduce the heat to low and add the sugar, peanut oil (if using), and salt. Cook, stirring, until sugar is dissolved. Raise heat to medium-low and cook, stirring often, until mixture is thickened and glossy, with both whole and half-crushed beans, 3 to 5 minutes. Remove from heat and let cool to room temperature before using as directed in the recipe. Completely cooled paste can be refrigerated, covered, up to 1 week.

{PER SERVING} (per about 2 tablespoons, or 1/16 of recipe, without oil) Calories 89 · Protein 3g · Total Fat 0g · Sat Fat 0g · Cholesterol 0mg · Carbohydrate 20g · Dietary Fiber 2g · Sodium 1mg

Litchi and Fresh Fruit Salad with Orange

Canned litchis make quick work of this easy yet elegant salad, a light and refreshing conclusion to a special meal. While you can vary the fresh fruits according to the season—for instance, strawberries can replace the cherries—try to include kiwifruit, the national fruit of China, to where it is native. Chinese marmalade, typically made from kumquats, is available in Asian markets.

MAKES 4 TO 6 SERVINGS

> 2 tablespoons orange juice, preferably freshly squeezed
> 2 tablespoons orange marmalade, preferably a Chinese variety, at room temperature
> 1 tablespoon Grand Marnier or other orange liqueur, or brandy (optional)
> ½ tablespoon light brown sugar
> 1 (10-ounce) can whole peeled seedless litchis, drained
> 2 cups fresh cubed pineapple
> 2 kiwifruit, peeled and thinly sliced
> 1 cup pitted Queen Anne cherries or white cherries, halved (optional)

In a large bowl, combine the orange juice, marmalade, liqueur (if using), and sugar, stirring until marmalade is dissolved. Add the remaining ingredients, tossing gently yet thoroughly to combine. Serve at once, or cover and refrigerate a minimum of 1 to 24 hours, and serve chilled.

{PER SERVING} Calories 155 · Protein 1g · Total Fat 1g · Sat Fat 0g · Cholesterol 0mg · Carbohydrate 40g · Dietary Fiber 3g · Sodium 10mg

Steamed Peaches in Syrup

This refreshing summertime dessert is ideal for relaxed entertaining, as it can be prepared a day ahead of serving.

MAKES 4 TO 6 SERVINGS

4 medium ripe yet firm peaches (about
    6 ounces each), halved and pitted
1 cup water
3 tablespoons white sugar
1 tablespoon brown sugar
Chopped fresh mint, for garnish (optional)

Place the peaches in a steaming basket set over about 2 inches of water; bring to a boil over medium-high heat. Reduce the heat to medium, cover, and steam about 10 minutes, or until fork-tender but not mushy. Peel and cut each in half again. Transfer to a serving bowl and let cool to room temperature.

In a small saucepan, bring the water and sugars to a brisk simmer over medium heat, stirring until the sugar dissolves. Reduce the heat slightly and simmer until the mixture is reduced to about ¾ cup, stirring occasionally. Set aside to cool to room temperature.

Pour the syrup over the peaches and toss gently to combine. Serve at room temperature, garnished with the mint, if desired. Alternatively, cover and refrigerate a minimum of 2 hours or up to 1 day and serve chilled, or return to room temperature.

{PER SERVING} Calories 105 · Protein 1g · Total Fat 0g · Sat Fat 0g · Cholesterol 0mg · Carbohydrate 27g · Dietary Fiber 3g · Sodium 1mg

Persimmon Cakes

These tasty little treats are sold throughout Xi'an's popular Muslim market. The softer, sweeter pulp from the fully ripened, acorn-shaped Hachiya variety of persimmon is required here—you will probably need about 2 large persimmons. If unavailable, substitute with canned pumpkin puree and see the Variation, below. Dried jasmine or chamomile flowers (or any other dried flower commonly used in herbal teas) can replace the sweet-scented osmanthus flowers, available in Chinese herbal medicine stores and Asian markets. Make sure you use glutinous rice flour, also known as sweet rice flour, and not regular rice flour; the former is made from short-grain sticky rice, which creates the essential chewiness of the cakes. Though not traditional, powdered sugar lends a festive touch.

MAKES 20 PIECES

1½ cups glutinous rice flour, plus
    additional, if necessary
⅓ cup all-purpose flour
¼ cup sugar
¾ cup persimmon pulp
1 tablespoon dried osmanthus flowers
6 to 8 tablespoons hot water, plus
    additional, if necessary
Peanut oil, for frying
Confectioner's sugar (optional)

Line a large baking sheet with several layers of paper towels and set aside.

In a medium bowl, mix together the rice flour, wheat flour, and sugar until well combined. Add the persimmon pulp and osmanthus, mixing until thoroughly blended (mixture will resemble coarse meal). Add hot water a few tablespoons at a time, kneading after each addition (add an extra table-spoon, or more, of hot water if dough seems too dry; this will depend largely on how much moisture is in the persimmon pulp; alternatively, add a bit more rice flour if mixture is too moist). Turn dough out onto a lightly floured work surface and knead until smooth, about 5 minutes. Form dough into a ball and return to bowl; cover with a damp kitchen towel and let rest 10 minutes.

Divide dough in half. Form each half into 10 balls about 1½ inches in diameter, for a total of 20 balls. Flatten each ball with your palm into a tiny cake about 2 inches in diameter and ½ inch in thickness. (At this point, cakes can be covered with plastic wrap and refrigerated up to 24 hours before continuing with the recipe.)

In a small heavy-bottomed, deep-sided skillet, heat about ½ inch of oil over medium heat. When a small piece of dough can sizzle (after about 5 minutes of preheating), reduce the heat to medium-low and add 4 or 5 cakes. Cook until golden and swollen, about 2 minutes per side. Transfer to prepared baking sheet to drain. Repeat with remaining cakes. Serve at once, sprinkled with confectioner's sugar, if using.

{PER SERVING} (per 1 cake, or 1/20 of recipe) Calories 90 • Protein 1g • Total Fat 3g • Sat Fat 1g • Cholesterol 0mg • Carbohydrate 15g • Dietary Fiber 1g • Sodium 0mg

{VARIATION}

To make Pumpkin Cakes, replace the persimmon pulp with ¾ cup canned pumpkin puree and increase the sugar by 2 tablespoons. Omit the osmanthus flowers and proceed as otherwise directed in the recipe.

Black Glutinous Rice Pudding

Black rice comes in both long-grain and glutinous form. Make sure you select the latter for this exotic, luxurious rice pudding. Pandan leaves are available in Asian markets; if you can't locate them, omit from the recipe and stir in ¹⁄₁₆ teaspoon of pandan essence or pure vanilla extract just before adding the cooked rice.

MAKES 6 TO 8 SERVINGS

1 cup black glutinous (sticky) rice
1⅓ cups water
⅔ cup sugar
1 pandan leaf, tied in a knot
1 cup regular coconut milk
1 cup light coconut milk
¼ teaspoon salt

Bring a large stockpot filled halfway with salted water to a boil over high heat; add the rice and reduce the heat slightly. Cook, stirring occasionally, until just tender, 30 to 35 minutes. Drain well in a colander (do not rinse).

In a large saucepan, bring the water, sugar, and pandan leaf to a boil over medium-high heat Add coconut milks and salt and let come to a brisk simmer; reduce the heat to medium and simmer, stirring occasionally, 8 to 12 minutes, or until reduced by about half. Remove the pandan leaf. Add the rice and reduce the heat to medium-low; cook, stirring, until heated through and thickened, about 5 minutes. Serve warm or at room temperature. Alternatively, completely cooled pudding can be covered and refrigerated up to 2 days and served chilled, or returned to room temperature.

{PER SERVING} Calories 306 • Protein 4g • Total Fat 10g • Sat Fat 9g • Cholesterol 0mg • Carbohydrate 52g • Dietary Fiber 1g • Sodium 118mg

Coconut-Pumpkin Sticky Rice Pudding

Pumpkin appears frequently in desserts throughout China. This scrumptious rice pudding firms as it cools.

MAKES 6 TO 8 SERVINGS

1 cup sticky (glutinous) rice

2 cups water

1½ cups canned light coconut milk

½ cup canned pumpkin puree

½ cup sugar

¼ teaspoon ground cinnamon

¼ teaspoon salt

⅛ teaspoon ground ginger

Rinse the rice in cold water twice; drain. Transfer to a medium saucepan and add the water. Bring to a boil over high heat. Reduce the heat to medium and cook, stirring occasionally, until thick and soupy, about 8 minutes. Add the coconut milk, pumpkin puree, sugar, cinnamon, salt, and ginger. Bring to a gentle simmer over medium-high heat. Reduce the heat to low and cook, stirring constantly, 5 minutes. Remove from the heat and let cool about 15 minutes, stirring a few times. Serve warm or at room temperature. Alternatively, cover and refrigerate completely cooled pudding up to 3 days and serve chilled.

{PER SERVING} Calories 246 · Protein 4g · Total Fat 5g · Sat Fat 4g · Cholesterol 0mg · Carbohydrate 47g · Dietary Fiber 2 g · Sodium 116mg

Eight-Treasure Glutinous Rice Cake

Known as ba bao fan, this gluten-free Chinese New Year favorite can be enjoyed any time of the year. Feel free to experiment with your favorite dried fruits, so long as the number, when included with the red bean paste, equals the fortuitous 8. For a festive red-hued cake, use about ½ cup chopped dried scarlet pink dragon fruit in lieu of one of the other chopped fruits—its red pigment acts as a natural food coloring, while its tiny black seeds resemble sprinkles.

MAKES 8 TO 10 SERVINGS

1½ cups glutinous rice

¼ cup chopped dried apricots, soaked in warm water to cover 20 minutes, or until softened, drained well

¼ cup chopped dried pears, soaked in warm water to cover 20 minutes, or until softened, drained well

¼ cup chopped dried mango, soaked in warm water to cover 20 minutes, or until softened, drained well

¼ cup chopped dried pineapple, soaked in warm water to cover 20 minutes, or until softened, drained well

¼ cup chopped dried peaches, soaked in warm water to cover 20 minutes, or until softened, drained well

¼ cup chopped dried pitted red dates (jujubes), soaked in warm water to cover 20 minutes, or until softened, drained well

2 tablespoons raisins

½ tablespoon peanut oil or canola oil

1 cup prepared sweet red bean paste (adzuki) or Sweet Red Bean Paste (page 182)

1 cup water

3 tablespoons sugar

2 teaspoons cornstarch mixed with 2
    teaspoons water

Bring a medium stockpot filled with salted water to a boil over high heat; add the rice and reduce the heat slightly. Cook, stirring occasionally, until just tender, about 12 minutes. Drain well. Transfer the rice to a large bowl and add the dried fruits, mixing well to thoroughly combine.

Grease a steam-proof 8-cup/2-quart bowl with the oil. Place half the rice mixture in the bowl. Using the back of a wet spoon, pack it down firmly and make a slight indentation in the center for the red bean paste. Place the red bean paste in the center and spread it evenly along the indentation. Top with the remainder of rice mixture, packing it down firmly and making it level and smooth. (At this point, completely cooled mixture can be covered and refrigerated up to 24 hours before continuing with the recipe.)

Place a steamer basket in a tall stockpot filled with about 2 inches of water. Place the bowl of rice in the steamer basket and bring the water to a boil over high heat. Immediately reduce the heat to medium, cover, and steam 25 minutes (add about 10 minutes if mixture was refrigerated). Uncover and let cool a few minutes.

In a small saucepan, bring water and sugar to a boil over high heat. Stir in the cornstarch mixture and reduce the heat to medium. Cook, stirring constantly, until thickened into thin syrup, about 5 minutes. Remove from heat and keep syrup warm.

Carefully remove rice bowl from the steamer basket. Let stand about 10 minutes to allow rice grains to harden slightly. Pass the tip of a dinner knife around the edge of the rice cake to loosen it. Invert onto a warmed deep-welled serving platter. (The cake should slip out easily.) Pour half the

syrup evenly over the cake. To serve, cut into wedges using a sharp knife and transfer with a pie wedge to deep-welled serving plates. Either drizzle each serving with equal amounts of remaining syrup, or pass the syrup separately.

{PER SERVING} (includes syrup) Calories 317 · Protein 6g · Total Fat 2g · Sat Fat 0g · Cholesterol 0mg · Carbohydrate 73g · Dietary Fiber 4g · Sodium 8mg

Five-Spice Sweet Rice Cake with Sesame Seeds

This gluten-free rice cake is nice with a cup of tea and conversation.

MAKES 8 SERVINGS

1 cup glutinous or sticky rice, soaked in
    warm water for 3 hours, drained
½ cup water
½ cup coconut milk
⅓ cup sugar
1 teaspoon five-spice powder
¼ teaspoon salt
¼ cup toasted sesame seeds

In a medium saucepan, combine the rice, water, coconut milk, sugar, five-spice powder, and salt; bring to a boil over medium-high heat. Immediately reduce heat to low, stir, and cover tightly; cook about 15 minutes, or until rice has absorbed the liquid and is tender.

Meanwhile, line an 8-inch-square baking dish with foil and sprinkle with half the sesame seeds. Toss the rice mixture with a fork and then pack into the pan, pressing firmly. Sprinkle evenly with remaining sesame seeds. Let cool to room temperature before cutting into 16 (2-inch) squares. Serve at once. Mixture can be refrigerated, covered, up to 4 days before returning to room temperature and serving.

{PER SERVING} Calories 179 · Protein 3g · Total Fat 6g · Sat Fat 4g · Cholesterol 0mg · Carbohydrate 29g · Dietary Fiber 1g · Sodium 71mg

Sesame Balls Filled with Red Bean Paste

While delicious recipes for sesame balls abound, this sweet potato variation is my favorite. To ensure the proper consistency, make sure you use glutinous rice flour, also known as sweet rice flour, which is made from sticky rice. The balls can be assembled 24 hours ahead before rolling in the sesame seeds and frying; for best results, serve shortly after cooking.

MAKES 20 PIECES

1 medium sweet potato (about 6 ounces), peeled, cut into small chunks

1½ cups glutinous rice flour

⅓ cup all-purpose flour

2 tablespoons sugar

½ cup hot water, plus additional, if necessary

6 tablespoons plus 2 teaspoons red bean (adzuki) paste or Sweet Red Bean Paste (page 182)

About ½ cup sesame seeds

Peanut oil, for frying

Confectioner's sugar, for dusting (optional)

In a small saucepan, bring the sweet potato and enough water to cover to a boil over high heat. Reduce the heat slightly and boil until tender, about 10 minutes. Drain and mash well with a fork (you should have about ¾ cup). Set aside to cool slightly.

In a medium bowl, mix together the flours and sugar until well combined. Add the sweet potato, mixing with a fork until thoroughly blended (mixture will resemble coarse meal). Add hot water a few tablespoons at a time, kneading after each addition (add an extra tablespoon, or more, of hot water if dough seems too dry). Turn dough out onto a lightly floured work surface and knead until smooth, about 5 minutes. Form dough into a ball and return to bowl; cover with a damp kitchen towel and let rest 10 minutes.

Divide dough in half. Form each half into 10 balls about 1½ inches in diameter, for a total of 20 balls. Flatten each ball with your palm into a circle about 2¾ inches in diameter. Place 1 level teaspoon of the red bean paste in the center of each circle; form back into balls. (At this point, balls can be covered with plastic wrap and refrigerated up to 24 hours before continuing with the recipe.)

Fill a small bowl with cold water. Place sesame seeds in a small bowl or deep-welled plate. Dip each dough ball into the cold water and then roll in sesame seeds to thoroughly coat.

Line a large baking sheet with several layers of paper towels and set aside.

In a small heavy-bottomed, deep-sided skillet, heat about ½ inch of oil over medium heat. When a small piece of dough can sizzle (after about 5 minutes), reduce the heat to medium-low and add about 5 dough balls. Cook until golden and swollen, turning frequently to evenly cook, 3 to 5 minutes. Transfer to the prepared baking sheet to drain. Repeat with remaining dough balls. Serve at once, sprinkled with the confectioner's sugar, if using.

{PER SERVING} (per 1 ball, or 1/20 of recipe) Calories 121 · Protein 2g · Total Fat 5g · Sat Fat 1g · Cholesterol 0mg · Carbohydrate 18g · Dietary Fiber 1g · Sodium 2mg

Snow Fungus Soup with Red Dates, Longan, and Ginkgo Nuts

Popular at Chinese New Year, this unusual and exotic dessert is surprisingly simple to make—I especially enjoy it cold, more as pudding than soup. White fungus, also known as snow fungus and silver ear, is a yellowish-white, almost translucent, gelatinous mushroom that is used in desserts, herbal soups, salads, and Chinese medicine. Indeed, scientific research has shown that white fungus may help to increase the body's immune system, fight and prevent cancers, and slow down the aging process—cosmetically, it is a popular skin toner, a type of "edible botox." Of course, as with most medicinal foods, moderate consumption of white fungus is highly recommended to avoid any negative side effects—therefore, eating this remarkable mushroom for breakfast, lunch, and dinner is probably not a good idea. If pandan leaves are unavailable, add ⅛ teaspoon of pandan essence, available in Asian markets, or pure vanilla extract along with the rock sugar.

MAKES 6 TO 8 SERVINGS

1½ ounces dried snow fungus or white fungus, soaked in very hot water to cover 20 minutes, or until softened

8 cups water

20 pitted dried red dates (jujubes)

5 pandan leaves, tied in a knot

10 canned peeled longans or whole seedless litchis, drained

½ cup canned or vacuum-packaged ginkgo nuts, rinsed and drained (about 3 ounces)

2 tablespoons dark brown sugar

½ cup rock sugar (lump sugar, lump candy), yellow or clear, or ⅓ cup granulated white sugar, or to taste

Drain the mushrooms well; remove and discard the stems. Using kitchen scissors, remove and discard any hard or discolored parts. Rinse and drain again. Cut into small pieces and place in a medium stockpot. Add the water, dates, and pandan leaves; bring to a boil over medium-high heat. Reduce the heat to medium and simmer, partially covered, 20 minutes, stirring occasionally. Add the longans, nuts, and brown sugar; simmer, uncovered, 10 to 15 minutes, or until the mushrooms are very tender and translucent, stirring occasionally.

Remove from heat and add the rock sugar; stir until the rock sugar is completely dissolved, about 2 minutes. Remove and discard the pandan leaves. Serve warm. Completely cooled soup can be refrigerated, covered, up to 4 days before serving chilled or reheating gently over low heat.

{PER SERVING} Calories 112 · Protein 1g · Total Fat 0g · Sat Fat 0g · Cholesterol 0mg · Carbohydrate 28g · Dietary Fiber 2g · Sodium 42mg

Watermelon in Ginger Wine

For adults only, this refreshing chilled dessert will make a superb ending to a special summer meal. Ginger wine is a fortified wine made from a fermented blend of ground ginger and raisins, originally produced in England. Dry sherry or port can be substituted; in this instance, double the amount of ginger in the recipe.

MAKES 4 SERVINGS

½ cup water
¼ cup ginger wine, dry sherry, or port
1 to 2 tablespoons chopped crystallized ginger
1 tablespoon sugar
Pinch salt
4 cups cubed or balled seedless watermelon
Chopped fresh mint, for garnish (optional)

In a small saucepan, bring the water, wine, half the ginger (½ tablespoon if using ginger wine, 1 tablespoon if using sherry), sugar, and salt to a boil over medium heat. Remove from heat and stir in the remaining ginger (½ tablespoon if using ginger wine, 1 tablespoon if using sherry). Set aside to cool to room temperature.

Place the watermelon in a medium bowl and add the wine mixture; toss gently to combine. Cover and refrigerate a minimum of 2 hours or up to 1 day, tossing a few times. Toss gently and serve chilled, garnished with mint, if desired.

{PER SERVING} (with dry sherry and 2 tablespoons crystallized ginger) Calories 98 · Protein 1g · Total Fat 1g · Sat Fat 0g · Cholesterol 0mg · Carbohydrate 15g · Dietary Fiber 1g · Sodium 41mg

Taro-Tapioca Soup

This rich and creamy soup is popular in southern China. Peel the taro with a vegetable peeler under cold running water to avoid any skin sensitivity to its sticky juices.

MAKES 6 SERVINGS

1 pound taro root, peeled, cut into ½-inch pieces
2 cups water
1 cup unsweetened coconut milk
½ cup sugar
3 tablespoons instant tapioca

Bring a medium stockpot filled with water to a boil over high heat. Add the taro and cook until tender, about 20 minutes. Drain, return to the stockpot, and mash well; set aside.

In a medium saucepan, combine the water, coconut milk, sugar, and tapioca; let rest 5 minutes. Cook over medium heat, stirring constantly, until mixture comes to a full boil. Remove from heat and add to the taro, whisking until smooth. Serve warm or at room temperature. Alternatively, cover and refrigerate completely cooled mixture up to 3 days and serve chilled.

{PER SERVING} Calories 254 · Protein 2g · Total Fat 10g · Sat Fat 9g · Cholesterol 0mg · Carbohydrate 43g · Dietary Fiber 3g · Sodium 15mg

METRIC CONVERSION CHARTS

COMPARISON TO METRIC MEASURE

When You Know	Symbol	Multiply By	To Find	Symbol
teaspoons	tsp.	5.0	milliliters	ml
tablespoons	tbsp.	15.0	milliliters	ml
fluid ounces	fl. oz.	30.0	milliliters	ml
cups	c.	0.24	liters	l
pints	pt.	0.47	liters	l
quarts	qt.	0.95	liters	l
ounces	oz.	28.0	grams	g
pounds	lb.	0.45	kilograms	kg
Fahrenheit	F	⁵⁄₉ (after subtracting 32)	Celsius	C

FAHRENHEIT TO CELSIUS

F	C
200–205	95
220–225	105
245–250	120
275	135
300–305	150
325–330	165
345–350	175
370–375	190
400–405	205
425–430	220
445–450	230
470–475	245
500	260

LIQUID MEASURE TO LITERS

¼ cup	=	0.06 liters
½ cup	=	0.12 liters
¾ cup	=	0.18 liters
1 cup	=	0.24 liters
1¼ cups	=	0.30 liters
1½ cups	=	0.36 liters
2 cups	=	0.48 liters
2½ cups	=	0.60 liters
3 cups	=	0.72 liters
3½ cups	=	0.84 liters
4 cups	=	0.96 liters
4½ cups	=	1.08 liters
5 cups	=	1.20 liters
5½ cups	=	1.32 liters

LIQUID MEASURE TO MILLILITERS

¼ teaspoon	=	1.25 milliliters
½ teaspoon	=	2.50 milliliters
¾ teaspoon	=	3.75 milliliters
1 teaspoon	=	5.00 milliliters
1¼ teaspoons	=	6.25 milliliters
1½ teaspoons	=	7.50 milliliters
1¾ teaspoons	=	8.75 milliliters
2 teaspoons	=	10.0 milliliters
1 tablespoon	=	15.0 milliliters
2 tablespoons	=	30.0 milliliters

· INDEX ·